Managing the Magic of Old Places

Managing the Magic of Old Places

Crafting
Public
Policies for
People-Centered
Historic
Preservation

Jeremy C. Wells

The University of Tennessee Press / Knoxville

Copyright © 2025 by The University of Tennessee Press / Knoxville.
All Rights Reserved.
FIRST EDITION.

Library of Congress Cataloging-in-Publication Data

Names: Wells, Jeremy C. author
Title: Managing the magic of old places : crafting public policies for
   people-centered historic preservation / Jeremy C. Wells.
Description: First edition. | Knoxville : The University of Tennessee
   Press, [2025] | Includes bibliographical references and index. |
Summary: "From 1849 to the early 1980s, fewer than one hundred
   highly educated, White, European and American men created
   what became today's US federal historic preservation policy.
   Jeremy C. Wells argues that the orthodox historic preservation
   doctrine that this lineage formulated has too long dominated
   federal policy and watered down the richness of laypeople's
   relationships to their own heritage. Instead, Wells envisions a
   more just and inclusive public preservation policy grounded in
   community-based participatory practice and the social sciences-
   especially environmental psychology-to understand and actualize
   the experiential work of preservation and the "magic of old places"
   that is its object"—Provided by publisher.
Identifiers: LCCN 2025005556 (print) | LCCN 2025005557 (ebook)
   | ISBN 9781621909774 paperback | ISBN 9781621909798 adobe
   pdf | ISBN 9781621909781 kindle edition
Subjects: LCSH: Historic preservation—Government policy—
   United States | Historic preservation—United States—Citizen
   participation | Environmental psychology | United States—
   Cultural policy
Classification: LCC E159 .W443 2025 (print) | LCC E159 (ebook) |
   DDC 363.6/90973—dc23/eng/20250430

LC record available at https://lccn.loc.gov/2025005556
LC ebook record available at https://lccn.loc.gov/2025005557

Contents

	Preface	ix
	Acknowledgments	xix
	Introduction	1
CHAPTER ONE	Challenging the Authorized Discourse on Built Heritage Conservation: Why Doctrine and Policy Are Not People- or Human-Centered	45
CHAPTER TWO	Being Affected by Old Places and the Person-Patina Relationship	89
CHAPTER THREE	Pure and Naked Heritage: Revealing the Vulnerability of Orthodoxy	111
CHAPTER FOUR	Transforming Historic Preservation Policy to Manage Charm	147
CHAPTER FIVE	Overcoming Historic Preservation's "Resistance to Research": Creating an Informed Policy	191
CHAPTER SIX	Time for Change	209
	Appendix A. Authors of Built Heritage Conservation Doctrine	221
	Appendix B. Conducting a Guided First-Person Existential Phenomenology	249
	Index	253

Illustrations

FIGURES

0.1.	Disciplinary Composition of ACHS Members	11
0.2.	The Zócalo in Córdoba, Mexico	17
0.3.	Internal Courtyard of Heritage Building in Córdoba, Mexico	18
0.4.	Rationale for the Content and Organization of This Book	32
1.1.	World Heritage Site of Macau, China	52
1.2.	Seventeenth-Century Temple, Hong Kong, China	52
1.3.	"Certificate of Appropriateness"	59
1.4.	Cemetery Sign, Deadwood, South Dakota	60
1.5.	Sketch of the Town Hall in Ballarat, Australia	71
2.1.	Physical Decay and Perception Scale	96
2.2.	Decay or Patina?	97
2.3.	Process of the Perception of Patina, Decay, or Forgery	98
2.4.	Al Capone's Cell, Eastern State Penitentiary, Philadelphia	100
2.5.	Eastern State Penitentiary Historic Site, Philadelphia	101
2.6.	Ghost Towns are Places of Magic	104
3.1.	Racial or Ethnic Identity of Federal Preservation Policymakers	135
3.2.	Gender identity of Federal Preservation Policymakers	135
3.3.	Educational Attainment of Federal Preservation Policymakers	136
3.4.	Elite University Degrees Among Federal Preservation Policymakers	136
4.1.	Typical Layout for a Public Meeting Emphasizing Front of the Room	153
4.2.	Meeting Layout with Adjusted Power Differentials	154
4.3.	Three-Step Process to Convert Community-Driven Recommendations into Public Policy	165
4.4.	Sketch of Peace Pagoda, San Francisco's Japantown	182

TABLES

0.1.	Content Analysis of "Magic," "Magical," "Charm," and "Charming"	21
1.1.	Canadian Provinces and Rules for Listing Historical Buildings and Places	77
4.1.	Orientations in Phenomenological Research, Themes, and Origins	171
5.1.	Built Heritage Publications in Common Social Science Disciplines	201
6.1.	Five Problems and Five Potential Solutions	219

Preface

This book intersects public policy and "magic" to creatively explore how historic preservation (a.k.a. built heritage conservation) might function better in its efforts to help people. It is the culmination of my nearly three decades of research, observations, and experiences in historic preservation practice in the United States and abroad. Given what appears to be an unusual conflation of topics, I think it's important to provide the reader with some perspective on the journey that informed my writing.

POLICY MAGIC

On a warm summer afternoon about a decade ago, I was sitting on the porch of a grand old mansion with the executive director of a statewide historic preservation organization. We were chatting about the preservation field, and she made a comment about "how nice it would be to actually have detailed statistics on the exact kind of work people do in historic preservation." Feeling motivated, I responded about a study I recently completed that provided these kinds of data. I described how the field can broadly be broken into people who work in interpretation, advocacy, construction and architecture, and regulatory compliance. I ended my summary by mentioning that "70% of the paid work in historic preservation is in that latter category—regulatory compliance." When I said this, the director choked on her iced tea, then cleared her throat and said: "You can't say that. You can't say that most of the work in historic preservation is in 'regulatory compliance.' You'll make us look like our stereotype—that we're the 'no' people. That would be terrible." To be sure, I was not surprised by the director's reaction, because professionals who work in historic preservation have long tried to undermine the stereotype of being the "no" people (e.g., Howard, 2023, p. 127; Lyon & Brook, 2003, p. 107; Meeks, 2016, p. 260), even if the data don't actually fit the denial.

A few days later, when I was meeting with my dean, I mentioned that the results of this same study showed that only about 10% of the paid work in the historic preservation field was directly related to architecture or construction. His response was simply, "I don't believe it." By denying the result of the study, it was clear that my dean—who was trained as an architect, liked older buildings, and directed a school of architecture—wanted the majority of the work in historic preservation to be in *his discipline*, regardless of the facts. At the time, I didn't know how to respond, because he wasn't challenging my methodology or the accuracy of the results; instead, my dean appeared to wish away the results because the study's findings appeared to challenge his desired paradigm.

Several months after my study was published, I was having a similar chat with a professor who taught in an environmental studies program. He mentioned that many of his graduates went on to work in the environmental compliance field and that this area of employment was one of the largest for his students. He went on to say how important it was, in an environmental studies curriculum, for students to understand public environmental policy, especially the regulations for the National Environmental Policy Act, the Clean Air Act, and the Endangered Species Act. Enthusiastically, I mentioned that in my study on historic preservation work, many employers were searching for potential employees who understood and could apply the regulations that stemmed from the National Historic Preservation Act *and* the National Environmental Policy Act. In response, the professor tilted his head and looked at me quizzically, saying "Really? I always thought historic preservation was about architecture. But, you're telling me it's actually more similar to environmental compliance? That's really surprising."

The study that was the center of these discussions was a unique design based on a yearlong census (i.e., not a survey) of all historic preservation job postings in the United States (Wells, 2018). What it was able to establish, for the first time, was the type of and way in which paid work in the historic preservation field was conducted. As my chats with the executive director and the dean demonstrate, many built environment professionals were not happy with the result that 70% of the work of paid historic preservation professionals is driven by regulatory compliance. And, of this 70% of regulatory-based practice, about 40% of the employers of historic preservation professionals were from workplaces that specialized in environmental compliance work; most importantly, many of these latter employers wanted to hire employees who were skilled in the implementation of regulations from both the historic preservation and environmental conservation fields. But, in my experience, as a kind of antipode to architecture, many professors who teach environmental compliance seemed to be largely unaware of this natural alliance. Thus, what appears to be the most natural ally of regulatory compliance in historic preservation—environmental compliance—is largely unacknowledged by professionals, from any discipline.

These are just a few examples of how I have experienced people's perception of public preservation policy and its disproportionately large influence on paid work in the historic preservation field: fear, denial, and unawareness. Unfortunately, what I have almost never perceived is a desire to reform historic preservation education in recognition of what employers actually need rather than catering to what professors enjoy teaching. Over the past thirty years, I have worked as a preservation practitioner in the public, private, and nonprofit sectors and have researched and taught in historic preservation programs at several universities; my multifarious efforts have covered the broad area of preservation practice from interpretation and advocacy to regulatory compliance and architectural design and construction. Through these experiences, I have made additional personal observations in relation to the historic preservation field's relationship with public policy, especially within the context of higher education.

One of my most important observations is how the historic preservation discipline seems decidedly unable to differentiate between the concepts of "law," "policy," "regulation," "rule," and "guideline." For instance, I have found that the graduates of historic preservation degree programs are often unable to define these terms, including the critical difference between "law" and "policy." This phenomenon could be an important reason why I have found that many professionals—and academics—use historic preservation "law," "policy," and "regulation" as synonyms in their speeches and writing, when they are clearly not. When I look at the syllabi for "preservation law" or "preservation policy" courses in the degree programs across the country (there are less than 100), the focus is overwhelmingly on case law, not public policy. Perhaps most surprising is that some historic preservation degree programs have no requirements for any coursework in laws, regulations, or public policy; I should know because I am a graduate from such a program.

Perhaps this lack of focus and consistency on public preservation policy in higher education is a reason why, in every meeting I have had with state historic preservation officers, the most common complaint is that new graduates from historic preservation degree programs do not understand how to apply federal preservation regulations in their work. If a degree program is focusing more on the constitutional implications of design review (e.g., Penn Central Transportation Co. v. New York City) while ignoring how 36 CFR 800 (the regulation for Section 106 of the National Historic Preservation Act) works, then such graduates are expected to learn, on the job, how most of the work of the historic preservation field happens. Knowing the constitutionality of takings, for instance, isn't going to help a prospective employee apply the Secretary of the Interior's Standards to a design review application.

Similarly, scholarly literature on public historic preservation policy is very thin, indeed. While there are a handful of textbooks on historic preservation law, which, again, emphasize case law and are targeted at law students as opposed to historic preservation students, there are essentially no scholarly books on public preservation policy. If this category of literature existed, it would detail analyzing the effectiveness of specific aspects of public preservation policy, including the use of data analysis tools and research methods, politics and governance, and budgeting and finance; these topics would be in addition to the specific rules, regulations, and guidelines relevant to federal, state, and local governmental preservation programs. But, most importantly, a focus on public policy would explain the relationship between politics and governance that establishes the primary framework for work in the historic preservation field.

Given this context, it should not, therefore, be surprising that there has never been a center for research on public preservation policy in the United States. Nor has there ever been funding for research on or the implementation of public preservation policy in this country. There is not a single public policy program in higher education that has ever focused on historic preservation—either through analyses or in coursework. Compare this to the tens of such centers across the country that address urban planning or the many funders of research on urban and regional planning policy. Similarly, there are hundreds of research centers for public environmental policy as well as for research funding. Again, in this broader context, the lack of *any* research or funding focus—ever—in the United States on public preservation policy is, for lack of a better word, strange.

Policy leaders and policy analysis experts in historic preservation have also been notably absent from government—with one important and recent exception. The former Chair of the Advisory Council on Historic Preservation, Sara Bronin, has used her expertise in law and regulations to advance some of the first research that answers basic questions on the ubiquitousness of federal preservation policy, even when not required, at the local governmental level (Bronin & Irwin, 2023). For decades, the US House's Preservation Caucus has largely focused on increasing or maintaining government funding for historic preservation, but discussions on other aspects of policy are mostly absent. Analyses on federal preservation policy by the Congressional Research Service—an entity that ostensibly informs elected leaders on policy matters—consistently omits or glosses over preservation policy issues and are written by employees with no education or experience in historic preservation. The National Park Service—the home of preservation policy in the United States—and the Advisory Council for Historic Preservation have never conducted an analysis on the overall effectiveness of public preservation policy.

Through these experiences and observations, it has been difficult for me to ignore that the historic preservation field seems to be in a persistent state of denial about the fundamental role public policy plays in the majority of its paid work. This observation is, in part, what drove me to write this book, which just might be the first of its kind ever published on the holistic analysis of public historic preservation policy in the United States.

What of "magic," then? Why conflate magic with policy? As I will explain in this book, for fifty years, public preservation policy has been quite effective in eviscerating local knowledge, sociocultural meanings, and emotional connections from its practice. Bolstered by its ancient foundational doctrines, public preservation policy is a fundamentally positivistic (i.e., fact based) and objective endeavor that leaves no room for subjectivity. In a word, by inherent design, there is no "magic" in orthodox public preservation policy. And, in that gap is lost a monumental potential to connect old places with the public, which may serve to dramatically increase public support for historic preservation. In sum, "magic" in historic preservation is essentially recognizing that the way in which the public perceives, experiences, and wants to protect historic places should inform public policy.

MOTIVATIONS FOR WRITING THIS BOOK

When I began writing this book, I was an assistant professor on the cusp of receiving tenure (which I did obtain). At the time, I had no idea that my work environment would become increasingly toxic—an untenable situation that would force me to walk away from my job, and, most importantly, to leave my career in higher education. I originally thought that this book would be the scholarly achievement that would lead to my promotion to a full professor. Unfortunately, my best laid plans went awry when I least expected it. No one wants to be a whistleblower for your workplace, much less a field of practice. There is a personal price to pay.

Beyond status for my career, I always had altruistic goals in mind with this book, based on the observation that US public policies and associated doctrines that address heritage reliably assume that the act of heritage conservation primarily benefits things—e.g., buildings, places, or objects. After many years of work and research on how old places affect people, I came to the conclusion that the act of heritage conservation should, instead, primarily benefit people. By taking a social science and action research focus, I therefore wrote this book to inspire leaders to move public preservation policy toward this people-centered focus using tools to increase participatory democracy and to value local knowledge. As I have learned, however, this people-centered idea for historic preservation can be a dangerous, heretical idea that opened me to persecution. A number of practitioners and academics in the historic preservation field are not particularly open to a shift from prioritizing fabric to prioritizing people, which is why I am motivated to at least try to open more people's minds to change.

In this effort to open more minds, I also wrote this book to connect US preservation practitioners and academics with progressive developments in Europe, Asia, Africa, Latin America, and Australia. With a few notable exceptions, as a historic preservation scholar in the United States, I have had great difficulty connecting with like-minded colleagues in this country. This has not been the case in other parts of the world, which is reflected in my citation metrics which, predictably, are primarily European. As I will explain shortly, my practice and academic journey through the historic preservation field has been troubling, and, most importantly, devoid of a community. No one wants to feel that their work is not important to others in the field or to be isolated from colleagues and their work, but that was my situation, which is part of the reason why I left higher education.

Initially, there is a thrill at being the first person to answer a research question, to provide useful data, or to help students in a way others have not done previously, but when this pattern becomes the norm, it leads to increasing feelings of isolation. To wit, some of my career "firsts" were:

- The first US scholar to inform historic preservation practice through environmental psychology (Wells, 2014; Wells, 2017; Wells & Baldwin, 2012);
- With my co-editor, the first scholar to publish a book on historic preservation education (Stiefel & Wells, 2014); notably this book emphasized a people-centered and social science approach to preservation education;
- The first US scholar to categorize US-based historic preservation practice based on a content analysis of employers' needs and job descriptions, including statistics on the percentage of work in each of these practice areas (Wells, 2018);
- The first scholar to analyze the scholarly productivity of tenure-track historic preservation professors, in the United States, including a statistical breakdown of topical areas of these scholars' publications (Wells, 2021b);
- The only scholar to have conducted an analysis of US public preservation policy to holistically identify issues of structural bias (Wells, 2021a);
- The only person to have published a guide for how to become a professional historic preservationist, geared toward prospective students (Wells, 2019);
- The only scholar to have published a comprehensive analysis of public preservation policy in the United States (this book).

To date, I remain the only person to have published on these topics with the exception of preservation education.

In assessing this list, what should be readily apparent to the reader is how unusual it is for a field's scholars to show so little interest in understanding a field's areas of practice, how its work affects people, how effective its public policies are, how it should engage in educational innovation, and what a preservation "scholar" actually is (or should be). (For another, similar perspective on this situation, see Ned Kaufman's [2019] analysis of the preservation field.) When fundamental questions about a field's work appear to lay unanswered for decades by its scholars, finding one's "community" as a scholar, by answering these questions, is a difficult endeavor, indeed. It's hard not to come to the conclusion that some scholars may simply not care, but I think this is probably not accurate. What I think is a stronger possibility is that some "preservation" scholars may not be particularly aware of the origins of the field or its policies. Most tenure-track professors associated with historic preservation degree programs in the United States don't have a degree in the field, have limited or no work experience in the field, and identify with another discipline, such as architecture, history, planning, or archaeology (see Wells, 2021b). In sum, I have long been baffled by a field that seems to show so little curiosity for the nature of its own work and the impact of its policies on the public.

My original hope, in addressing these research questions, was to build a community of like-minded scholars for discussion, collaboration, and teaching innovation. To a limited extent, I did find this in Europe, but the distance from the United States makes maintaining these international relationships rather difficult. (Funding is also an issue for non-European scholars working with European scholars.) But, in the United States, what instead has happened, with distressing frequency, is that rather than collaborating, some scholars have chosen to attack the fundamental people-centered basis of my work, and sometimes, me, personally.

My first realization that my people-centered focus seemed to threaten other preservation scholars was from a letter I received, via regular mail, from a well-known historic preservation professor. He laid out a diatribe on how my focus on people and the social sciences should *never* be a part of historic preservation research or practice. Instead, he advocated for "doubling down" on preservation's traditional focus on fabric and things. At the end of the letter, the professor wrote that I should seriously consider changing my research focus as it was "not helpful" and could "hurt the field."

Additional letters and emails started arriving, with similar themes. There was the preservation professor from an Ivy League institution who threatened to "destroy my career" if I continued publishing on the importance of the social sciences in preservation education. Or the practitioner who was "disgusted" with my work because it "threatened" to overturn existing preservation policy and would result in a "free-for-all" of widespread destruction of the historic built environment. And then there were the scholars who questioned the very need to look for racial and ethnic bias in public preservation policy because public policy was already "objective" and "without any cultural context."

To be sure, there were (and are) cryptic supporters of my work, who were afraid of being fired for working with me, but would try their best to collaborate without their home institutions finding out about their participation. A good example of this phenomenon were the preservation planners who would contribute to conferences I organized, but would fold over the part of their name badges with their city's name because, in their own words, "I can't be seen as a representative of my city questioning its preservation policies."

Even some of my professors who, as a student, I admired, were doubtful of the value of my people-centered work. During the Covid pandemic, as an alumnus, I remember the former director of my graduate program in historic preservation, via a Zoom call, addressing a question I asked. He responded to the small, virtual audience that he was deeply suspect of this "people-centered" approach in historic preservation. He then proceeded to proudly say, "I unabashedly remain a staunch materialist." Similarly, colleagues who were initially supportive of my people-centered work eventually changed their perspective, including a senior professor in my program who said that my research and teaching focus "threatened white material culture." This professor then proceeded to block all attempts at discussing potential curriculum changes that would reflect a more people-centered focus on practice.

These constant attacks and lack of support—especially a lack of support from administrators in my home institution—took a mental and physical toll on my health. Shortly after I walked away from my job as a tenured professor, as I lay in the emergency room, on the threshold of death, I couldn't escape the thought that my detractors had "won" by not only trying to erase my work, but by literally erasing *me*. I didn't hold malice toward my detractors, but rather an overwhelming sense of peace because of my escape from the maelstrom.

But, as you, my dear reader, are likely to conclude, I did not die. By leaving higher education, I found a place to recover. I came very close to abandoning this book, because every time I returned to the manuscript, my trauma returned as well. With therapy and self-care, and my family's support, I was able to work through these feelings and complete what I had started, so many years ago. While this book will obviously not advance my cause to full professorship, my hope is that it will do something far better: compel more people in the historic preservation field to think, contemplate, and act in the name of human interest.

One last goal, in publishing this book—another small hope, however unrealistic—is that someone reading this tome might join in an effort, with others, in building a community of like-minded, people-centered preservationists that I was not able to accomplish.

May you find peace, courage, and balance in your own (preservation) life.

Works Cited

Bronin, S. C., & Irwin, L. R. (2023). Regulating history. *Minnesota Law Review*, 108(1), 241-331.

Howard, J. M. (2023). *Buying time for heritage: How to save an endangered historic property*. University of North Carolina Press.

Kaufman, N. (2019). Resistance to research: Diagnosis and treatment of a disciplinary ailment. In J. C. Wells & B. L. Stiefel (Eds.), Human-centered built environment heritage preservation: Theory and evidence-based practice (pp. 309-316). Routledge.

Lyon, E. A., & Brook, D. L. S. (2003). States: The backbone of preservation. In R. E. Stipe (Ed.), *A richer heritage: Historic preservation in the twenty-first century* (pp. 81-116). University of North Carolina Press.

Meeks, S. (2016). *The past and future city: How historic preservation is reviving America's communities*. Island Press.

Stiefel, B. L., & Wells, J. C. (Eds.). (2014). Preservation education: Sharing best practices and finding common ground. University Press of New England.

Wells, J. C. (2014). A methodological framework for assessing the "spirit and feeling" of World Heritage properties. In T. R. Gensheimer & C. L. Guichard (Eds.), World heritage and national registers: Stewardship in perspective (pp. 19-32). Transaction Publishers.

———. (2017). How are old places different from new places? A psychological investigation of the correlation between patina, spontaneous fantasies, and place attachment. International Journal of Heritage Studies, 23(5), 445-469.

———. (2018). Challenging the assumption about a direct relationship between historic preservation and architecture in the United States. Frontiers of Architectural Research, 7(4), 455-464.

———. (2019). A guide to becoming an historic preservation professional: The work you can do, what employers want, and educational considerations. National Trust for Historic Preservation. https://savingplaces.org/stories/guide-to-becoming-a-historic-preservationist

———. (2021a). 10 ways historic preservation policy supports White supremacy and 10 ideas to end it. University of Maryland, College Park faculty papers. https://doi.org/10.13016/hyol-8vgp

———. (2021b). Does intra-disciplinary historic preservation scholarship address the exigent issues of practice? Exploring the character and impact of preservation knowledge production in relation to critical heritage studies, equity, and social justice. International Journal of Heritage Studies, 27(5), 449-469.

Wells, J. C., & Baldwin, E. D. (2012). Historic preservation, significance, and age value: A comparative phenomenology of historic Charleston and the nearby new-urbanist community of I'On. Journal of Environmental Psychology, 32(4), 384-400.

Acknowledgments

A number of people have been indefatigable supporters of my work, for whom I am extremely grateful. In no particular order, I would like to thank: Cari Goetcheus who, as a member of my dissertation committee, was one of my earliest champions in my quest for a more people-centered preservation practice; Barry Stiefel, for his wisdom, compassion, and trustworthiness—an exceptional colleague; Philip Marshall, for always being there for me and instilling an infectious positivity in life; Richard Hutchings for reminding me that there is, indeed, life after academia; Neil Silberman, for having faith in people-centered preservation and journeying with me to try and bring it to the masses; and Clara Irazábal-Zurita, for extending support to me when I needed it most.

Introduction

> Memories and memorializing, identities (kin, clan, nation, class, gender, sexuality and so forth), ideologies, aesthetics, nation building, [and] commerce[—]none of these adequately explains all of the dimensions of the dialogic relationship between heritage places and its visitors. It goes most of the way, but not quite all of the way. The magic is missing. (Staiff, 2014, p. 163)

> I don't want realism. I want magic.
>
> — BLANCHE DUBOISE character in Tennessee Williams's play, *A Streetcar Named Desire* (1947)

Writing in the seventh century A.D., Saint Bede chronicled the death of King Oswald of Northumbria, who, through his pious deeds, became venerated as a saint. As G. R. Evans (2007, p. 72) describes, the King

> died in battle at the hands of a heathen, and subsequently many miracles took place as a result of even indirect contact with his corpse. A sick horse rolled on the spot where his body had fallen and was miraculously cured. ... When the bones were eventually honorably received and washed before being placed in their shrine, the very water in which they were washed became holy and so did the earth on which it was poured away.

To be sure, Bede's account focuses on the numinous. People perceive numinous places and objects as containing some kind of embedded spirit or essence; the term acquired its modern connotations in the early twentieth century and was first associated with holy places and relics (Otto, 1917). In this story, King Oswald's corpse and the objects it touched are numinous. In a similar sense, historic places become important by "bearing witness" to the people and events around them; these environments can also be numinous (e.g., Agard, 1875; Cameron & Gatewood, 2000; Jones, 2009; Langelier, Tach, & Wood, 1906; Smith, 2006). This basic idea, which is at the heart of built heritage conservation/historic preservation doctrine (Muñoz Viñas, 2005; Waterton, Smith, & Campbell, 2006), treats fabric that has experienced such history with increased reverence or "significance." We believe (or at least assume) that something unusual has happened to this fabric. As a result, embedded in the fabric is some unique, indefinable essence of the past, which invites a cognitive dissonance that is ubiquitous in built heritage conservation doctrine and policy: We treat historic objects as if they contain a numinous essence from the past while simultaneously denying this possibility of the subjective. It is acceptable to treat—in *de facto*—historical places and objects as if they are numinous and magical, but not to actually refer to them as such or acknowledge this essence directly. Instead, we use metaphors, such as an object bearing witness to the past. The point is that in practice and research, we often refuse to acknowledge the magic of old places because we are afraid of leaving the comfort of detached, objective positivism (Wells, 2017a).

A Note on the "Preservation" and "Conservation" Terminology Used in This Book

Throughout this book, there are several interchangeable terms that will be used that reference some aspect of the built environment and its treatment. Unfortunately, these terms have not been standardized in the English-speaking world and, as such, can be confusing for the reader. Because so much of the referenced literature in this book relates international (i.e., English-speaking countries other than the United States) scholarship and practice with scholarship and practice in the United States, it is difficult to only use one term for this book. To avoid confusion, I will define these "conservation" and "preservation" terms and their relationship to each other, below. Similar terms are grouped together.

Conservation/preservation. In widely accepted and broadly applied international practice, but *only* in niche practice contexts and narrowly defined statutory terms in the US (e.g., Secretary of the Interior's Standards [36 CFR 68]), "preservation" is exclusively the act of retaining, to the highest degree possible, older or "historic" materials that comprise a building, structure, or place; in this book, however, "preservation" will not be limited to its narrow, international sense.

As used in this book, "preservation" (common to usage in the United States) and "conservation" (more common internationally) apply to the broader recognition, protection, and treatment of older (or "historic") buildings, places, structures, and landscapes. These terms will be used interchangeably, varying primarily with geographic context, with "conservation" predominating in discussions with international relevance and "preservation" predominating in discussions primarily relevant to the United States. As opposed to "preservation," however, in international contexts the word "conservation" often relates to the entire scope of cultural heritage; in the rare cases where these broader discussions are made in this book, the single-word modifier of "heritage" will be added to "conservation"—as in "heritage conservation." Unless this broader scope is readily identified, however, "conservation" is synonymous with "built heritage conservation" (refer to the next set of definitions, below).

In the United States, "conservation" is most often assumed to mean environmental conservation, while internationally—especially in Europe—this term is more often synonymous with the recognition, protection, and treatment of cultural heritage; in this book, unless modified with the word, "environmental," the word "conservation" is not applicable to environmental conservation, but only to the human-modified environment or, where identified specifically, cultural heritage.

Built heritage conservation/historic preservation. More often used internationally, "heritage conservation" (without the "built" modifier) can refer to *any* aspect of the recognition, protection, and treatment of tangible or intangible aspects of culture. In this book, however, "built" will consistently be used as a modifier to narrow this context to tangible or intangible aspects of the human-modified environment (i.e., the aspect of the environment that is "built" or constructed by people and is generally not readily movable, such as buildings or places). "Historic preservation" is a phrase that is *only* used in the United States and, unlike heritage conservation, is almost always assumed to be equivalent to built heritage conservation, with a rare few exceptions, such as work that addresses printed materials, such as books. This book will use the phrase "historic preservation," however, *only* to address the built environment, echoing its popular meaning.

The contextual basis for the use of these terms. "Conservation"/"preservation," and "built heritage conservation"/"historic preservation" are used interchangeably in this book to describe the recognition, protection, and treatment of the human-modified environment. The choice of word, however, will convey the geographical context with "built heritage conservation"/"conservation" meaning an international context and "historic preservation"/"preservation" meaning a context specifically relevant in the United States. In a few instances, the phrase "heritage conservation" will be used, which means both an international context and a broad application to all tangible and/or intangible aspects of culture.

What Is "Doctrine"? What Is "public policy"? Who Makes Doctrine and Policy?

Throughout this book, the terms "doctrine" and "public policy" or, in its shortened form, "policy," are frequently used. "Doctrine" refers to a guiding document of principles, directives, and/or goals of some aspect of heritage conservation, which has been authored by conventional experts, such as architects, art historians, or archaeologists. In built heritage conservation, experts author these documents as part of international or national meetings organized under a specific theme, and they are often referred to as "charters," the contents of which are the result of a consensus of the participants. While doctrines guide both practice and the development of policy, they are not, in and of themselves, policy, nor do they carry the weight of law. "Public policy" is defined as the laws, regulations, guidelines, and/or official actions of local, state or provincial, or federal government. Policy is made by "policy makers," who are elected officials, political appointees, or supervisors within government agencies.

For instance, in 1931, a group of architects and archaeologists met in Athens, Greece, to discuss the appropriate way to treat historical monuments in order to conserve their authenticity. As a result of this meeting, they produced a document of principles and directives called the "Athens Charter." Many decades later, in 1964, a similar group of people met in Venice, Italy, to discuss the same topic; they also produced a document of principles and directives, based on the Athens Charter, which became known as the "Venice Charter." The Athens Charter and the Venice Charter are two examples of doctrines.

In 1976, the US Congress passed the Federal Rehabilitation Tax Credit (colloquially known as the "Historic Tax Credit") in order to provide financial incentives for property owners to rehabilitate historic buildings; this act is an example of a law. In the act, the Department of the Interior (via the National Park Service [NPS]) was asked to create a list of standards to "certify" whether the historical integrity of rehabilitated buildings had been retained. The NPS responded by tasking two employees, W. Brown Morton III and Gary L. Hume, with writing these standards. The result was the creation of a regulation (36 CFR 68) called "The Secretary of the Interior's Standards for the Treatment of Historic Properties," which these authors based on the Venice Charter, a doctrine. In order to help people understand how to apply the Standards, other employees at the NPS created *The Secretary of the Interior's Standards for the Treatment of Historic Properties with Guidelines for Preservation, Rehabilitation, Restoration, and Reconstruction of Historic Buildings* (Weeks & Grimmer, 1995), which is an example of guidelines. Several years later, the NPS adopted a policy, in the form of an official action, to include a focus on sustainability in historic preservation, which led to an updated version of these guidelines. Collectively, the Federal Rehabilitation Tax Credit, the Secretary of the Interior's Standards, *The Secretary of the Interior's Standards for the Treatment of Historic Properties*, and the official action of the NPS to focus on sustainability define one part of federal historic preservation policy.

For millennia, numinism, or the belief of the divine being present in a physical object, has been a part of many religious traditions, including Christianity. Miracles are thus associated with being in the presence of the bones of saints, and protection is offered by anointing with holy water: there is something fundamentally intangible in these objects that makes them more than what they are objectively. What if the experience of old places has a similar quality and that embedded in these places (or, more accurately, in the minds of those who experience them) is something "extra" that makes them more real, authentic, and vicarious? This is not a new concept in heritage conservation; Salvador Muñoz Viñas (2005) is perhaps the first person to connect numinism with heritage conservation in this way. Sîan Jones's (2009, p. 138) ethnographic research reveals that people describe built heritage in a way that has a "magical, almost numinous, aura." Many others have written about the connection between numinism and historic places, as well (e.g., Cameron & Gatewood, 2000; Silva, 2011; Smith, 2006; Snyder, 1990). To be sure, there is ample evidence that some people perceive older places to be magical and charming through their numinous qualities, but this recognition is largely absent from discussions and policy that intersects with the applied aspects of preservation/conservation practice.

Using what is known about this normal human behavior in context with old places, this book is therefore based on three fundamental premises. The first premise is that many laypeople perceive older (or historic) places as numinous, and as such, full of "magic" and "charm." Moreover, this experience is fundamental to the value and meanings that laypeople give to these places. The second premise is that built heritage conservation doctrine and policy—specifically public historic preservation policy in the United States—is deeply compromised by its purposeful ignorance of this normal human, psychological experience. The third premise is that unless built heritage conservation doctrine and policy change to recognize normal human experiences associated with the older built environment, the public will become increasingly hostile to the well-meaning, but naïve, endeavors of heritage conservation practitioners whose work is largely driven by policy.

In exploring these issues, this book provokes orthodox conservation doctrine and policy with social science evidence from anthropology, sociology, and especially psychology. This human-centered, bottom-up perspective naturally upends the detached objectivity and top-down processes of conventional preservation/conservation practice because it requires understanding the psychological effect of the physical age of places on laypeople. In this sense, I will explore the psychology of *senescent* environments, or the way in which the changes associated with patina and decay engender unique psychological responses in people.

This book also makes three rather important assumptions based on widely available knowledge about built heritage conservation:

- It is a useful endeavor that benefits the public;
- Its practice directly affects hundreds of millions of people across the globe; and
- Its practice needs to change through reformed public policy.

I will explore each of these three areas in order to provide a foundation to help defend why an investigation into the psychology of senescent environments is even necessary, much less desirable.

Why is there a need to substantiate the existence of built heritage conservation? Surely, the benefits of this activity are self-evident. Not all readers of this book, however, will identify with this area of research and practice, and it would be erroneous to make this assumption. This context is even more important given that the intent of this book is to appeal to a broad audience, including planners, architects, landscape architects, policy makers, and social scientists. These latter groups often have a benign or adversarial relationship with heritage conservation, so it is critical to not take these professionals for granted or be overly dismissive of their perspectives.

To be sure, built heritage conservation/historic preservation practice is a balkanized endeavor and those external to the field are frequently dismissive of its aims and importance. There are fundamental barriers in how built heritage conservation/historic preservation practitioners can collaborate with their other built environment colleagues. These barriers are sustained through a lack of organizations that specifically support the professional interests of conservation professionals and through the way in which nonconservation practitioners sideline the work of these individuals (Wells, 2009). For instance, in the United States, the American Planning Association has not updated its guidelines for historic preservation planning since 1997 (APA, 1997). According to Minner and Holleran (2016), the flagship journal of this organization, the *Journal of the American Planning Association*, only published three articles on historic preservation from the mid-1990s until these individuals helped edit a special issue in this journal on this topic in 2016. *The Journal of Architectural Education* has shown a similar neglect of historic preservation practice (Wells, 2018). Deborah Berke (2018, p. 207), Dean of the Yale School of Architecture, seems to deny the need for heritage when she writes that "historic preservation, as it is currently understood, will not ... be an essential tool [for] transforming old buildings." And the Historic Resources Committee of the American Institute for Architects (AIA) has struggled, since 1890, for the acceptance and relevancy of historic preservation in the field of architecture; according to the AIA's own numbers, only about 6% of its members have chosen to belong to this committee. Further, there is other empirical evidence that the field of architecture and its practitioners, as a whole (with some notable exceptions), have remarkably little interest in historic preservation, including failing to require any education on the subject for students (Wells, 2018).

Other fields, including many of the social sciences (especially psychology) have little knowledge or apparent interest in built heritage conservation or its connection to people, place, and flourishing. Until the Association for Critical Heritage Studies (ACHS) was created in 2012, there was no organizing entity for heritage conservation research in the social sciences. Heritage conservation psychology is still not recognized to any significant degree by the ACHS or the American Psychological Association. And, for most well-trained experts who are not associated with history or the built environment in some way, historic preservation is little more than a bricks-and-mortar endeavor driven by nostalgic, antiquarian impulses (Denslagen, 2009). In this light, it becomes more understandable why, when communicating to a professional or academic audience not familiar with built heritage, one must begin with a defense for its need. In one sense, those of us in this field often find ourselves fighting for our very existence. It is a luxury that architects and urban planners do not have to engage in similar rhetoric.

Likewise, outside of the academy, built heritage practitioners frequently have to defend their work in a world predisposed to mass consumerism, new construction, and unsustainable development that manifests as a bias against the sustainable reuse of the existing built environment. Research in cognitive psychology and consumer behavior consistently indicates that people prefer to purchase new goods rather than reused or recycled ones, including those items associated with building construction (Mahpour, 2018; van Weelden, Mugge, & Bakker, 2016); people also prefer new residential building construction over old (Bajec, 2007; Garrison, 2014). Public policy incentivizes new construction over the reuse of existing buildings (Frey, Dunn, & Cochran, 2011); developers and lenders prefer the predictability of new construction over building reuse (Al-Mansoori, 2000; Denhez, 1994, p. 194); and even architects and developers seeking LEED certification also prefer new construction over the retrofit of existing buildings (van der Heijden, 2018). This practice environment exists even when we now have ample evidence that the conservation of the existing built environment is not only inherently sustainable (Young, 2012), but should be considered an activity central to slowing the advance of climate change (Cassar, 2009).

Moving beyond sustainability arguments and toward direct effects on people, we know that globally each year, the conservation of historic buildings and places is responsible for nearly a trillion US dollars of economic activity that sustains tens of millions of jobs (Gilderbloom et al., 2009; Historic England, 2014; Nypan, 2007). The rules, laws, and regulations that undergird built heritage conservation in nearly every country through numerous national, regional, and local laws, directly or indirectly impact large numbers of people living in urbanized and rural areas. For instance, in the United States, nearly three-quarters of all built heritage conservation practice is the direct result of rules, laws, and regulations (Wells, 2018); or in another sense, without these regulations, three-quarters of built heritage conservation practitioners would be unemployed. It is likely that similar numbers exist for many other countries as well. But these observations provide a superficial assessment, at best, of the economic and regulatory effects of built heritage conservation. What do we know of the important sociocultural and psychological benefits that heritage provides? It is important to recognize that this question has only begun to be asked with any frequency in the twenty-first century, so while intriguing answers to this question have started to arrive, there is still much that needs to be accomplished, especially from a psychological perspective.

In my own work, and especially in my grant-seeking activities, I am frequently challenged by experts external to the field on the basic need for built heritage conservation. For instance, I quickly discovered in applying for government social science research grants (in the United States), and even similar grants from my own university, that if I failed to make a case for the fundamental need for historic preservation/built heritage conservation using quantifiable data, I would invariably receive critical comments or a denial on my application. How many architects would receive comments on their grant applications such as "I don't see why architecture is an important activity. You've not made a case for why we need to construct buildings?" The answer is probably not many. Yet, these are the kinds of questions to which I am challenged to respond because of the relative obscurity of my field. Similarly, my academic colleagues from the social sciences are warned against focusing on research topics and questions that are too applied (and often central to preservation/conservation work), which, if undertaken, may jeopardize a tenure case. The fact is that the underlying values of built heritage conservation are far from universal, and its proponents need to be careful in assuming that others think similarly. We are not yet in a world that takes for granted that human beings *need* heritage for reasons of continuity, memory, and identity among many possibilities (Mayes, 2018).

Considering these issues, which are inherent to a balkanized field, there is a glimmer of light. While built heritage conservation has long been understood to be closely associated with design, architecture, and history, leaders in the field are increasingly reconceptualizing it as a social science endeavor, as explained by Thompson Mayes (2018, p. 211), Vice President of the National Trust for Historic Preservation:

> The feelings of continuity, memory, and identity from old places give us a sense of who we are. The experience of beauty and the awe of the sacred at old places deepens our connections to a broader world and fosters a sense of empathy with others. Knowing the places where our ancestors are from gives people a deep sense of belonging. Learning history at the places where history happened is a viscerally memorable experience that stays with us for the rest of our lives. . . . The bottom line is that old places matter for more reasons that we generally assume. As such, the preservation of old places is not just something "nice" to do; it provides profound material, emotional, sociological, and spiritual benefits for all.

It is critical to emphasize that the meanings and values that Mayes enumerates are not normally considered to be a part of orthodox built heritage conservation doctrine and policy, which instead relies on connoisseurship and art/historical facts as primary considerations. Indeed, the field has an ingrained bias against the meanings and experiences of laypeople in understanding why old or "historic" places are important (King, 2009; Pannekoek, 1998; Smith, 2006; Wells, 2015). This situation has led to the rise of critical heritage studies and the creation of the ACHS in the early 2010s. The ACHS frames heritage as a "political act" and encourages inquiry centered on the effects of "nationalism, imperialism, colonialism, cultural elitism, Western triumphalism, social exclusion based on class and ethnicity, and the fetishizing of expert knowledge" on the creation and use of heritage in all forms. ACHS's manifesto has a Marxist tone in its emphasis of both "ruthless criticism" and the effect of class and power on heritage (ACHS, 2012). Interest in critical heritage studies from 2010 onward has increased dramatically. ACHS went from zero members to nearly 1,000 across the globe; the flagship refereed journal for the field of study went from two issues per year to four; and the cornerstone texts for the critical heritage studies field, chiefly Laurajane Smith's *Uses of Heritage* (2006) and Rodney Harrison's *Heritage: Critical Approaches* (2013), collectively have nearly 10,000 citations as of early 2023, according to Google Scholar, which is a remarkable number for such a small field.

The richness of the research from critical heritage studies researchers has revealed some fundamental characteristics about people and their relationship with heritage, including:

- Heritage can be found everywhere (Schofield, 2014, p. 3);
- Everyone is a heritage expert (Schofield, 2014, pp. 7-8);
- Heritage is neither natural nor cultural; it is both with different aspects of each emphasized in different ways (Dyer, 2007; Harrison, 2013, p. 4);
- People come to understand and value heritage through shared cultural meanings and experiences that rarely align with the objective art/historical values used by experts in the field (Harrison, 2013; Smith, 2006);
- Heritage values are constantly created and destroyed in the present through a process of group and cultural conflict and, as such, are unstable and constantly changing (Holtorf & Schadla-Hall, 1999, p. 243; Smith, 2006; Sommer, 2009, p. 103);
- Heritage is intimately intertwined with personal and group identities (Breglia 2006; Harrison, 2013; Smith, 2006);
- Laypeople are less concerned about material authenticity than is demanded by orthodox conservation doctrine and public policy thereof (Wells, 2010, 2020);
- Heritage can be therapeutic and cathartic (Ander et al. 2013; Smith & Campbell 2015);
- The destruction or creation of heritage is used for political ends by various state and other groups (Breglia 2006; Logan 2012).

Most researchers in critical heritage studies are trained in anthropological (or closely associated archaeological) theory and methods, which is then reflected in their published research. To wit, in 2017, I performed a census of all members of the ACHS that list their official position title on the ACHS website, which should accurately represent their research specialization or expertise. When several areas were mentioned, I only used the first area to

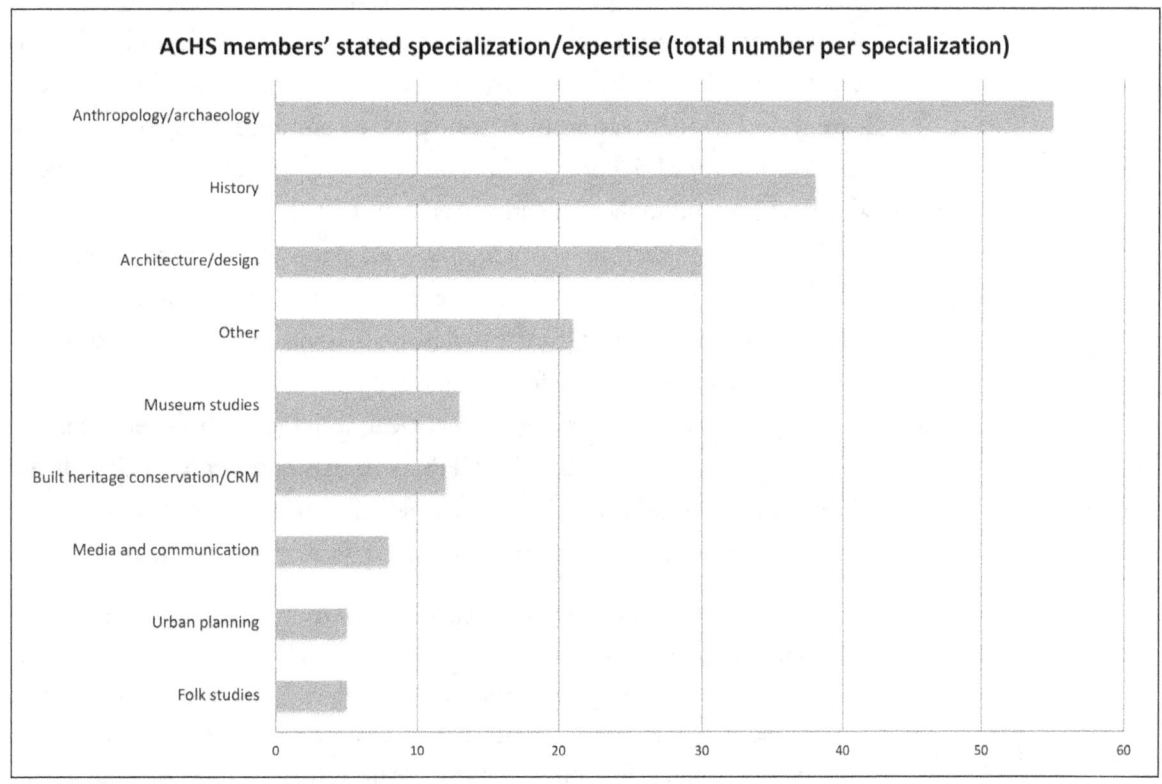

FIGURE O.I. Disciplinary composition of ACHS members

avoid duplicate entries with the assumption that the first area mentioned was the dominant one. While one cannot assume that the specializations/expertise of ACHS members mirrors that in the published scholarly literature, I would argue it ought to be a reasonable approximation of reality. The results are in Figure 0.1.

Not surprisingly, the membership in the ACHS shows the same dominance of an anthropological and archaeological perspective (about 30%) that I have noticed in the published critical heritage studies literature. History is a close second (about 20%) in terms of area of research/expertise, yet I find no such representation from the discipline of history in critical heritage studies literature defined by the themes above. Indeed, I have found very few scholarly publications written by self-identified historians that are clearly positioned in a subfield of history other than public history (i.e., no representation from art history, social history, political history, etc.) that clearly address critical heritage studies. While pure supposition on my part, I assume that the discipline of history has yet to (or is unwilling to) fully embrace critical heritage studies because it would require a divorce from an objective historical reality through at least some kind of philosophical, poststructuralist detour. In other words, history is too grounded in objective history (i.e., the recreation of a "real" past) to embrace many of the philosophical and social science precepts embodied in critical heritage studies in which understanding an objective past is not a primary goal. Similarly, the discipline of architecture is well represented in the ACHS membership, but this field, as a whole, has not embraced either the social sciences or even evidence-based or people-centered design, making architecture and critical heritage studies strange bedfellows, indeed.

Yet, what is clearly missing from critical heritage studies—either in the literature or membership of the ACHS—is psychology, and specifically environmental psychology. A literature review that meets the following criteria associated with the psychology of senescent environments is very thin indeed:

- A central focus on the historic environment from a theoretical and/or empirical research perspective;
- Research methods primarily associated with environmental psychology (especially compared with other social science disciplines), such as behavioral mapping, environmental attitude measurement, phenomenologies, visual preferences, simulated environments, postoccupancy evaluations, and neuroscience, among other possibilities;
- A theoretical construct based on place identity, place attachment, environmental perception, and the settings in which certain behaviors occur. (These are common themes in environmental psychology.)

As of the date I am writing this chapter, there are no monographs or edited books that meet these criteria, but there are just a handful of refereed articles that do (Ahn, 2013; Askari, Dola, & Soltani, 2014; Herzog & Gale, 1996; Herzog & Shier, 2000; Levi, 2005; Uzzell, 2009; Wells, 2017b; Wells & Baldwin, 2012). The evidence clearly indicates that there is a large gap in critical heritage studies literature from the perspective of psychology. These criteria are not necessarily intended to ignore the literature that does address the historic environment from the perspective of environmental psychology to some extent, of which there is a much larger body, but the theme is a central, primary focus on the individual's relationship with the historic environment, not a tangential side note.

To be sure, a psychological approach has much to offer in terms of addressing many of the problems that critical heritage studies researchers have identified in built heritage conservation practice. For instance, a review of this literature reveals the following fundamental themes for change:

- Respect for local or situated knowledge and bottom-up as opposed to top-down approaches (Schofield, 2014; Wells, 2015);
- Recognition of the dynamic quality of heritage by replacing static lists/registers of historic buildings and places with some kind of dynamic system that gives more agency to stakeholders (Handler, 2003; Wells & Lixinski, 2017);
- Conversion of heritage experts into facilitators trained in conflict negotiation/resolution techniques (Wells, 2015);
- Changing the requirement that laypeople speak/write/document in the language of the expert to the expert needing to speak/write/document in the language of laypeople (Wells, 2015; Wells & Lixinski, 2017);
- Recognition that while heritage conservation is a creator of social justice issues, it can also present some novel solutions to these kinds of issues (Gibson, Hendricks, & Wells, 2018);
- Respect that when a group of people believe an old building or place is important—for any reason(s)—then, it is important (King, 2009).

Generally speaking, what all six of these themes reveal is a need for a more holistic, social-science-based perspective on built heritage conservation doctrine and policy that is less reliant on an exclusive art/historical perspective. In essence, these themes impose a requirement on the expert to understand built heritage from the perspective of laypeople on the terms of laypeople. While we have a number of ethnographic techniques to understand group meanings and values as applied to place, there is a dearth of recognized methods for understanding the individual's relationship with older or historic places. Of the six items above, all have some kind of requirement for a psychological perspective to help understand people and their behavior. In particular, a heritage facilitator trying to diffuse conflict between individuals and attempting to communicate with laypeople in their language/meanings would greatly benefit from cognitive psychology. And understanding why people find place meaningful and, most importantly, emotionally significant is fundamentally the domain of environmental psychology. Continuing under the *status quo*, which equates to an imposed ignorance of the human perspective on heritage, is not only naïve, but enervates the potential tools that could change practice. And one place to start is by understanding how old places psychologically affect people, by exploring how they are "magical."

WHAT ARE "MAGICAL" AND "CHARMING" PLACES?

It is not possible to discuss "magic" in the context of old places without also introducing the related word "charming" as these two words are intimately associated with each other. In my studies (e.g., Wells, 2010; Wells & Baldwin, 2012), laypeople use these words interchangeably, which makes sense when one references the Oxford English Dictionary, revealing that "charming" means "to act upon with or as with a charm or magic, so as to influence, control, subdue, bind, etc.; to put a spell upon; to bewitch, enchant." To clarify, this book is *not* an exploration of the paranormal nor do I personally make the unscientific assumption that magic is real. Regardless, the veracity of these phenomena matters little in my endeavor to understand others' use and interpretation of these words in context with old places: I therefore make no attempt at an objective inquiry into "magic" because it has little bearing on this research. Instead, I trust that when people, in describing their experience of older or historic places, use these words, they mean what they say. If people believe certain places to be full of magic and charm, then for all intents and purposes they *are full of magic and charm* in whatever way they choose to define these terms. In assuming this frame, I therefore abstain from imposing my objective authority on others and instead assume a perspective that inherently values people's lived experiences and local knowledge without bias. My endeavor here is to understand the experiences of others on their own terms, even if I do not necessarily believe the nature of the reality that is being presented. Or, in another sense, *my reality is not the one that is important.* This is a book about the magical reality of others and how built heritage conservation doctrine and policy can be informed by understanding this psychological experience.

How, then, do laypeople express magic and charm in the context of old places? In my work understanding the "revitalization culture" of Main Street (downtown revitalization) programs, an unpaid volunteer resident shared how downtown Anderson, South Carolina, is both magical and charming (Wells, 2010, p. 429):

> Downtown has a tradition, it's got sort of an Old World charm that says, hey a hundred years ago this was the epicenter of business in this part of the state.... And there is some little magical thing that goes on in my mind that as I see these old pictures of what Anderson was with all the buggies and carriages and the boom and the buzz and then they brought in the electricity, and it was just ... everything of this part of the state.... And so here I sit in the same place, in this building that has been here since 1870, and it allows me to kind of somehow feel in touch with the historical significance. ... It's more emotional than anything else.

Because of the way this resident experiences the "history" of his town, its magic facilitates his emotional bond with its physical places—or, using terminology from environmental psychology, the magic of old places results in place attachment. With consistent regularity, in my research involving questions of meaning, significance, and historic places for laypeople in Anderson and Charleston (South Carolina) and in Allentown (Pennsylvania; Wells, 2010; Wells et al., 2016), the people I spoke with described the older places in which they lived and worked as charming and magical, linking these words to a specific emotional state.

Other researchers, such as from public history and folklore, have also noticed the way in which emotional experiences in older places are frequently associated with magic and charm (Samuel, 1990). More specifically, in her work with laypeople in the United Kingdom, Siân Jones (2009, pp. 137, 144) observes that historical objects have a "powerful magical or enchanting quality" in which "the authenticity of [historical] objects is experienced and negotiated as a magical, almost numinous, quality." Handler and Saxton (1988, p. 245) describe how in their work with military reenactors that their goal is to achieve "magic moments" in which the recreated event "seems really real."

Folklore and popular media include many references to magic and charming places. In Celtic traditions, for instance, there is the concept of "thin places" that are locations where the perceived barrier between the physical and mystical world begins to dissolve. These are often sacred places, such as churches and shrines, but many historical sites (especially particularly ancient ones) are thought to have similar qualities. Keven Koch (2018, p. 12) explains that "Thin Places [are] those places of Celtic lore where the veil between this world and the Otherworld is thin and permeable. In a modern context, the Thin Places are those locations that shimmer with the mystical presence of the storied past." Movies and television are also fruitful places to find examples of charming and magical places. Indeed, what would *Harry Potter* be without Hogwarts and its deep layers of decay and patina as evidence of great age? Lost, for certain, because it is inconceivable to imagine Hogwarts in some kind of contemporary corporate tower. Similarly, J. R. R. Tolkien's *The Hobbit* would lose much of its magical impact if it took place in a contemporary world instead of one filled with vast layers of antiquity. To be sure, these examples are not exceptions: An inventory of the top movies based on magic in the Internet Movie Database shows that the vast majority take place in old buildings and old places (IMDb, n.d.). Similarly, Mexico's Secretariat of Tourism has taken full advantage of this layperson's association with magic and old places by promoting many of its small colonial-era towns that have remained largely unchanged in the past 100 years as "Pueblos Mágicos" (Magical Towns; Secretaría de Turismo, 2020).

Case Study: Mexico's Pueblos Mágicos Program: When Government Policy Recognizes "Magic"

In 2001, Mexico's Secretary of Tourism launched the Pueblos Mágicos (Magical Towns) program as a way to promote these towns' economic development, through tourism, by capitalizing on what the Secretary describes as "the magic that emanates from their attractions" (trans. Secretaría de Turismo, 2020). The program emphasizes how these towns express their "magic" through symbolism, legends, and continued cultural traditions in addition to the qualities of their historic built environments (SECTUR, 2017). While economic development is a major goal of the Pueblos Mágicos program, Mexico's federal government clearly indicates that it wants to sustain intangible heritage and protect and maintain the cultural landscapes of these towns (Balslev Clausen & Gyimóthy, 2016; Pérez-Ramírez & Antolín-Espinosa, 2016). In the more than two decades the program has been in operation, a handful of recognized towns has grown into 174 (177 recognized minus 3 that were removed from the program) as of the end of 2023.

Any town can ask to be considered for inclusion in the program, based on a formal application that requires the formation of a Pueblos Mágico Committee, consisting of volunteer (unpaid) residents of the town, broadly representing diverse interests and identities, who help to guide the program in collaboration with government officials. Local and state elected leaders need to approve the application and commit to funding the conservation of the town's tangible and intangible heritage. The application should include a plan that clearly identifies how the town is "magical," its symbolic associations, what makes it unique, and why this heritage needs to be sustained. Lastly, the application needs to include evidence that the town has an infrastructure that can support tourists (e.g., health facilities, security, hotels, restaurants; SECTUR, 2017). It is important to note that a strict emphasis on material integrity, in architectural conservation work, such as an adherence to guidelines similar to the Venice Charter, is not a requirement of the program. While the town should have "some" listed historic buildings or places, it is not a requirement of the program for a town to identify and list more of these resources.

The reception of the Pueblos Mágicos program by scholars has been mixed, such as López-Levi's (2015) assertion that it is nothing more than the "political manipulation" of "magic" to cater to tourist interests and dupe local residents into compliance. Other researchers, however, have, through qualitative studies, come to the conclusion that the program can offer direct benefits to local residents, including indigenous peoples in Cuetzalan del Progreso (Puebla; Navarro Gamboa et al., 2019). In a survey of residents of Cuitzeo del Porvenir (Michoacán), the majority of respondents believed that their town was indeed "magical" and agreed that it should be part of the Pueblos Mágicos program, although 95% of the people surveyed indicated that they did not directly participate in the program's formation (García Vega & García Roja, 2014). In this survey, more than half of the residents indicated that there were clear social and cultural benefits to the program, as well as economic ones.

Moreover, in many of these towns, such as

FIGURE 0.2. The Zócalo (town square) in Córdoba, Mexico, an official Pueblo Mágico (photo by author)

Coatepec (Veracruz), there is a long tradition of storytelling about supernatural or magical phenomena that are associated with specific places, both outside and inside buildings (Guillén Ortiz, 2016). In oral traditions in Mexico, these stories are called "leyendas" (legends), which is a term that is also found in the official guidelines for the Pueblos Mágicos program (SECTUR, 2017). In Adriana Guillén Ortiz's research (trans. 2016, p. 212) based on interviews with local residents, she finds that the people of Coatepec believe it "is a magical place, where the supernatural gains strength in the apparitions that take to the streets, like La Llorona, the woman in white, the souls of purgatory or even the black charro; or inside the houses, where a shadow almost chokes a girl or invisible beings move everyday objects."

What is unique about Mexico's Pueblos Mágicos program is the way in which it not only recognizes the public perception of "magic" being embedded in place, but it capitalizes on residents' beliefs in this magic. While not ignoring the tangible elements of heritage or traditional cultural practices that can be more objectively described, the inclusion and celebration of "magic" in the promotion of these towns' identities show the potential of listening to, understanding, and then acting on local residents' beliefs to conserve their places of importance in ways that are congruent with their values.

FIGURE 0.3. Internal courtyard of heritage building in Córdoba, Mexico, an official Pueblo Mágico (photo by author)

But, are these examples isolated instances? The answer is readily available on social media, especially the tripadvisor.com site where thousands of people have shared their personal impressions upon visiting old and historic places across the globe. An example of some of the meanings that people share related to magical and charming places is in Table 0.1. While this is by no means an exhaustive analysis, nor is it necessarily generalizable to a larger population, the intent is to provide evidence that people do associate magic and charm with older or historical places and that this phenomenon, resting on psychological principles, is understudied within the fields of built heritage conservation/historic preservation, critical heritage studies, and heritage conservation, more generally. The fact is that this phenomenon exists, and moreover, as I will explain later in this book, orthodox conservation doctrine and policy has not and cannot accommodate this natural human experience without changes. For all purposes and intents, the three-quarters of built heritage conservation practice that is driven by policy sidelines or ignores the possibility that one reason people find old or historic places meaningful is because they are full of magic and charm.

One can also find much older examples, prior to World War II, where laypeople, preservation architects, and historians refer to old buildings and places in magical and charming terms, relating the emotional experience of the place with its perceived physical age. It is obligatory to mention John Ruskin (1849, p. 304) here, long considered the godfather of built heritage conservation, who was clearly enchanted by gothic cathedrals and who referred to the physical age of buildings as "their chief charm." Similarly, Frederick Rogers (1886, p. 10), an architect, referred to the ancient Wells Cathedral more as a product of the magic of time than the mere representation of human labor. And, Alois Riegl (1903/1996), another progenitor of orthodox built heritage conservation theory, while not using words associated with magic, was, however, quite clear that the experience of age value "affected the emotions directly" in opposition to historical value, which was objective (or factual) in quality. Camilo Boito (1893, pp. 56, 205), the Italian architect credited with synthesizing a middle ground between the scrape and anti-scrape theories of the nineteenth century, recognized the magical qualities of old buildings as well as how they had a kind of spirit or soul that resided within. The argument here is that some of the founders, and their contemporaries, of orthodox built heritage conservation doctrine were writing in terms that emphasized the magical qualities of old buildings. To be sure, this phenomenon was likely in their minds as their doctrines were being developed, even if the way in which their directives manifested did not explicitly make reference to enchanted environments.

Evidence for magic and old places exists in popular media going back hundreds of years. For instance, in a *Scribner's Magazine* essay by Armistead Gordon (1923, p. 77), he attributes a long list of historical places in Virginia (USA), such as Williamsburg, the College of William and Mary, and Jamestown, with "kindling" his mind with "magic"; Gordon admits that without the associated age of these places, there would be no "magic." Similarly, the well-known English preservation architect, Sir Charles Reed Peers (1931, p. 311), is quite clear that ordinary places become charming with signs of physical age:

> An old town which shows no trace of its age in its buildings, however well designed they may be, is definitely less interesting and attractive, to any thinking person, than one which still displays the outlines of its mediaeval aspect. Time adds to most things a charm of which the eye and mind are equally conscious, and if we are not always at the pains of analyzing our admiration, and speak of beauty when we mean human interest, the quality remains and cannot be ignored.

What is remarkable about Peers's interpretation of age is that he indicates that the act of "analyzing" impairs the ability to perceive charm; or, in another sense, the logical mind has the power to destroy the emotional aspects of charm through the process of objectification. David Lowenthal (1985, p. 368) is more succinct in his similar observation that "factual fidelity may dispel some of the past's enchantment." In this way, without explicitly indicating so, Peers considers the relationship between the perception of physical age in a place with a pleasing emotional experience of something having "charm."

To be sure, the magic and charm of old places have long been fundamental reasons why people like to visit and reside and work within them. History—as objective fact—is boring, dry, and dull. When one wraps historical facts in the shroud of the imagination, history comes alive, as related by Columbia University historian William Archibald Dunning (1914, p. 220):

> Many a fact of history is like the grain of sand that intrudes within the shell of the pearl oyster. Tiny and insignificant, it is quickly lost to sight and knowledge; but about it are deposited the ensphering layers of myth and

TABLE 0.1.

Content analysis of the words "magic," "magical," "charm," and "charming" in context with historic or older places in social media

Place	Sentiment
The Headland Hotel & Spa–Newquay, Wadebridge, UK	"It was such a magical old building it made me want to run around and explore like a child . . . and we did!"
Manastirea rupestra Sinca Veche, Sinca Veche, Romania	"One of my favorite places in Romania, where peace will take over your emotions and fill you with good energy and joy. This magical place is debated to be a [D]acian sanctuary, going back to centuries B.C. or an old church from the 1700s."
Chaco Culture National Historical Park, New Mexico, USA	"Chaco is a magical place. Understanding the history of Chaco and then visiting it make the hair on my arm stand up."
Torre di Bellosguardo, Florence, Italy	"A magical, historic oasis. . . . I seek out historic and unique hotels, and Torre di Bellosguardo is certainly at the top of my list. It is an experience to stay here, and well worth the splurge. It is a glorious trip back in time."
Fort House Museum, Waco, TX	"A charming place full of history. I am happy to have gone and visited that charming little museum downtown Waco. Inside, one feels in a past century as the decor and the furniture are well organized to introduce visitors to the Waco early history."
The Citadel, Damascus, Syria	"everything about Damascus is enchanting. the most magical place i have ever visited. . . . The street of straight runs through the old town and you will find magical experiences."
Izamal, Mexico	"Magical magestic [sic] historical place of interest. . . . I hope if you intend on experiencing magic, you will enjoy Izamal as much as we did."
Grand Hotel Villa Igiea, Palermo, Sicily, Italy	"Magical old building with so much history!"
Hollywood Cemetery, Richmond, Virginia, USA	"Strolling through Hollywood cemetery is truly magical."
La Guerida, Havana, Cuba	"Amazing Visual and Emotional experience. Charming location. The restaurant is in an old, arty building in Vedado area. . . . The old stairways and the broken entrance is very charming and it is not easy to put into words."
The Courtyard Kells, Kells, Ireland	"The courtyard is an absolutely magical place from the moment you get out of your car. . . . I cannot recommend this place enough, you will . . . get lost in the magic."
Port of Charlestown, Charlestown, Nevis	"Charming History. It is a quaint town with a lot of pirate history. The buildings look original and you can also catch the ferry to St. Kitts."
The Dome, Edinburgh, Scotland	"Wonderfully magical old building, takes you back a few eras."
Old Nessebar, Bulgaria	"Charming historical town. Old Nessebar is a charming place with narrow streets. There is love, romance and history in the air."
Dar Finn, Fes, Morocco	"We had a wonderful time at Dar Finn, magical old building filled with history, exquisite architecture and detail from a bygone era."
Wizards Thatch at Alderley Edge, Liverpool, UK	"[The proprietors] have done an amazing job restoring this magical old building and you actually imagine a wizard at work in its wonky old rooms."

legend till a glimmering treasure is produced that excites the mightiest passions of men. Under the charm of its beauty, art, religion, civilization, is developed; through the lust to possess it a dynasty is overthrown, an empire falls into ruin. The historian may crush the pearl and bring to light the grain of sand; but he cannot persuade us that the sand made all the intervening history.

In a similar sense, historical places also come alive to people through the imagination and the charming qualities associated with the vicarious experience of old places. This unique quality of old places has long been recognized and discussed in a variety of literature through the past several centuries. An early twentieth-century example is from Princeton University historian Julian P. Boyd (1938, pp. 33–34). In discussing the interpretation of history through the built environment, he emphasizes the importance of the emotional experience in connecting people with authentically old buildings and places:

> Let us forget the idea that history is a dull recording of dates and names, that it can be taught only in books. Here we have history before us, instinct with all the charm and feeling of living personalities. These ancient buildings of ours, no less than written documents, are the materials by which, through the alembic of time and a common experience, we may identify ourselves with our ancestors and their history. We have before us, scattered all over the country, an incomparable agency for educating ourselves in our past. History, as most of us learned it in school, can be a dull and painful experience. But this new method which we are privileged to employ for ourselves and our children, is nothing short of entrancing. Moreover, it is tremendously effective. Who can stand in the library of Ralph Waldo Emerson and not feel his calm and genial presence—and who can forget the experience so easily as he could forget anything that he might read about Emerson?

Nineteenth century literature, in particular, teems with stories of visits to old places where one can stand in the footsteps of some great historical person and, through this vicarious experience, make a direct connection to the past. These places are frequently referred to as "hallowed ground" and endowed with a unique kind of time travel magic as the Rev. John Chelwode Eustace (1813, pp. 567–568; original author's emphasis) relates:

> Nothing can more strongly shew [*sic*] the commanding influence of genius over the minds and hearts of men in all ages and climes than the homage which every traveler, who lists Naples, hastens to pay to the tomb of Virgil.

> To a classical scholar this is a scene of enchantment, and we should have but an ill opinion of that man's taste and affections, who was not enchanted with the scene. It is hallowed ground, and so it will be *felt* by every man who has the nerves to feel. Those who have no nerves, on which *the genius of the place* can breathe any of its inspiration, will perhaps laugh at the idea that the heart should vibrate with more pleasure or more regret at the tomb of Virgil than at that of a ploughman or a parish clerk. But it is vain to attempt to reason men into feelings which the coarse structure of their frame, or cold nature of their temperament will not permit them to entertain. What is felt on these occasions is a spontaneous excitement from within, rather than the effect of argument from without.

What is critical to point out in Eustace's passage is that exposure to the "enchantment" of hallowed ground is a deeply emotional experience that requires dismissal of detached objectivity; to be sure, in his reference to the *genius loci* of the place, the reader has a sense that hallowed ground contains a literal spirit of someone from the past: magic indeed. Moreover, Eustace accurately captures how these emotional experiences catalyzed by old places are spontaneous, a psychological phenomenon that I will explore in depth in chapter 2.

More commonly, especially toward the latter half of the nineteenth century, the magic of hallowed ground was most closely associated with patriotism, both in the United States as well as Canada. More than sixty years after Eustace's writing, at an Ohio Medical Society meeting at Put-in-Bay Island, Ohio (USA), Dr. A. H. Agard (1875, p. 7) spoke of how their meeting took place on the enchanted ground of patriots who gave their lives in defense of liberty:

> Gentlemen, we meet here to-day upon hallowed ground, environed by consecrated waters; upon ground rendered immortal in history by successful deeds of heroism, done in a noble cause deeds so far-reaching, that we, living a half century away, and in the full enjoyment of their fruits, can scarcely appreciate their worth to the country, which they largely helped to develop; their worth to the cause of civil liberty, which they served to establish, both here and abroad, will be acknowledged with feelings of gratitude, while we have a country, and will be recognized by patriotism everywhere, so long as oppression is known, and there are found patriots to resist its encroachments. It should draw out aspirations for the development of a truer manhood; strengthen and ennoble the purposes of life, and elevate all its aims to stand here on this hallowed spot, so sacred to the

cause of our national independence, and nurse in the heart, the memory of the heroes, who so struggled here for the right, that their achievements became a bright epoch in our nation's history, and threw an unfading halo of glory over all these charmed and enchanting surroundings.

Agard claims that simply standing on such magical, hallowed ground could make one a better person, able to resist oppression and truer to the great ambition of an ennobled life. This is essentially the same argument made by Wendell Phillips, a well-known orator and abolitionist, when he argued for the preservation of the Old South Meeting House in Boston (Committee on Federal Relations 1878, p. 9). Similarly, the argument for creating King Edward Park in Cove Fields, Quebec, rested on the ability of the ground hallowed by "Celtic blood" in the Battle of the Plains of Abraham to communicate its patriotic message regardless of the fact that a rifle factory had irrevocably changed the contour and appearance of the original battlefield (Langelier, Tach, & Wood, 1906). What is curious, in a contemporary light, is that these arguments for historic preservation relied much more on recognizing the quality of the spirit of the place than in defining and documenting physical fabric.

DO "MAGICAL" AND "CHARMING" PLACES EXIST OUTSIDE OF COLONIZED CONTEXTS AND WHITE MATERIAL CULTURE?

To be sure, because highly educated White men from Europe and America developed orthodox built heritage conservation doctrine and policy (see chapter 3), significant parts of this book speak from the perspective of the colonizer and the dominance of White material culture. But, it is essential to emphasize the perspectives that were omitted, which include historically marginalized groups, such as African American people, Asian American people, Latinx people, and Indigenous people, not only in the United States, but across the globe. How does "magic" and "charm" in relation to older places manifest in these contexts? While the full scope of this endeavor is outside the scope of this book, it is still important to provide this context.

In the field of heritage conservation, professionals who work with Indigenous peoples often state the necessity for the respect of local knowledge and customs; to be sure, the desire for diverse perspectives are often an important part of practice and are reinforced by many organizations and institutions (although certainly not universally). Yet, quite often, when these professionals encounter traditions, such as magic, that are not "normal" from the perspective of the colonizer, their response is to try and reduce these meanings into objective facts that are easier to digest within the professional expert's own cultural traditions. And, indeed, this is most readily manifest through the US National Park Service's (NPS's) Bulletin 38, which directs professionals, who are assessing the historical significance of places important to Indigenous cultures, to translate local knowledge into the objective knowledge expected by Western science (Parker & King, 1992). Byrne, Brockwell, and O'Connor (2013, p. 9) explain how this treatment might manifest in practice, especially within religious places, where magic is not an accepted part of the conventional expert's worldview:

> Conservation scientists tend to focus on the "rational" elements of popular religion in places like Thailand; they appear to be uncomfortable with the magical and supernatural dimension of religion. Byrne [the first author] suggests this represents a projection onto non-Western popular religion of the secular-rationalist "disenchanted" worldview that has been predominant in the West since the Protestant Reformation and the Enlightenment.

For instance, in Laos, when an ancient temple was abandoned and decayed, local people began to believe that the place was inhabited by spirits (known as *phii*). These spirits guarded the ruins from desecration, but they also served as a powerful disincentive to intervene in the continuing decay of the site (Karlström, 2013, p. 148). Western conservationists wanted to excavate, document, and restore the site back to use, but local people hesitated for fear that the *phii* might retaliate. In this kind of situation, it is all too common for the Western, objective perspective to colonize local knowledge and disempower local people. In this specific case, however, at Viengkham, there was compromise and the ruined temple was kept to "protect the prestige of the village and its residents [as] empowered and magic objects" (Karlström, 2013, p.148).

According to Wöss (1992), in Japan, three-quarters of all teenagers believe that ghosts are real, which may be related to the prevalence of the Shinto religion in this country. A core belief of Shinto is that spirits (called *kami*), from various malevolent and benevolent forces of nature, exist in many places and are accessed in shrines. In this way, a shrine is considered to be "the place where the spirit of Kami can be contained" (Yamakage, 2006, p. 80). Many of these shrines are some of the oldest wooden buildings in the world, dating back nearly 1,000 years. Religious sites, such as these, seem to often be associated with connotations of magic, including the idea that "spirits" are somehow embedded in the fabric of the place. Considering that many non-Abrahamic religions are equally as ancient, their related sites of practice are often quite old as well. What is not clear, from the literature, is whether the age of these places is somehow connected with the perception of magic or whether this correlation might simply be coincidental.

Another example of magic and place comes from the Marquesas Islands (Donaldson, 2018), whose indigenous people have lived there since 1,000 A.D. The Marquesans believe that certain ancient places have *tapu* or sacred meanings conveyed by the spirits that inhabit these areas. These places have *mana* or a kind of spiritual power that can be either benevolent or malevolent; a person can use this power for good or ill. On these islands are the ancient stone ruins, called *paepae*, of houses and ceremonial buildings where people used to live and practice their cultural beliefs. The Marquesans often fear these places because of the association of malevolent spirits with these *paepae*, but not always, as such places can be associated with belonging and identity. Emily Donaldson (2018, p. 15) describes how a Marquesan knows that a place has *tapu* because

> you get goose bumps; your hair stands on end; you feel a weight on your shoulders or back; your head feels like it is growing large or heavy; or you hear mysterious voices, sounds, or a strange, phantom rooster call.

These embodied descriptions of magical places are surprisingly similar across cultures and supported in my own research in Charleston, South Carolina (USA; see chapter 2).

Similarly, in Bolivia, traditional communities are understood to have their own *wak'a*, or spirit, that is embedded in the fabric of the community (Mamani-Bernabé, 2015). To be sure, wherever one looks, the supernatural's relationship with old places is a part of cultural traditions across the globe, including various traditional cultural groups representing Native Americans (Basso, 1996; Milholland, 2010), Africans (Parrinder, 2002), Afro-Caribbeans (Murrell, 2010), and Indonesians (Forshee, 2006).

In the United States, people with minoritized racial or ethnic identities frequently use the words "charm" and "magic" to describe the older communities in which they live. For instance, a participatory project in Brownsville,

Texas (USA), focused on the "magic moments" that older places instilled in people so as to create a "magical, and just future where Black people, culture, and spaces matter and thrive" (Osore, 2020, p. 146). In African American communities, the "charm" of historical neighborhoods can be both a positive asset and a threat to these places' demographics, such as when Charles Whitaker (2001, p. 142) points out that the "charm" of the "historical architecture" of Harlem, New York, which has long had a large African American population, is under threat from gentrification. And, in my research on the Latinx community living and working in Allentown, Pennsylvania (USA), many of the people I interviewed described the older buildings with words such as "charm" and how the places they experienced were "magical" because of their age (Wells et al., 2016).

Public Preservation Policy and Diversity, Equity, and Inclusion (DEI)

Throughout this book, I will discuss issues around diversity, equity, and inclusion (DEI) in relation to paid work in the historic preservation field, especially as they relate to preservation policy. This theme is associated with the overarching goal of exploring ways to make public preservation policy more responsive to the needs, perceptions, and values of the public through bottom-up, grassroots approaches that elevate the value of local knowledge on par with the knowledge of conventional heritage experts.

While many fields lack the same level of racial and ethnic diversity as the American population, compared to other fields, historic preservation is notable for its substantial lack of racial and ethnic diversity (Wells, 2021):

- About 1% of the people who work in the historic preservation field have a minoritized racial or ethnic identity;
- According to the US Department of Education (using standardized US census categories), 1.0% of college students are American Indian, 2.3% are Asian, 2.8% are African American, and 6.4% are Latino.
- A similar lack of racial and ethnic diversity exists for tenure-track faculty with at least a 50% teaching appointment in historic preservation degree programs.

In a discussion of DEI work in historic preservation, it is essential to begin with an overview of what the work of "historic preservation" actually is, to avoid inevitable stereotypes and unfounded assumptions. The fact is that more than 70% of the paid work in the historic preservation field, in the United States, directly relates to implementing rules and regulations, as required by local, state, and federal laws; and, more than 95% of this regulatory work consists of environmental review (e.g., Section 106 review) at the federal and state levels and design review at the local level (e.g., private property owners obtaining permission to make changes to a listed historic building; Wells, 2018). Of the remaining 30% of paid work in historic preservation, only about 10% addresses the interpretation (and associated documentation) of historic buildings and sites, yet it is this latter area, especially outside the context of public policy (i.e., in the private and nonprofit sectors), which has received the most attention.

For instance, it has become increasingly expected that when visiting a historic site, a visitor will learn how the lives of historically marginalized people intersected with the history of the site. Examples of this include the National Trust for Historic Preservation's emphasis on interpreting the lives of enslaved African Americans, including opening formerly closed areas of historic sites for public visitation, such as the rooms in which enslaved people slept and worked (NTHP, n.d.). Another equally important effort, which more readily overlaps with public policy, is local, state, and federal governments' efforts to encourage the revision and submission of new nominations for historic properties to recognize the excluded histories of marginalized peoples. An example of this work is the NPS's "Underrepresented Communities" grant that provides funding to increase the diversity represented in National Register of Historic Places nominations (NPS, n.d.).

But, to date, the way in which governmental entities have addressed the diversity deficit in historic preservation has largely been limited to this interpretation of historic sites and documentation, such as encouraging more diverse nominations for historic places. While these efforts are certainly not unimportant, there has been little work on exploring, much less making, changes to public policy in relation to DEI that are directly relevant to the 70% of paid preservation stemming from environmental review and design review.

For a sample of what DEI work looks like in relation to public preservation policy that does focus on environmental review, one of the few examples is the National Conference of State Historic Preservation Officers (NCSHPO) report on recommended changes to federal historic preservation policy (NCSHPO, 2023). An important recommendation this report makes is to change the NPS's policy guideline for the evaluation of the "historical integrity" of vernacular buildings and places. This is an important issue because the majority of historic places of importance to people with minoritized racial and ethnic identities are vernacular (e.g., not high style; not primarily valuable for their aesthetics). The net effect of the current public preservation policy is to exclude far more buildings and places associated with marginalized groups from being historically significant compared to places associated with White people, who have historically tended to be wealthier. As of mid-2024, however, the NPS has not responded to the content of this report and has not, at least publicly, considered revisions to this or other related preservation policies. As of this date, the NPS has undertaken no public-facing work addressing how public preservation policies impact DEI beyond increasing representation in interpretation and documentation; potential changes to core policies, such as the National Register of Historic Places criteria and the Secretary of the Interior's Standards remain unexplored, yet these policies embody centuries of bias that this book explains, in detail, especially in chapter 3.

The dominance of policy-based practice in the paid work of historic preservationists is an important reason why, instead of focusing on how sites are interpreted or nominations are written, this book emphasizes preservation doctrines. Preservation doctrines are the foundation of public preservation policy, and by exploring their genesis, we can begin to understand the innate bias that underpins all public preservation policy. Thus, rather than accepting public preservation policy as unbiased and that there are no significant structural issues—which is the perspective many preservation practitioners and academics appear to have taken—this book undertakes a structural analysis, starting with fundamental ideas that form public preservation policy and how these ideas fail to represent the way in which the majority of Americans perceive, experience, and value the older built environment. Moreover, as is explored in chapter 3, preservation doctrine, and the public policy that resulted from this doctrine, appears to have, in part, been developed to intentionally sustain White supremacy; it is therefore likely that this intended structure is still operating in the present because, in the United States, the doctrines and resulting rules stemming from these doctrines have been largely unaltered for a half century or more. While increasing diversity and inclusion in the interpretation and documentation of historic places is sorely needed, the elephant in the room—public policy that sustains injustice through environmental review and design review—still needs to be recognized and addressed.

BRINGING IT TOGETHER: THE PURPOSE OF THIS BOOK AND WHAT IT WILL COVER

What are we, then, to make of these case studies of the magic associated with older places? When one looks at the entirety of people's experiences, across the globe, a homogeneity emerges where many people believe in the magic of older places, independent of cultural context—a characteristic that strongly implies that there may be a psychological phenomenon at work. While the chief way that this experience manifests is through a belief in spirits (or ghosts) that inhabit landscapes, buildings, and ruins (e.g., Franz, 2021; Holloway, 2010; Jawer et al., 2020; Wells, 2010), there are many other ways the magic of older places can manifest. But the key characteristic of the magic of older places is the *affective experience* of being in older places, or, in another sense, "Being Affected by Old Places" (BAOP). The logical conclusion, therefore, is that perhaps the experience of magic and charm in relation to old places may be a universal human characteristic, more rooted in individual psychology than cultural meanings. To be sure, I make no claims of generalizability in my observations; I only state that among all cultures that I have looked at across the globe, there always appears to be *some* people who experience the magic of old places in very similar ways. I do not purport to know what percentage of people have this experience in various contexts, nor is this essential to establish the premise of this book, which is that some people have magical experiences catalyzed by being in old places.

Exploring this experience through a psychological lens, however, opens a new chapter in critical heritage studies, which, as a field of study, has largely failed to incorporate this social science perspective in its work. Thus, understanding the magic of old places is only one aspect of the psychology of senescent environments. Because few people have taken this path, my endeavor is a wide-open one, but I have chosen this rather narrow focus on the perception of magic and charm in old places because I think it forms not only the core of why many people believe old places are important, but offers an intriguing way to manage the authenticity of place.

Orthodox built heritage conservation doctrine and public policy approach authenticity through a fabric-based perspective. Critical heritage studies looks at this kind of authenticity through an anthropological and sociological lens, focused on discourse and the use and abuse of power. The psychology of senescent environments instead approaches authenticity as personal experience; in this sense, what is historically "authentic" *feels real* to the individual who experiences a place. To be sure, none of these perspectives would exist without a desire to understand *from* practice and to *change* practice. One of the most powerful ideas to come from a critique of built heritage conservation practice is Laurajane Smith's (2006, pp. 29–30) "Authorized Heritage Discourse" (AHD), which frames practice in terms of who has power and how it is used. The AHD describes how

> the proper care of heritage, and its associated values, lies with the experts, as it is only they who have the abilities, knowledge and understanding to identify the innate value and knowledge contained at and within historically important sites and places. This is an embedded assumption within the discourse that has a legacy in antiquarian understandings of knowledge and material culture. Principally, it is architects, historians and archaeologists who act as stewards for the past, so that present and future publics may be properly educated and informed about its significance.

The AHD is therefore based on the connoisseurship of rare heritage objects whose values and meanings are defined by the dominant professional social group who have long been highly educated, Eurocentric, White males, as I will discuss in chapter 3. Because this group controls the meanings of heritage, they also control the nature of discourse about heritage such that the values of laypeople are often unintentionally "sidelined" (Smith, 2006, p. 106). In other words, in order for laypeople to be understood by heritage experts, they must use the language and meanings of heritage conservation doctrine and associated rules and regulations or else risk being delegitimized (King, 2009).

The AHD is the basis of the need for this book: the meanings and values of the public, at large, have been sidelined in deference to expert rule. Thus, we have a system whereby built heritage conservation is performed primarily to benefit architectural historians, historians, and archaeologists, but not the public, even though the laws, rules, and regulations make claims to the contrary in their preambles (Wells, 2017a). To be sure, the idea that historic places can be significant for their association with magic and charm is patently heretical in many conservation circles (cf. Perry, 1935; Weeks & Jandl, 1996). In essence, this book is about a new discourse to, in effect, sideline expert rule through an "unauthorized discourse" on built heritage that seeks changes to orthodox doctrine and policy. In this unauthorized discourse, everyday people conceptualize and experience built heritage and cultural landscapes through imagination, and most importantly, feeling or affect.

The power of this knowledge has important and potentially profound impacts on the management of historic places and especially public policy. What if we could manage the authenticity of historic places based on how people experience and perceive this authenticity in addition to conventional, fabric-based approaches? If the purpose of built heritage conservation is to benefit humanity then should not we learn about the fundamental human experience of being in a "historic" or older place? To date, we cannot adequately answer questions about the basic psychological experience of authenticity, much less the experience of magic and charm that older places instill in people. Few people have bothered to conduct research in this area and even fewer have tried to take basic psychological principles in this area and inform conservation/preservation practice. This objective is what this book aims to achieve.

I have organized the chapters in this book in a logical, progressive order, proceeding from problem definition, to theory, informing practice with this theory, and concluding with how to change research to substantiate, inform, and drive changes to orthodox policy. Refer to Figure 0.4 for a flow chart for an overall rationale for the content and organization of this book.

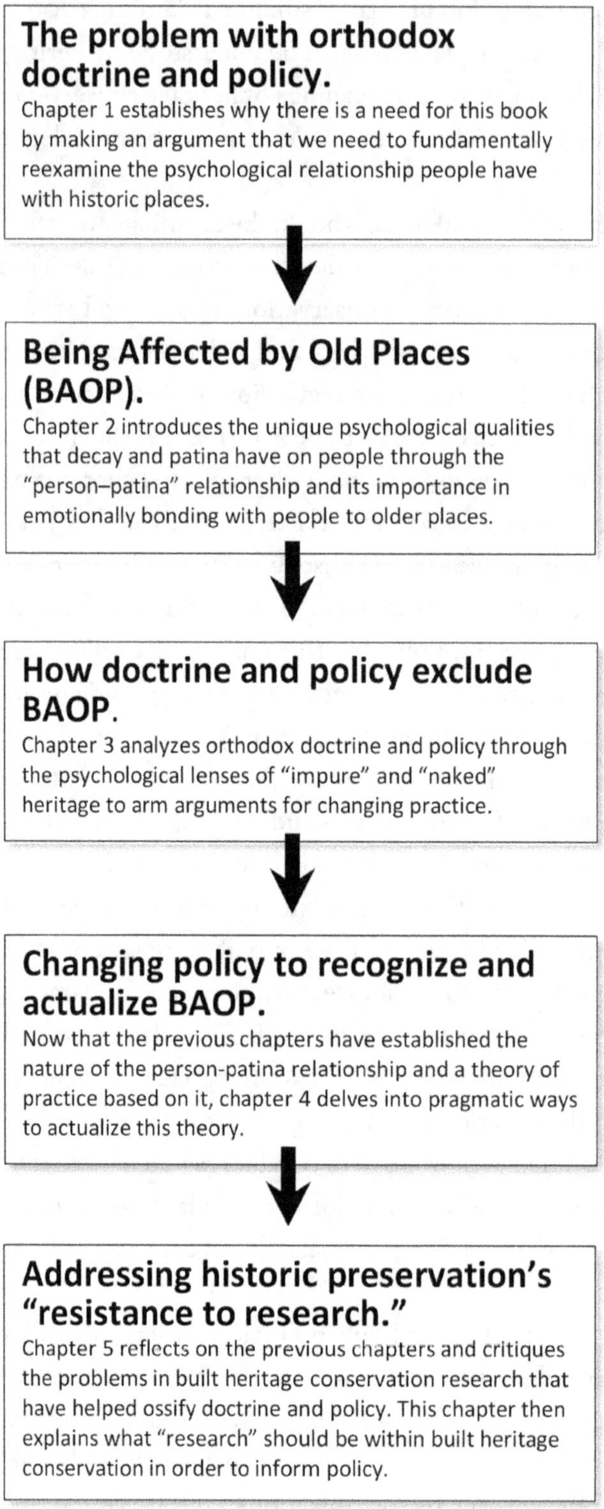

FIGURE 0.4. Rationale for the content and organization of this book

The problem with orthodox doctrine and policy.
Chapter 1 establishes why there is a need for this book by making an argument that we need to fundamentally reexamine the psychological relationship people have with historic places.

Being Affected by Old Places (BAOP).
Chapter 2 introduces the unique psychological qualities that decay and patina have on people through the "person–patina" relationship and its importance in emotionally bonding with people to older places.

How doctrine and policy exclude BAOP.
Chapter 3 analyzes orthodox doctrine and policy through the psychological lenses of "impure" and "naked" heritage to arm arguments for changing practice.

Changing policy to recognize and actualize BAOP.
Now that the previous chapters have established the nature of the person-patina relationship and a theory of practice based on it, chapter 4 delves into pragmatic ways to actualize this theory.

Addressing historic preservation's "resistance to research."
Chapter 5 reflects on the previous chapters and critiques the problems in built heritage conservation research that have helped ossify doctrine and policy. This chapter then explains what "research" should be within built heritage conservation in order to inform policy.

Chapter 1 establishes why there is a need for this book by making an argument that we need to understand the fundamental psychological relationship people have with historic places. In the early part of the twenty-first century, there are over 150 years of well-established doctrine on the identification, protection, and treatment of built heritage founded on the ideas of aristocratic, White, European men from the nineteenth century. These individuals' ideas became doctrines which, in turn, directly led to the development of orthodox policy by the mid-twentieth century that remains largely unchanged a half century later. But while conservation/preservation doctrine and scholarship on people and historic places have been evolving since the mid-twentieth century to become less focused on fabric and more focused on the meanings, values, and experiences of everyday people, orthodox built heritage conservation policy has failed to incorporate these later developments.

This chapter also discusses how, in the current century, there are four areas of scholarship that are attempting to change built heritage conservation practice. They are critical heritage studies, values-centered preservation/conservation (sometimes called values-based preservation/conservation), people-centered conservation, and human-centered conservation. Critical heritage studies is largely based on anthropology and archaeology while values-centered conservation has its origins in urban planning. People-centered conservation borrows concepts from all these areas while human-centered conservation is largely focused on the individual's relationship with old places through the lens of environmental psychology. While these strands of scholarship are promising in terms of influencing built heritage conservation practice, in reality, only planning activities not directly associated with regulatory compliance have been affected.

Lastly, chapter 1 establishes that the role of policy in defining practice is essential to the arguments laid out in this book because about 70% of built heritage conservation practice is driven by policy, which can be divided into three primary areas: identification of historical buildings and places, design review, and environmental assessments. The laws that control these activities are remarkably consistent across the United States, the United Kingdom, Australia, and Canada, which is not surprising given their collective genesis in doctrine such as the Venice Charter. These regulatory systems are based on expert rule, top-down approaches, and a colonizer mindset in which objective facts and positivism are used to displace how the public emotionally experiences places. Because of the dominance of orthodox built heritage conservation policy in driving the practice of built heritage conservation, it is necessary to change public policy in order to make practice more people- and human-centered, which is a daunting task. The first place to start, however, is with a fundamental reconsideration of the relationship people have with historic places.

Chapter 2 introduces the unique psychological qualities that decay and patina have on people through the "person–patina" relationship and its importance in emotionally bonding people to older places through BAOP. How do human beings experience the older or "historic" built environment? Orthodox built heritage conservation doctrine and policy, because of their inherent positivism, cannot answer this kind of question. One common approach, however, to understand place and affect, used since the mid-twentieth century, is a phenomenology, but places specifically defined by their physical age have escaped the attention of researchers that use this methodology. This chapter therefore explores the meanings behind age value and the individual's experience of being in a "historic" environment. Evidence suggests that age value is the core concept in understanding people's emotional attachment to historic places and that a phenomenological reduction can be useful in exploring the experience behind age value; in the absence of signs of age in the built environment, such as patina or decayed surfaces, attachment to place is less evident and more simplistic in its expression.

This chapter reveals the long history of people writing about the way that the historic environment emotionally impacts them, especially before the mid-twentieth century. The impact of environmental patina—or the way that surfaces of built environment decay and change over time—has a significant psychological effect on people, especially in terms of how the historical authenticity of a place is perceived. The decay must not be so extreme so as to evoke negative feelings of dirt, disintegration, and death, but enough decay needs to be extant so that an object is perceived as being authentically old. For many people, environmental patina is highly desirable, evoking a "peculiar beauty" (Vergara, 1999) and "ruinmood" that makes us "shudder with delight" (Ginsberg, 2004).

Chapter 2 also discusses some of my research, where I have been able to establish a statistical correlation between the appearance of decay (or, in a more positive sense, "patina") in the built environment and a person's tendency to experience a "spontaneous fantasy." Spontaneous fantasies only occur in places with the right kind and degree of decay or patina, and much as the name suggests, the person who experiences this phenomenon has no direct control over its manifestation. But, the experience of such fantasies is a highly emotional one and results in a greater degree and diversity of emotional attachment with places. There is therefore a unique psychological relationship between decay or patina in the built environment and the ability of this patina to increase people's emotional bonds to old places through spontaneous fantasies.

Chapter 3 redefines heritage conservation theory, doctrine, and policy through the psychological lenses of "impure" and "naked" heritage as a prelude to arguments for changing policy. This chapter explores the meanings and values that define the ontological and epistemological bases of orthodox built heritage conservation doctrine and policy, and in the process, reveals what has been excluded in the development of the discipline's paradigm. The key takeaway from this discussion is that, as the discipline of historical preservation developed, it acquired a strong sense of morality and a desire for purity in its practices, especially around the need for the presence of authentic building fabric and an ethical prerogative to protect this fabric from adulteration. As historic preservation doctrine, and later, policy developed, it focused on creating an increasingly purer version of an authorized heritage discourse. This process is defined through fabric purity, ontological purity, epistemological purity, and social purity. What remains are therefore the "impure" ideas, meanings, and values of built heritage, which orthodox doctrine, and later regulations, discarded.

The development of orthodox doctrine and policy cannot be separated from the people who developed these areas over the past 150 years, especially in terms of the biases that they introduced—intentionally or unintentionally. Ninety-four White European and American men are identified through a strict methodology that empirically establishes their role in creating doctrine and/or policy, with a focus on the US National Register of Historic Places criteria and the US Secretary of the Interior's Standards. As this chapter shows, not only is this a rather small group, they are defined not only through their racial identity, but also through their very high levels of education and documented racial biases.

If, as chapter 3 substantiates, most people do not value heritage places based on their objective visual and art/historical facts, then the entire premise upon which the orthodox built heritage policy is based becomes a kind of illusion. If one removes the false veil of objectivity from practice, nothing much remains underneath upon which a heritage practitioner can latch. In this scenario, heritage conservation practice becomes *naked* and therefore highly vulnerable to change and criticism. The remaining chapters will explore practice and research through this vulnerability that fundamentally challenges core, accepted notions of conservation practice.

Now that the previous chapters have established the nature of the person–patina relationship and a theory of practice based on it, chapter 4 delves into pragmatic ways to actualize this theory. This chapter focuses on the importance of community-based participatory research and environmental psychology research in transforming policy that assumes that people must help older places to policy that shows how preservation/conservation benefits, or potentially harms, people. In this chapter, I discuss the role of civil experts in coproducing policy, which assumes that the public benefits achieved through public policy are better maximized by conventional experts working, in tandem, with civil experts (e.g., residents, stakeholders) through a process that equalizes the distribution of power in recognizing the way in which BAOP should be actualized in policy.

Community workshops have been used by urban planners to inform comprehensive and small area plans and to help make decisions about what is important about heritage. Many disciplines use these community workshops as a way to engage defined groups in an open atmosphere that encourages sharing and participatory democracy. In this context, I have learned that there are some techniques that are essential to being an effective facilitator as well as a more effective historic preservation practitioner. In this chapter, I describe the process of converting community-driven recommendations into new or reformed public policy. In addition, I discuss the potential for historic preservation policy to begin to embrace intangible heritage, which it does not do today, for the most part. I also describe the potential in using a phenomenological reduction in the context of grass-roots participatory processes. The phenomenology is a well-established and reliable methodology to access the precognitive, emotional meanings associated with being in certain places. It also has close associations with gestalt psychology upon which the Italian school of architectural conservators based their theories, which then informed the Athens and Venice charters and the US Secretary of the Interior's Standards (see chapter 3). This technique is also of particular relevance when dealing with the questions of significance for preservation.

Chapter 5 describes how preservation policy has long been ossified and highly resistant to change, especially change that considers the magic of old places and the importance of this phenomenon to the public. Part of this issue is due to the field's "resistance to research" and the biases inherent in its policies. Thus, this chapter discusses the premise for centering social justice issues in historic preservation policy, as well as the need for policy research that intersects environmental psychology and the older built environment in order to inform public policy. Policy research, informed by the social sciences—especially environmental psychology—needs to be normalized in the historic preservation field; otherwise change will likely not occur. There is a role for everyone in the field to play in normalizing research in the historic preservation field, including preservation advocacy organizations. The NPS and the Advisory Council on Historic Preservation (ACHP), because of their centrality in establishing and promoting orthodox policy in the United States, should play a leading role in normalizing policy analysis as a tool in the field, potentially even providing funding for it; and preservation education programs need to be teaching the policy analysis.

Lastly, chapter 6 argues for a needed shift in public preservation policy, advocating for a more people-centered and inclusive approach. It critiques current preservation practices and calls for a focus on understanding and addressing the public's lived experiences and values. While the federal government—largely due to the NPS's intransigence—appears unable to address the contemporary needs of the public, local municipalities are uniquely empowered to lead this change; they can do so by crafting their own policies, independent of federal oversight and control. Higher education also needs to assume responsibility for how future preservation professionals are equipped to address these policy reform challenges. Ultimately, these changes will help to create more relevant and equitable public preservation policies that benefit the public and better reflects their needs and desires.

MANAGING THE MAGIC OF OLD PLACES

Not so long ago, Blaine Cliver (1992, p. 177), an influential historical architect at the NPS and former Chair of the International Centre for the Study of the Preservation and Restoration of Cultural Property (ICCROM) in Rome, warned preservation practitioners that "age can invoke fantasy, and in the fantasy is seen what is thought to be an illustrious past. Reality is lost in this desire to create a false image and a . . . romanticized vision of our past." In contrast to Cliver's appeal to objectivity, consider Robert Ginsberg's (2004, p. 317) deeply emotional description of how old places inspire "a fantasy that dances in the moonlight. Ruinmood excites wonder. Enthralled, we are captivated by inchoate feelings that come to light like moonbeams and then sink behind the shadows of primitive walls. Shudder with delight." To be sure, Cliver is dismissing normal human emotional responses in his appeal for detached objectivity, while Ginsberg fully acknowledges the emotional depth of the subjective experience of being in old places. As such, this book is a direct challenge to Cliver's warning; rather than being afraid of the relationship between the physical age of the built environment and people's fantasies, this book seeks to embrace and understand this relationship to a depth heretofore unexplored. I am not afraid to go where I have been told by preservation doctrine and policy not to go; indeed, I am emboldened to understand what has for far too long been ignored in this field: *people do perceive old places as magical*. This is a valid research area and one which deserves far greater attention than it has received to date.

Yet, how do we, as researchers, practitioners, and policy makers in built heritage conservation, reconcile the fundamental differences in Cliver's and Ginsberg's perspectives? Moreover, why is this question even important? These two questions are where I will begin my exploration of the inherent bias against normal human psychological responses to the older built environment that permeates doctrine and policy in built heritage conservation.

Works Cited

Agard, A. H. (1875). Address of welcome. In *Transactions of the thirtieth annual meeting of the Ohio State Medical Society held at Put-in-Bay, June 15th, 16th and 17th, 1875* (pp. 6-7). A. H. Poundsford & Co.

Ahn, Y.-K. (2013). Adaptive reuse and historic churches. *Preservation Education & Research*, 6, 25-40.

Al-Mansoori, M. J. (2000). Government low-cost housing provision in the United Arab Emirates. Implications of standards of construction and conditions of tenure. *Newcastle University Forum Ejournal*, 3(1), 25-30.

American Planning Association (APA). (1997). APA policy guide on historic and cultural resources. https://www.planning.org/policy/guides/adopted/historic.htm

Ander, E., Thomson, L., Noble, G., Lanceley, A., Menon, U., & Chatterjee, H. (2013). Heritage, health and well-being: Assessing the impact of a heritage focused intervention on health and well-being. *International Journal of Heritage Studies*, 19(3), 229-242.

Askari, A. H., Dola, K. B., & Soltani, S. (2014). An evaluation of the elements and characteristics of historical building façades in the context of Malaysia. *Urban Design International*, 19(2), 113-124.

Association for Critical Heritage Studies (ACHS). (2012). 2012 manifesto. https://www.criticalheritagestudies.org/history

Bajec, J. F. (2007). Architectural heritage: An important element of identity in the Karst Region of Slovenia. *Lithuanian Ethnology: Studies in Social Anthropology & Ethnology*, 7(16), 157-171.

Balslev Clausen, H., & Gyimóthy, S. (2016). Seizing community participation in sustainable development: Pueblos Mágicos of Mexico. *Journal of Cleaner Production*, 111(3), 318-326.

Basso, K. H. (1996). Wisdom sits in places: Notes on a western Apache landscape. In S. Feld & K. H. Basso (Eds.), *Senses of place* (pp. 53-90). School of American Research Press.

Berke, D. (2018). Against historic preservation: Transforming old buildings for new (sustainable) futures. *Journal of Architectural Education*, 72(2), 205-207.

Boito, C. (1893). *Questioni pratiche di belle arti; restauri, concorsi, legislazione, professione, insegnamento*. Ulrico Hoepli.

Boyd, J. P. B. (1938). The preservation of historic buildings. Pennsylvania Arts and Sciences 3(1), 32-53.

Breglia, L. (2006). *Monumental ambivalence: The politics of heritage*. University of Texas Press.

Byrne, D., Brockwell, S., & O'Connor, S. (2013). Introduction: Engaging culture and nature. In S. Brockwell, S. O'Connor, & D. Byrne (Eds.), *Transcending the culture-nature divide in cultural heritage: Views from the Asia-Pacific region* (pp. 1-12). Australian National University Press.

Cameron, C. M., & Gatewood, J. B. (2000). Excursions into the un-remembered past: What people want from visits to historical sites. *The Public Historian*, 22(3), 107-127.

Cassar, M. (2009). Sustainable heritage: Challenges and strategies for the twenty-first century. *APT Bulletin*, 40(1), 3-11.

Cliver, E. B. (1992). Revisiting past rehabilitation projects. In A. J. Lee (Ed.), *Past meets future: Saving America's historic environments* (pp. 175-180). Preservation Press.

Denhez, M. (1994). *The Canadian home: From cave to electronic cocoon*. Dundurn Press.

Denslagen, W. (2009). *Romantic modernism: Nostalgia in the world of conservation*. Amsterdam University Press.

Donaldson, E. C. (2018). Place, destabilized: Ambivalent heritage, community and colonialism in the Marquesas Islands. Oceania, 88(1), 1-21.

Dunning, W. A. (1914). Truth in history. *American Historical Review*, 19(2), 216-230.

Dyer, A. (2007). Inspiration, enchantment and a sense of wonder... can a new paradigm in education bring nature and culture together again? In P. Howard & T. Papagiannēs (Eds.), *Natural heritage: At the interface of nature and culture* (pp. 86-97). Routledge.

Eustace, J. C. (1813). A tour through Italy. *The Critical Review*, 3(6), 561-577.

Evans, G. R. (2007). *The church in the early Middle Ages*. I. B. Tauris & Co.

Forshee, J. (2006). *Culture and customs of Indonesia*. Greenwood Press.

Franz, M. K. (2021). Haunted intimacy: Spectral and vital space within a historic house museum. *Museum & Society*, 19(3), 382-394.

Frey, P., Dunn, L., & Cochran, R. (2011). *The greenest building: Quantifying the environmental value of building reuse*. National Trust for Historic Preservation.

García Vega, D., & García Roja, H. R. G. (2014). El programa "Pueblos Mágicos": Análisis de los resultados de una consulta local ciudadana El caso de Cuitzeo, Michoacán, México. *Economía y Sociedad*, 18(31), 71-94.

Garrison, Trey. (2014, May 6) Trulia: American homebuyers prefer new homes 2 to 1. *Housingwire*. https://www.housingwire.com/articles/29915-trulia-american-homebuyers-prefer-new-homes-2-to-1.

Gibson, J., Hendricks, M., & Wells, J. C. (2018). From engagement to empowerment: How heritage professionals can incorporate participatory methods in disaster recovery to better serve socially vulnerable groups. *International Journal of Heritage Studies*, 25(6), 596-610. https://doi.org/10.1080/13527258.2018.1530291

Gilderbloom, J. I., Hanka, M. J., Ambrosius, J. D. (2009.) Historic preservation's impact on job creation, property values, and environmental sustainability. Journal of Urbanism, 2(2), 83-101.

Ginsberg, R. (2004). *The aesthetics of ruins*. Rodopi.

Gordon, A. (1923). Thomas Nelson Page—An appreciation. *Scribner's Magazine,* 73(1), 75-80.

Guillén Ortiz, A. (2016). Personajes y espacios sobrenaturales en la tradición oral de Coatepec, Veracruz [Master's thesis, El Colegio de San Luis, A.C.]. Repository Colsan. http://colsan.repositorioinstitucional.mx/jspui/handle/1013/643

Handler, R. (2003). Cultural property and culture theory. *Journal of Social Archaeology*, 3(3), 353-365.

Handler, R., & Saxton, W. (1988). Dyssimulation: Reflexivity, narrative, and the quest for authenticity in "living history." *Cultural Anthropology,* 3(3), 242-260.

Harrison, R. (2013). *Heritage: Critical approaches*. Routledge.

Herzog, T. R., & Gale, T. A. (1996). Preference for urban buildings as a function of age and nature context. *Environment and Behavior*, 28(1), 44-72.

Herzog, T. R., & Shier, R. L. (2000). Complexity, age, and building preference. *Environment and Behavior*, 32(4), 557-575.

Historic England. (2014). Heritage counts 2014: The value and impact of heritage. English Heritage.

Holloway, J. (2010). Legend-tripping in spooky spaces: Ghost tourism and infrastructures of enchantment. *Environment and Planning D: Society and Space*, 28(4), 618-637.

Holtorf, C., & Schadla-Hall, T. (1999). Age as artefact: On archaeological authenticity. *European Journal of Archaeology*, 2(2), 229-247.

Internet Movie Database (IMDb). (n.d.). Search on term, "magic." https://www.imdb.com/find/?q=magic&ref_=nv_sr_sm.

Jawer, M. A., Massullo, B., Laythe, B., & Houran, J. (2020). Environmental "gestalt influences" pertinent to studies of haunted houses. *Journal of the Society for Psychical Research*, 84(2), 65-92.

Jones, S. (2009). Experiencing authenticity at heritage sites: Some implications for heritage management and conservation. *Conservation and Management of Archaeological Sites*, 11(2), 133-147.

Karlström, A. (2013). Local heritage and the problem with conservation. In S. Brockwell,

S. O'Connor, & D. Byrne (Eds.), *Transcending the culture–nature divide in cultural heritage: Views from the Asia-Pacific region* (pp. 141-156). Australian National University Press.

King, T. F. (2009). *Our unprotected heritage: Whitewashing the destruction of our cultural and natural resources*. Left Coast Press.

Koch, K. (2018). *The thin places: A Celtic landscape from Ireland to the Driftless*. Resource Publications.

Langelier, F., Tach, E. E., & Wood, W. (1906). *First report of the Quebec Landmark Commission; the subject of this report is the preservation of the Heights and Plains of Abraham*. Quebec Landmark Commission.

Levi, D. J. (2005). Does history matter? Perceptions and attitudes toward fake historic architecture and historic preservation. *Journal of Architectural and Planning Research*, 22(2), 149-159.

Logan, W. (2012). Cultural diversity, cultural heritage and human rights: Towards heritage management as human rights-based cultural practice. *International Journal of Heritage Studies*, 18(3), 231-244.

López-Levi, L. (2015). Pueblos mágicos mexicanos: magia, hechizos e ilusión. *URBS, Revista de Estudios Urbanos y Ciencias Sociales*, 5(2), 13-26.

Lowenthal, D. (1985). *The past is a foreign country*. Cambridge University Press.

Mahpour, A. (2018). Prioritizing barriers to adopt circular economy in construction and demolition waste management. *Resources, Conservation and Recycling*, 134(July), 216-227.

Mamani-Bernabé, V. (2015). Spirituality and the Pachamam in the Andean Aymara worldview. In R. Rozzi, F. S. Chapin, J. B. Callicott, S. T. A. Pickett, M. E. Power, J. J. Armesto, & R. H. May (Eds.), *Earth stewardship: Linking ecology and ethics in theory and practice* (pp. 65-76). Springer.

Mayes, T. M. (2018). *Why old places matter*. Rowman & Littlefield Publishers.

Milholland, S. (2010). In the eyes of the beholder: Understanding and resolving incompatible ideologies and languages in US environmental and cultural laws in relationship to Navajo sacred lands. *American Indian Culture and Research Journal*, 34(2), 103-124.

Minner, J., & Holleran, M. (2016). Introduction to the special issue [on historic preservation planning]. *Journal of the American Planning Association*, 82(2), 69-71.

Muñoz Viñas, S. (2005). *Contemporary theory of conservation*. Elsevier.

Murrell, N. S. (2010). *Afro-Caribbean religions: An introduction to their historical, cultural, and sacred traditions*. Temple University Press.

National Conference of State Historic Preservation Officers (NCSHPO). (2023). *A report of the National Historic Designation Advisory Committee: Recommendations for improving the recognition of historic properties of importance to all Americans*. https://ncshpo.org/wp-content/uploads/2023/04/NHDAC-Full-Report.pdf

National Trust for Historic Preservation (NTHP). (n.d.). Stories of African American cultural heritage. https://savingplaces.org/stories-of-african-american-cultural-heritage

Navarro Gamboa, M., Vazquez Solís, V., Van´t Hooft, A., & Reyes Agüero, J. A. (2019). Participación comunitaria y turismo alternativo en zonas indígenas en el contexto mexicano: cuatro estudios de caso. *El Periplo Sustentable*, 36, 7-33.

Nypan, T. (2007). Cultural heritage monuments and historic buildings as value generators in a post-industrial economy (excerpts). In P. Lehtovuori, K. Schmidt-Thomé (eds).

Economics and built Heritage—Seminar proceedings (pp. 43-50). Nordic Council of Ministers.

Osore, E. (2020). Blackspaces: Brownsville codesigning Black neighborhood heritage conservation. In Avrami, E. (Ed.), *Preservation and social inclusion* (pp. 137-146). Columbia University Press.

Otto, R. (1917). *Das heilige: Über das irrationale in der idee des göttlichen und sein verhältnis zum rationalen*. Trewendt & Granier.

Pannekoek, F. (1998). The rise of the heritage priesthood or the decline of community based heritage. Forum Journal, 12(3), 4-10.

Parker, P. L., & King, T. F. (1992). *Guidelines for evaluating and documenting traditional cultural properties*. US Department of the Interior, National Park Service.

Parrinder, E. G. (2002). *West African psychology: A comparative study of psychological and religious thought*. James Clarke & Co.

Peers, C. R. (1931). The treatment of old buildings. *RIBA Journal*, 38(10), 311-320.

Pérez-Ramírez, C. A., & Antolín-Espinosa, D. I. (2016). Programa pueblos mágicos y desarrollo local: Actores, dimensiones y perspectivas en El Oro, Mexico. *Estudios Sociales*, 25(47), 219-243.

Perry, W. G. (1935). Notes on the architecture [of Colonial Williamsburg]. *The Architectural Record*, 78(6), 363-382.

Phillips, W. (1878). *Speech of Hon. Wendell Phillips for aid in the preservation of the Old South Meeting-House [Speech to Massachusetts Legislature, Committee on Federal Relations]*. Alfred Mudge and Son.

Riegl, A. (1996). The modern cult of monuments: Its essence and its development. In N. S. Price, M. K. Talley, Jr., & A. M. Vaccaro (Eds.), *Historical and philosophical issues on the conservation of cultural heritage* (pp. 69-83). The Getty Conservation Institute. (Original work published 1903)

Rogers, F. (1886). *Specifications for practical architecture: A guide to the architect, engineer, surveyor, and builder*. Crosby Lockwood and Co.

Ruskin, J. (1849). *The seven lamps of architecture*. Smith, Elder, and Co.

Samuel, R. (1990). *The myths we live by*. Routledge.

Schofield, J. (2014). *Who needs experts? Counter-mapping cultural heritage*. Ashgate Publishing.

Secretaría de Turismo. (2020). Pueblos Mágicos de México. Gobierno de México. https://www.gob.mx/sectur/articulos/pueblos-magicos-206528

SECTUR. (2017). Guía para la integración documental Pueblos Mágicos. Secretaría de Turismo. https://www.gob.mx/cms/uploads/attachment/file/273030/Gui_a_2017_de_Incorporacio_n_2017.pdf

Silva, K. (2011). Mapping meaning in the city image: A case study of Kandy, Sri Lanka. *Journal of Architectural and Planning Research*, 28(3), 229-251.

Smith, L. (2006). *Uses of heritage*. Routledge.

Smith, L., & Campbell, G. (2015). The elephant in the room: Heritage, affect and emotion. In W. Logan, M. N. Craith, & U. Kockel (Eds.), *A companion to heritage studies* (pp. 443-460). Wiley-Blackwell.

Snyder, G. (1990). *The practice of the wild*. Counterpoint.

Sommer, U. (2009). Methods used to investigate the use of the past in the formation of regional identities. In M. L. S. Sørensen, & J. Carman (Eds.), *Heritage studies: Methods and approaches* (pp. 103-120). Routledge.

Staiff, R. (2014). *Re-imagining heritage interpretation: Enchanting the past-future*. Routledge.

US National Park Service (NPS). (n.d.). Underrepresented Communities grants. https://www.nps.gov/subjects/historicpreservationfund/underrepresented-community-grants.htm.

Uzzell, D. (2009). Where is the discipline in heritage studies: A view from environmental psychology. In M. L. S. Sørensen & J. Carman (Eds.), *Heritage studies: Methods and approaches (pp. 326–333)*. Routledge.

van der Heijden, J. (2018). Voluntary programs for low-carbon building development and transformation. In S. Wilkinson, T. Dixon, N. Miller, & S. Sayce (Eds.), *Routledge handbook of sustainable real estate*. Routledge.

van Weelden, E., Mugge, R., & Bakker, C. (2016). Paving the way towards circular consumption: Exploring consumer acceptance of refurbished mobile phones in the Dutch market. *Journal of Cleaner Production, 113*(1), 743–754.

Vergara, C. (1999). American ruins. Monacelli Press.

Waterton, E., Smith, L., & Campbell, G. (2006). The utility of discourse analysis to heritage studies: The Burra Charter and social inclusion. *International Journal of Heritage Studies, 12*(4), 339–355.

Weeks, K., & Grimmer, A. (1995). *The Secretary of the Interior's standards for the treatment of historic properties with guidelines for preservation, rehabilitation, restoration, and reconstruction of historic buildings*. US Department of the Interior, National Park Service.

Weeks, K. D., & Jandl, H. W. (1996). The Secretary of the Interior's standards for the treatment of historical properties: A philosophical and ethical framework for making treatment decisions. In S. J. Kelley (Ed.), *Standards for preservation and rehabilitation* (pp. 7–23). ASTM.

Wells, J. C. (2009). Historic preservation: Challenges to collaboration with other disciplines. In M. Chapin, J. Bissell, M. A. L'Heureux, K. D. Moore, M. Rashid, & K. Spreckelmeyer (Eds.), *Proceedings of the Environmental Design Research Association (EDRA) 40 conference: Re: The ethical design of places, Kansas City, MO, May 27–May 31* (pp. 83–91). Environmental Design Research Association.

———. (2010). Our history is not false: Perspectives from the revitalisation culture. *International Journal of Heritage Studies, 16*(6), 417–438.

———. (2015). In stakeholders we trust: Changing the ontological and epistemological orientation of built heritage assessment through participatory action research. In B. Szmygin (Ed.), *How to assess built heritage? Assumptions, methodologies, examples of heritage assessment systems* (pp. 215–265). International Council on Monuments and Sites (ICOMOS) International Scientific Committee for Theory and Philosophy of Conservation and Restoration; Romualdo Del Bianco Foundatione; Lublin University of Technology.

———. (2017a). Are we "ensnared in the system of heritage" because we do not want to escape? *Archaeologies: Journal of the World Archaeological Congress, 13*(1), 26–47.

———. (2017b). How are old places different from new places? A psychological investigation of the correlation between patina, spontaneous fantasies, and place attachment. *International Journal of Heritage Studies, 23*(5), 445–469.

———. (2018). Challenging the assumption about a direct relationship between historic preservation and architecture in the United States. *Frontiers of Architectural Research, 7*(4), 455–464.

———. (2020). Probing the person–patina relationship: A correlational study on the psychology of senescent environments. *Collabra: Psychology*, 6(1), 41.

———. (2021). 10 ways historic preservation policy supports White supremacy and 10 ideas to end it. University of Maryland, College Park faculty papers. https://doi.org/10.13016/hyol-8vgp.

Wells, J. C., & Baldwin, E. D. (2012). Historic preservation, significance, and age value: A comparative phenomenology of historic Charleston and the nearby new-urbanist community of I'On. *Journal of Environmental Psychology*, 32(4), 384-400.

Wells, J. C., Hirsch, A., Grimaldi, B. M., Pooley, K. B., & Sutherland, E. M. (2016). Latin Americans and heritage values in Allentown's 7th Street corridor. *Journal of Architectural and Planning Research*, 33(3), 181-198.

Wells, J. C., & Lixinski, L. (2017). Heritage values and legal rules: Identification and treatment of the historic environment via an adaptive regulatory framework (part 2). *Journal of Cultural Heritage Management and Sustainable Development*, 7(3), 345-363.

Whitaker, C. (2001, August). New money, new economic development, create new mood. *Ebony*, 136-142.

Williams, T. (1947). *A streetcar named desire*. New American Library.

Wöss, F. (1992). When blossoms fall: Japanese attitudes towards death and the otherworld: Opinion polls 1953-87. In R. Goodman, & K. Refsing (Eds.), *Ideology and practice in modern Japan* (pp. 72-100). Routledge.

Yamakage, M. (2006). *The essence of Shinto: Japan's spiritual heart*. Kodansha International.

Young, R. A. (2012). *Stewardship of the built environment: Sustainability, preservation, and reuse*. Island Press.

CHAPTER 1

Challenging the Authorized Discourse on Built Heritage Conservation

Why Doctrine and Policy Are Not People- or Human-Centered

INTRODUCTION

Don Norman cares a lot about people. As the head of UC San Diego's Design Lab and author of *The Design of Everyday Things*, he uses social science methods to learn the ways people interact with the objects in their world to facilitate better design (Wilson, 2017). This approach, known as "human-centered design," is common to many areas that focus on the invention of new consumer products, especially in Silicon Valley, ostensibly because easy-to-use technology is more profitable to its creators. The key to human-centered design, as William Rouse (2007, p. 5) explains, is "assuring that the concerns, values, and perceptions of all stakeholders in a design effort are considered and balanced"—an admirable goal, which is, unfortunately, rather difficult to achieve consistently. Indeed, Norman expresses discontent in the frequently top-down approach used by "traditional" designers who erroneously call their craft "human-centered"; these designers fail because they spend too much time "thinking *about* the people, which is not the same thing as using or testing *with* people" (Wilson 2017, para. 7). In a similar sense, heritage conservation pundits proclaim that we are now entering a world of "people-centered" or "values-centered" preservation/conservation, where, for the first time, practitioners should, *de rigueur*, consider the meanings of laypeople in planning processes (e.g., Gibson & Pendlebury, 2009; OWHC-AP, 2014; Silberman & Puser, 2012). There are two problems with this perspective: the first is the assumption that such a transition is actually occurring, and the second, when such an activity occurs, is to what extent and depth the meanings of laypeople are actually being considered. In the latter case, Norman's critique of design rings true for built heritage conservation, especially as it is driven by policy: we are spending too much time thinking *about* people and not enough time working *with* them, especially as individuals. And one of the fundamental reasons we fail to achieve a truly human-centered focus is due to the field's doctrinal and policy baggage of the past century.

Before proceeding, it is important to clearly differentiate what is meant by "people-centered" versus "human-centered" as they are used in this book. "People," as a plural concept, is very much based on sociocultural meanings, and as such, is most readily associated with anthropological and sociological concepts. On the other hand, the word "human" suggests the individual; therefore, something "human-centered" is rooted in psychological constructs as opposed to cultural ones. In the context of the older built environment, human-centered conservation addresses the intersection of environmental psychology with the individual's perception of and behavior in places defined by their physical age. In the broader sense, when joined with the verb "conservation," human-centered heritage conservation uses an environmental psychology perspective in the identification of what is, and is not, significant about old places. Further, human-centered conservation focuses on changes to old places that do not impair their perceived and experiential authenticity, again, defined from the perspective of environmental psychology.

ORTHODOX BUILT HERITAGE CONSERVATION DOCTRINES AND POLICY

Unique among the many fields that engage with the built environment is the depth to which doctrine has long played a primary role in built heritage conservation, architectural conservation, and historic preservation, starting with the education of students in universities and colleges. The only two bodies that address curricular standards in university degree programs are the Institute for Historic Building Conservation (IHBC) in the United Kingdom and the National Council for Preservation Education (NCPE) in the United States. The IHBC requires that educational programs provide training in all the doctrines adopted by the International Council on Monuments and Sites (ICOMOS) and in the Principles of the Conservation of

Historic Buildings (adopted by the British Standards Institution), which is in turn based on the ICOMOS doctrine known as the Venice Charter (IHBC, 2008, p. 9). Similarly, NCPE requires at least one course or module in the "history and theory of preservation." A survey of available syllabi from the 44 NCPE-associated bachelor's and master's programs reveals that the most commonly required textbooks in classes that address preservation/conservation philosophy are Robert Stipe's *A Richer Heritage* (2003) and Tyler, Ligibel, and Tyler's *Historic Preservation: An Introduction to Its History, Principles, and Practice* (2009). Both of these books treat doctrine, such as the Secretary of the Interior's Standards (US regulation 36 CFR 68), which is, in turn, based on the Venice Charter (ICOMOS, 1964), as received wisdom, questioning neither their aims or goals nor introducing the reader to the historical genesis of doctrine and law. The critical point to make here is that within the field of built heritage conservation, the two bodies that maintain curricular standards treat mid-twentieth century doctrine, such as the Venice Charter, and each country's interpretation of this charter, as received wisdom.

A survey of these built heritage educational programs also shows that they tend to emphasize the theories of highly educated, European, White men who wrote sometime between the mid-nineteenth and mid-twentieth centuries, such as John Ruskin, William Morris, Eugène Viollet-le-Duc, Camillo Boito, Alois Riegl, Paul Philippot, Cesare Brandi, and Giovanni Carbonara. (For more information on the authors of orthodox doctrine, see chapter 3.) While it is true that these individuals wrote some of the first philosophical examinations of the treatment of tangible heritage, and thus, are part of the important historical continuum that students should learn about in the field, again, the issue is the often uncritical way in which their ideas are introduced and discussed today. A more critical examination of these authors reveals a nearly total emphasis on fabric and a delegitimization of intangible heritage and arguments founded in scientism, positivism, connoisseurship, and colonialism (see Emerick, 2014; Muñoz Viñas, 2005; Sauvegrain, 2001; Swenson, 2013; Wells, 2007). To expect otherwise would be naive, however, because these men represented *au courant* thinking in their day. Only with the perspective of critical theory in the twenty-first century can we see the lopsided qualities of their rationalistic arguments. But the key point here is that higher education is not taking a twenty-first-century perspective on the doctrinal origins of the field, especially the first official doctrines of built heritage conservation—the Athens Charter (1931) and the Venice Charter (1964)—that were highly influenced by these individuals, some of whom directly participated in the writing of these documents.

The Athens Charter (Congress in Athens, 1931) was the outcome of a meeting in Athens, Greece, in 1931 associated with the International Committee on Intellectual Cooperation that was part of the League of Nations. Chaired by Jules Destrée, President of the International Museums Office, 120 mostly White, European men attended sessions in which experts presented papers on various approaches to the conservation of historical monuments in Athens, Greece (Jokilehto, 1999, p. 284). The Athens Charter, which represented the consensus of the participants, has a strong, central focus on the retention of fabric from previous periods of time and allowing restoration as an exception, rather than the rule. There is a strong appeal to the use of science both in the conservation process, but also in decision making. Indeed, recently uncovered archival documents provide evidence that objective, scientific approaches dominated the discussion, which is epitomized by the presentation given by Paul Léon, the Director General of Fine Arts of France, on the way that conservation work in France had become more scientific and "experimental" in its approach by the turn of the twentieth century (Ohba 2017, p. 101). According to Go Ohba, the entire second session of the conference focused on debating the "development of anti-unscientific interventions to conserve monuments in their original state"; in other words, interventions that could not be justified through scientific approaches and science in general, such as broader perspectives from the humanities or social sciences, were deemed to be unacceptable. To be sure, the men presenting at the Athens conference were heavily influenced by a bias against stylistic restorations that embraced the public consciousness in the late nineteenth and early twentieth centuries (e.g., "Anti-Restoration Movement," 1878; Editor, 1908; "Restoration of Paul Revere House," 1914; "Restoration of Westminster Hall," 1885; "Restoration of White House," 1903), so, in many ways, the Athens Charter is quite understandably a product of its time.

Similarly, the Venice Charter (ICOMOS, 1964)—born in the period of high Modernism—promotes science as central to the endeavor of conservation. This meeting was an outgrowth of an earlier UNESCO symposium in 1957 that convened architects and conservators, which later catalyzed an invitation by the Italian government to bring together these kinds of professionals in Venice in May of 1964. More than 600 people attended, again mostly representing White men from Europe, although there was significant representation from North America. The outcome of this conference was the Venice Charter, which was clearly conceived as a logical extension to the earlier Athens Charter (Jokilehto, 1999, p. 288). This doctrine has achieved great success in colonizing the world with the need for scientific conservation, expert rule, and making sure that buildings do not "lie" because it is the basis for the majority of contemporary public policy for built heritage conservation the world over (Erder, 1994; Hudgins, 2012; Jokilehto, 1999, p. 289; Silva, 1994; Starn, 2002; Wells, 2007). The need to be truthful is embodied in article 9 of the charter, which demands that any new fabric added to a building must not be misconstrued as being older than it really is—i.e., the need to differentiate the "old" from the "new." The premise upon which this article is based is that it is possible to make buildings lie, or convey what has become known as a "false sense of history" (Weeks & Jandl, 1996, p. 19). It is important to note, however, that the basic premise here is illogical because it dubiously assumes that a "false" object can exist; in reality objects always experience events (or history) over time, no matter how strenuously a person may try to alter the historical trajectory of said object (Muñoz Viñas, 2005, pp. 91-92). Instead, when interpreted in light of its inherent positivism, article 9 of the Venice Charter actually directs us to select and enforce one "true" way of interpreting the past through a design intervention while discarding other possibilities that may be equally as acceptable to disparate constituencies. As such, this is not science at work, but rather a subjective interpretation, which denies the possibility that there are multiple, and potentially equally valid, ways that a building can exist while still conveying its historical authenticity (Wells, 2007).

Thus, there are two key takeaways from the Athens Charter and the Venice Charter. The first is that both appeal to the singular value of "science"—or more accurately, scientism—and expert rule rather than the possibility of understanding and then using the public's values in defining the treatment of historical monuments. In this sense, they serve as top-down instruments to oppress viewpoints contrary to the professionals who drafted these doctrines, viewpoints which are, in fact, held by the majority of the human race. To be sure, they are documents of their time, embedded in the positivism of modernism, and they embody what Mikael Stenmark (2017,

p. 15) refers to as a complete faith that "science alone can solve all of our . . . problems." What is problematic in the twenty-first century is that the majority of global built heritage conservation practice that occurs is still based on a mid-twentieth century ontology that rejects pluralism and meanings that are not Western, White, or male in origin (Wells, 2007; Wells, 2015). And equally important is that these doctrines deny the possibility of community participation or, indeed, any kind of a ground-up approach to the conservation of built heritage.

The second key takeaway from the Athens Charter and the Venice Charter is their immutability, continued relevance to practice, and the pseudo-religious quality they have achieved in relatively short order, especially in regard to the second document. Cevat Erder (1994, p. 24) was especially prescient when, in 1977, he wrote that "the [Venice] Charter should be preserved as it stands, as an historic monument itself." In 1983, Roland Silva (1994, p. 40) declared that the Venice Charter was the equivalent of the "Magna Carta for the safeguarding of the monumental heritage of mankind for the sake of the generations of the present and the future [and] the ten commandments of conservation." Considering the era in which these statements were made, it is little wonder that orthodox policy regarding the preservation, conservation, and restoration of historic buildings, since the late 1960s, is inexorably based on the Venice Charter. For instance, in the United States, W. Morton Brown, III, the author of the Secretary of the Interior's Standards, which is the most widely required regulation that controls historic building interventions at both the national and local levels, is quite transparent in his use of this charter when he drafted the rule in 1976 (Hudgins, 2012). In sum, in the twenty-first century, the majority of local, regional, and national policy across the world's countries that directly addresses the intervention in the fabric of historic buildings remains highly derivative of the Venice Charter and its embrace of high-Modernism, positivism, and colonialism (Hardy, 2008; Semes, 2009); this includes many non-Western countries, such as India (Krishna, 2014), China (Zhao, 2006), and Japan (Akagawa, 2015), in which the Venice Charter's concepts are antithetical to local values and traditions and constitute what David Byrne (2012, p. 295) refers to as "a kind of twentieth-century soft imperialism which secured the West's global supremacy and which was a substitute for the gunboat diplomacy of an earlier era."

Case Study: The Dominance of the Venice Charter and European Values in the Heritage Policies of East Asia and Africa

While the colonization of East Asia and Africa by European countries is a well-known phenomenon, less effort has been spent by scholars investigating how traditional understandings of heritage were also colonized in these places, especially through public policy. Sometimes this colonization of heritage was imposed by external force, such as when colonial leaders in Africa created European-like heritage laws and regulations that are still in force, while in other cases, such as in Japan and China, some scholars and leaders chose to elevate Western heritage conservation theory and policy over traditional practice.

A useful place to start this exploration is with the concept of history, which is not universal. Scholars in Europe developed a positivistic (i.e., fact-based) concept of history based on continual, linear progress with a clear beginning, middle, and end; the past was assumed to be more primitive and unordered while the future symbolized progress and increased structure. This understanding is so basic that it is an innate and unquestioned part of Western culture. In China, on the other hand, the traditional view of "history" is cyclical, based on repeating patterns of building/collapse and order/disorder as exist in nature, such as the seasons (e.g., winter/summer). History existed as a way to learn societal lessons rather than as a manifestation of progress (Edwin, 1965). Thus, learning from the cycles of history was understood as an important way to uphold social order, ethical behavior, and filial piety (Wills, 1994) rather than to explain cause and effect. Traditional concepts of history in Japan are similar, with additional emphases on the role of mythology in explaining the cycles of history (Brownlee, 1997).

China's and Japan's heritage laws, starting in the twentieth century, adopted the Western concept of positivistic history to describe which buildings, places, and structures were of historical significance (Ho et al., 2014). As in European, and later, US practice, historical assets are considered significant for the facts associated with them related to historical events, people, scientific progress, and artistic achievements. The similarities between these countries' heritage laws in this regard and European heritage policy is obvious. In the later part of the twentieth century, as heritage experts from China and Japan started working with Western colleagues through ICOMOS and other international organizations, the use of Western frameworks for historical significance increased, especially in regard to World Heritage.

China and Japan have a well-established practice of "stylistic restoration" going back millennia, long before contact with Western peoples and their heritage theories. As opposed to European heritage conservation theory, in which the protection of material authenticity is of utmost importance, in many Asian countries, traditionally, conservators believe that the ability of a building or place to convey its intended meaning was of the greatest importance (Chung, 2005). In this sense, traditional Chinese and Japanese conservation practice is rooted in the protection of intangible, rather than tangible, heritage.

During the twentieth century, heritage conservation practitioners and academics from China and

FIGURE I.1. (*above*) World Heritage site of Macau, China, whose authenticity is addressed through the lens of European values (photo by author)

FIGURE I.2. (*right*) Seventeenth-century temple located in a World Heritage district in Hong Kong, China, whose authenticity is addressed through the lens of European values (photo by author)

Japan increasingly worked with their Western counterparts through international organizations, such as ICOMOS, and, through this interaction, these practitioners and academics adopted European ideas around authenticity and historical significance and, in the process, displaced traditionally accepted ways in which older buildings and places were conserved. Xi Chen (2016, p. 355), who has studied this phenomenon extensively in China, concludes that "Chinese architectural conservationists critically accepted, applied, and reflected on the Western conservation theory represented by the Venice Charter" while deprecating traditional Chinese concepts for the treatment of heritage buildings and places. Public heritage policy in China also incorporates Western conservation ideas through the adoption of the Venice Charter, especially in relation to World Heritage (Yang, 2021).

As with China, Japan is also a participant in the World Heritage Convention, and as such, is committed to using the Venice Charter in the management of these kinds of sites. But, as practitioners in China have found, the material authenticity tenets in the Venice Charter are at odds with traditional Japanese practice, as Knut Einar Larsen (1994, p. 62) explains:

> A major tenet in Japanese preservation thinking since 1897, when the government enacted the country's first law for the protection of cultural properties, has been to consider the original state of a historic building, or the most significant stage in its development, as the ideal aim for the restoration of that building. Consequently, structural or other members which have been added to a historic building during its life-time, are considered to be of lesser importance compared to original material. This view is fundamentally incompatible with international preservation standards which emphasize that the evaluation of the authenticity of a historic building does not limit consideration to original form and structure, but includes all subsequent modifications and additions over time, which in themselves possess artistic or historic value.

In Japan, although public policy can be lenient in terms of the treatment of historic buildings (as long as they are not listed as World Heritage), the professionals who are required to undertake this work are well educated in Western heritage theory, including international doctrines such as the Venice Charter, and regularly apply these concepts in their work. NGOs that advocate for the conservation of cultural property, such as the Association for Conservation of National Treasures and the Japanese Association for Conservation of Architectural Monuments, promote Western conservation theory and require their members to uphold Western ideals for conservation while trying to balance traditional approaches to conservation, especially with wooden architecture (ACNT, n.d.; JACAM, n.d.).

Countries like China and Japan have, for many decades, tried to balance traditional conservation theory with Western theory. International charters and documents such as the Nara Document on Authenticity (ICOMOS, 1994) and the Principles for the Conservation of Heritage Sites in China (China ICOMOS, 2004) have sought to assert the right of conservation professionals in these countries to use traditional conservation theory in their work. But, this endeavor is an imperfect one as Western concepts of authenticity are often at odds with traditional ones, making it difficult, if not impossible, to balance approaches. More often than not, it is the funding source's requirements, sometimes required by policy, for work on a historic building or place that dictate which approach or approaches are used. And, if this funding comes from an entity supported by UNESCO or ICOMOS, inevitably the use of Western conservation doctrine in an intervention is typically assumed.

Even considering this situation, in these countries, there continues to be an ongoing debate on Western versus traditional heritage theories and policies. But, especially when the listing of a World Heritage place or site in these countries is being considered, it is still mandatory to consider, through the Venice Charter, the material authenticity of the site. In this context, it is important to remember that members from East Asian countries were absent in the drafting of the Venice Charter in 1964, and thus East Asian conservation values are entirely absent from this document.

As opposed to China and Japan, public heritage policy in African and some Asian countries (such as India) tended to be externally imposed, starting in the nineteenth century, by European colonial rulers. The specific heritage policies mirrored the current policies of the colonizer's country, such as in Kenya, when in 1927, the colonial government passed the Antiquities and Monuments Act, which was, in turn, based on the United Kingdom's Ancient Monuments Consolidation and Amendment Act of 1913 (in force until 1979). Another example is in 1904, in India, when the colonial government passed the Ancient Monuments Preservation Act, which mirrored the United Kingdom's earlier Ancient Monuments Protection Act of 1900. As these heritage laws in various African and Asian countries changed, they continued to mirror the heritage laws of their colonizer's countries, even after gaining independence (Obafemi, 2017, p. 958). As most of these countries are now signatories to the World Heritage Convention, their heritage policies have broadly adopted Western policies related to historical significance and authenticity as promulgated by ICOMOS.

In the twenty-first century, scholars and leaders from several African countries have begun a dialog critical of the Western heritage policy regime imposed on them by former colonial rulers. In Nigeria, for instance, Olukoya Obafemi (2017, p. 955) describes how prior to colonization, "cultural heritage was perceived as an embodiment of cultural, cosmic and spiritual significance.... Cultural heritage places [are] part of [people's] cosmological environment with tendencies of connecting them with their ancestors and the spirit world." As opposed to the Western dichotomy of tangible/intangible, traditionally, cultural heritage in Nigeria intertwined these concepts in a way that was not separable, which contemporary Western heritage policy cannot adequately address (Obafemi, 2017, p. 959). Often, because the language and meanings of colonizers is part of public heritage policy in many African countries, there is an intentional or unintentional emphasis on preserving/conserving buildings and places built by colonizers while neglecting traditional structures, places, and landscapes (Lagae, 2008). To date, some policy changes have begun to be made, such as in Rwanda, where, in 2016, its legislature passed Law 28 "On the Preservation of Cultural Heritage and Traditional Knowledge" which recognizes the value of folklore and the protection of traditional knowledge (Rwanda Parliament, 2016). As these discussions continue, it seems inevitable that more African countries will embrace elements of their traditional cultural heritage in their heritage policies.

To be sure, the Athens Charter and the Venice Charter do not appear to have directly influenced the official way in which a historic building is recognized/inscribed/listed/registered in the United Kingdom, the United States, Canada, and Australia, and quite possibly in most other parts of the world. This conclusion is logical because neither of these charters directly address historical significance, values, or meanings. Indeed, prior to the Nara Document on Authenticity in 1994, international preservation/conservation doctrine did not directly address historical significance, which is probably why there is much greater variation across countries in terms of how historical significance is defined. For instance, in the United States, the National Register of Historic Places (36 CFR 60) is the official way in which the federal government recognizes historic buildings and districts. Created as part of the 1966 National Historic Preservation Act, it is in turn based on the way historic buildings were recognized in the Historic American Building Survey program established in the 1930s and thus has a long history of participation from historians, but few other disciplines, in the definition of what is, and is not, a historic building (Sprinkle, 2014).

In the United States, there are four criteria for historical significance, defined in a regulation (36 CFR 60): association with events from the past, association with a person or people from the past, architectural style or design, and archaeological value. In the United Kingdom, there have never been clearly defined criteria for historical significance; instead, a group of historians and archaeologists determines if a building is "of special architectural or historical interest" in a much more openly defined process that should consider aspects of age and rarity, aesthetic qualities, selectivity, national interest, and state of repair (DCMS, 2010). Of note is that in the United States any citizen can write and submit a National Register nomination, and the state and federal governments must assess and process it; while in the United Kingdom, all a citizen can do is recommend to the government that experts should consider investigating the building for possible listing.[1] Specifically, there is no requirement for the Secretary of State to consult with the English public in making a decision to list a building; the law only requires consultation with staff from the Historic Buildings

---

1. For instance, see https://historicengland.org.uk/listing/apply-for-listing/.]

and Monuments Commission for England and "persons . . . having special knowledge of, or interest in, buildings of architectural or historic interest" (Listed Building Act 1990, Part 1, Chapter 1, Section [4]). Other countries tend to use one of these systems or a combination thereof, but, overwhelmingly, the operational values for officially recognizing a historic building derive from experts in the disciplines of architecture, history, and archaeology. The broader humanities or social sciences are not represented at all, much less the values and meanings of the greater public.

State/regional and especially local governments may have their own authority to list historic buildings, either independently of, or in cooperation with national governments. It is beyond the scope of this chapter to perform an exhaustive evaluation of every local heritage building law in every country on the planet, which would warrant its own book, or perhaps several. In the literature that does attempt a less comprehensive cross-country comparison, such as Bonnici (2008), Fisch (2008), Pickard (2012), Aygen (2014), Ho et al. (2014), and Antons (2017), a clear theme does emerge, which is that expert rule and the values of historians, architects, and archaeologists dominate the discourse on the designation of historic buildings, monuments, and places at the local level in every country examined. Where policy allows it, public participation is minimal, token, or entirely absent.

A REACTION AGAINST ORTHODOX DOCTRINE AND POLICY: PEOPLE- AND HUMAN-CENTERED HERITAGE CONSERVATION

The push to reorient built heritage conservation from a top-down process dominated by expert rule into something more egalitarian and bottom-up originated from debates in archaeology/anthropology and urban planning and not in the field of built heritage conservation proper. This top-down/bottom-up debate has always been external to the fields of historic preservation, architectural conservation, and heritage building preservation, and as of the date of the writing of this chapter, still remains largely external. The primary reason for this situation is the way in which these fields focus on fabric instead of people, which is deeply rooted in practice and reinforced by public policy that in turn creates most of the need for this practice. This last point is critical: the world over, most built heritage conservation work is driven by public policy. For instance, in the United States, without the laws and regulations that define policy, 70% of all historic preservation practice would immediately vanish (Wells, 2021). The net effect is an insidious cycle where built heritage regulations require practitioners to ignore the public's heritage values and meanings which in turn feeds back into a practice that overemphasizes fabric over people. In government sectors that deal with regulatory compliance, a practitioner who wants to work with local members of the community is faced with breaking doctrine and even the law and will likely lose their job (Elliott, 2019). Pragmatically, this scenario is often not a choice because the government agencies in which these individuals work are typically underresourced and understaffed, leaving little time to ponder changing practice to be more responsive to community desires and needs. To be sure, the debate on top-down versus bottom-up processes has helped to inform overall planning processes that do not directly engage the regulatory environment, such as comprehensive plans, but this constitutes a significant minority of overall built heritage conservation practice.

In the 1970s, archaeologists in the academy initiated a debate on whether or not the discipline should be rigidly objective, scientific, and positivistic or whether a more subjective, postmodern approach grounded in the act of interpretation should redefine research and practice. This became known as the processual versus postprocessual debate (Hodder and Hutson, 2003), which still has not been resolved. In the 1970s, archaeology was taking the same "postmodern turn" that other areas of the humanities and social sciences were also undertaking, especially in anthropology, in which Clifford Geertz played a leading role (Engelstad, 1991). The key takeaway from the processual versus postprocessual debate is that it clearly defined top-down versus bottom-up approaches and thus who gets to be an expert. In conventional (processual) archaeology, the archaeologist is always the expert and has complete authority over process. In post-processual archaeology, the archaeologist gives away a bit of their power and autonomy to everyday people who are stakeholders, which is epitomized by community-based archaeology, in which laypeople are given authority to make decisions in an archaeological excavation—often participating in the dig themselves—and how the artifacts are removed, processed, and interpreted. In this sense, postprocessual archaeology is about a much higher degree of respect for people's heritage and deference to these stakeholders in the decision-making process; it also prioritizes local knowledge (Silliman, 2008).

While the processual/postprocessual debate was well underway, David Lowenthal, a humanistic geographer, published *The Past is a Foreign Country*

(1985), arguably one of the most influential books ever published in the field of built heritage conservation. In writing his monograph, Lowenthal appears to have been influenced by other humanistic geographers, such as Yi-Fu Tuan (1974), and their emphasis on subjective human experiences influenced by the environment, but there is no evidence that Lowenthal was influenced by the postprocessual debate; certainly nothing of the kind is mentioned in his book. *The Past is a Foreign Country* is, however, significant as one of the first attempts at a critical approach to built heritage conservation doctrine and the heritage industry, in general. Lowenthal tackles the supposed objectivity of the field, questions the irrational ways in which the past has been interpreted, and explores the experiences that everyday people have with the historic environment. For Lowenthal (1985, p. 356), heritage professionals control the past to placate people in the present: "we are conformable with a contrived past because it is partly a product of the present, of people like us—not wholly the work of strange folks of long ago, with their weird and outlandish ways." Professionals, in *The Past is a Foreign Country*, operating through orthodox doctrine, assume heritage is static and always situated in the past, but Lowenthal argues that heritage is continually manufactured in the present and that conservation is, in fact, an engagement more often with the present and future than the past (Lowenthal 1985, p. 410). It is this latter point that a group of anthropologists and archaeologists latched onto starting in the 1990s, building what has become known as the nascent field of critical heritage studies, combining a postprocessual perspective with Lowenthal's penchant for critique embedded in a discourse about power and control.

Case Study: David Lowenthal's Exposé on How Heritage Professionals Control the Past

In the world of heritage, perhaps no book has been more cited, analyzed, and critiqued than David Lowenthal's (1985) groundbreaking book, *The Past is a Foreign Country*. While it is a broad exploration of how society engages with the past, it often emphasizes how heritage professionals shape, and, at times, attempt to control that engagement. Critical approaches to heritage studies, which arose starting in the 1990s, were highly influenced by Lowenthal's work, and remain so, to the present, because of the controversial themes in *The Past is a Foreign Country* that reveal how professionals try to convey history "truthfully," but, instead, often acquiesce to the public's romantic and antiquarian desires while still promoting their discipline's agenda to "save" the past (Carman and Sørensen, 2009). In this book, three

FIGURE 1.3. A "Certificate of Appropriateness" is one example of how heritage professionals control the discourse on aesthetics in historic districts in the US through public policy (photo by author)

themes are particularly salient for how heritage professionals attempt to influence societal memory, sanitize the past, and moralize the protection of heritage:

Influence of societal memory. In their work to interpret the past to the public, Lowenthal argues that historians, museum curators, and historic preservationists play a critical role in influencing how a society understands, values, and protects heritage through their choices of what gets documented, exhibited, restored, or in some cases, erased or ignored. He exposes the fallacy that professionals use an objective "truth" to guide their decisions and instead shows how personal or disciplinary bias, an overreliance on the written record, and consumers' tastes influence how the past is interpreted, protected, and reified.

Sanitization of the past. Tragic, immoral, and horrendous events have characterized recorded human history for many millennia, but there is a natural human tendency to sanitize or romanticize this history to make it more acceptable, or in some cases, to serve a particular political agenda. Museums and historical sites tend to focus on the positive, highlighting advancements and social achievements, which feeds into the expected Western societal narrative of continual progress, while deprecating human suffering, social inequalities, or ethical complexities that, in many cases, are associated with these advancements. The stories of everyday people—especially those told from an oppressed perspective—are complex and difficult to simplify for public consumption, which results in glossing over messy historical realities, nuances, and controversies. This practice of sanitization also manifests in an overemphasis on the preservation of grand monuments with easy-to-convey high aesthetic or cultural value over vernacular buildings and places or sites with difficult memories.

Moralizing the protection of heritage. Lowenthal's book was one of the first analyses of how, in the protection of cultural heritage, heritage professionals often rely on moral, rather than scientific or objective, arguments. The destruction of cultural heritage is therefore not primarily a loss of information, experiences, or representations, but rather an act that should instill feelings of anger and disgust in the observer. This emotional motivation for justifying heritage conservation can result in choices that may selectively highlight contributions of certain groups, while ignoring others, in an effort to present a moral obligation to protect a legacy. In other cases, professionals present selective heritage conservation acts as essential for maintaining a community's or nation's identity. But, one of the most common ways of instilling morality in the discussions of heritage is in the context of the destruction of historical sites or artifacts, which professionals typically portray as a "loss," which emotionally connects with the public's understanding of loss through death. The professional's desire, in this case, is to instill a moral duty to safeguard these tangible links to the past.

Because Lowenthal tends to focus on the most egregious examples of these three behaviors, described above, it is important to note that not all heritage professionals undertake these actions in all situations. Rather than painting an absolutist picture, Lowenthal explains the general *tendencies* within professional heritage practice that impact how the public interacts with and understands the past.

FIGURE 1.4. Although the place-based histories promulgated by heritage experts and employed by governmental entities in the US are slowly becoming more diverse and inclusive, examples of neglected histories such as this sign in a cemetery in Deadwood, South Dakota, are commonplace. Missing from this narrative is how White people subjected Chinese immigrants to racist abuse. (Photo by author.)

The coalescence of these ideas around a field named "critical heritage studies" only happened in the second decade of this century. Laurajane Smith (2012, p. 537), who is one of the field's acknowledged leaders, recounts in an editorial that "Rodney Harrison [another prominent heritage studies researcher] may have first used this phrase in a 2010 publication" (she does not, however, cite this publication), but there are definitely earlier examples of its use. For instance, the phrase appears in Lisa Breglia's *Monumental Ambivalence* (2006, p. 12) and also appears even earlier in the title of a symposium hosted by the Centre for African Studies at University of Cape Town in 2002 (Murray, 2005, p. 58). But, the field achieved widespread recognition with the ACHS at the University of Gothenburg in 2012 during its eponymous inaugural conference. ACHS has since held conferences biannually: Canberra, Australia, in 2014; Montreal, Canada, in 2016; Hangzhou, China, in 2018; virtually in 2020 (due to the pandemic); and Santiago, Chile, in 2022. These conferences have drawn around 300-600 international attendees (FRH, n.d.; Smith, 2012, p. 533). According to the list of members on the ACHS website (www.criticalheritagestudies.org), about 30% are affiliated with anthropology and archaeology, and about 20% each are affiliated with history and the architecture and design fields. In total, there are more than 2,000 members as of 2023, which is a rather remarkable growth from the inception of ACHS in 2012.

Based on sheer numbers of citations from Google Scholar, it is readily apparent that the three canonical texts for the field of critical heritage studies are *The Past is a Foreign Country* by David Lowenthal (1985), *Uses of Heritage* by Laurajane Smith (2006), and *Heritage: Critical Approaches* by Rodney Harrison (2013). The *International Journal of Heritage Studies* is the acknowledged scholarly journal for the field. The five major themes contained in these texts and supported by associated literature are:

- Critical heritage studies is about the present, not the past (Emerick, 2014; Harrison, 2013, pp. 32, 165; Waterton, Watson, & Silverman, 2017, pp. 4, 8; Smith, 2006, p. 3);
- Critical heritage studies explores contemporary relationships between people, heritage, and power (Logan & Wijesuriya, 2015, p. 569; Smith, 2006, p. 281; Smith, Shackel, & Campbell, 2011, p. 4);
- Heritage is inherently dissonant and created through a continual process of conflict and negotiation (Tunbridge & Ashworth, 1996; Breglia, 2006, p. 3; Daly & Chan, 2015, p. 492; Smith, 2006, p. 82);

- Heritage is a process (not a thing) and inherently intangible (Emerick, 2014, p. 190; Harrison, 2010, p. 3; Smith, 2006, p. 43; Winter, 2013);
- Critical heritage studies engages with and attempts to correct or improve conservation practice (Emerick, 2014, p. 226; Winter, 2013; Witcomb & Buckley, 2013, p. 574).

One of the most cited theoretical concepts in critical heritage studies is Smith's (2006, pp. 29-30) "Authorized Heritage Discourse" (AHD) which describes the way in which conventional experts—principally, architects, historians, and archaeologists—control the discourse over the values of heritage. In the AHD, only these experts know how to identify, protect, and conserve heritage, and it is their role, duty, and obligation to inform the public about the correct ways in which heritage should be known, interpreted, and communicated. Smith's AHD is very much based on colonialism, in which a small group of individuals with power force others to adopt their unique values and behavioral system. The widespread acceptance of the AHD in heritage conservation practice makes it difficult to engage in discussion counter to its value system, making it unlikely that the processes for managing cultural heritage will change in the future (Smith, 2006, p. 154). This situation is partially due to the way in which the AHD assumes that heritage is "simple" and "conflict free" and that its meanings do not change over time (Smith, 2006, p. 166).

While critical heritage studies has illuminated many of the shortcomings of conventional built heritage conservation practice, it is not without its own issues. Too little of its scholarship has focused on policy (Rodenberg & Wagenaar, 2023), which is the fundamental tool that enforces the AHD (Lixinski, 2015). Heritage experts that work in the built environment are often forced to adopt the AHD because it is required by policy (Wells & Lixinski, 2016, 2017), which is a fact largely ignored by critical heritage studies scholarship. While, ostensibly, critical heritage studies is focused on changing conservation practice, too few of its authors relate their research to these kinds of changes; indeed, one is often left with the impression that the natural end of critical heritage studies is the morass of relativism, where there can never be any decisions because all values and meanings are equivalent (Wells, 2016). But, perhaps its most significant shortcoming is that while critical heritage scholarship embraces sociological and anthropological perspectives, a focus on the individual's relationship with the historic environment (e.g., environmental psychology) is seriously underrepresented.

The net effect is that while we know much about group (i.e., cultural) values associated with heritage, we still lack a significant understanding of the psychological relationship people have with heritage and place and how this should influence policy.

While anthropologists and archaeologists were debating the AHD and cultural understandings of heritage, urban planners in the United States and the United Kingdom created what is known as "values-centered preservation" or "values-centered conservation" Values-centered preservation/conservation is important because it opens the possible values to engage in preservation/conservation work beyond the official values in doctrine and law. More importantly, there is some emphasis on identifying and engaging with members of particular communities in an effort to understand their perspective, often through community workshops, interviews, and nonparticipant observation. Unlike critical heritage studies, which tends to focus more on museums and archaeological sites, values-centered preservation/conservation is very much associated with the built environment.

Probably the earliest literature on the subject of values is by William Lipe (1984) in which he outlines four primary values that can be associated with built heritage: associative/symbolic value, informational value, aesthetic value, and economic value. This led to later publications in which each author, in turn, attempted to expand on this value typology (e.g., Avrami, Mason, & Torre, 2000; Gibson & Pendlebury, 2009; Low, 2003; Nanda et al., 2001; Smith, Messenger, & Soderland, 2010; Worthing & Bond, 2008). This competitive process to uncover even more values makes it readily apparent that it is possible to create an infinite number of values that could be associated with cultural heritage. But this process still fails to inform historical significance because we do not understand what these values actually mean, as Fredheim and Khalaf (2016, p. 477) explain:

> The examination of published heritage value typologies ... suggests that values-based theory rests on an incomplete understanding of values. New value typologies continue to be proposed without thorough consideration of their implications for information gathering, synthesis and communication, or the actual requirements placed on statements of significance by conservation practice. The growing body of value typologies is symptomatic of a discipline increasingly concerned with critical reflection and introspection, but which rarely gives typologies the critical attention they deserve.

In the end, the larger question of "whose values are more important and why?" becomes ever more elusive. While focused more on practical applications than critical heritage studies, values-centered preservation/conservation still fails to adequately address policy or to offer practitioners useful new tools to engage with members of a community. Nigel Walter (2014) offers an additional critique of this values-centered approach, describing it as thinly veiled positivism, where the full richness of cultural experiences is reduced to convenient little boxes with labels. In the end, we have the names for the values but really do not fully understand what they mean to the communities from whom they have been gleaned.

The canonical text in values-centered preservation/conservation is *Values and Heritage Conservation* by Avrami, Mason, and Torre (2000) based on the sheer number of citations in other scholarly work. Part of the reach of this publication is the fact that the Getty (its publisher) released it for free download on its website, helping to guarantee its widespread availability. The impact of this work on spurring human-centered discussions on built heritage conservation is therefore significant as it has, in comparison to critical heritage studies, affected some practice, albeit subtly; unfortunately, there is no evidence that it has influenced public policy, especially in the United States. Some examples include the use of a values-centered framework by English Heritage (2008; now Historic England), which is the national governmental body for heritage planning in the United Kingdom, in its heritage protection discourse, emphasizing evidential value, historical value, aesthetic value, and communal value (English Heritage, 2008, pp. 27-34). And the National Park Service (NPS) in the United States uses a values-centered approach in its management of the Chaco Culture Heritage Site as a tool to help in community engagement (Little, 2014).

It is important to note that critical heritage studies and values-centered preservation/conservation both focus on sociocultural values and meanings and not individual or experiential meanings; or, in a simplistic sense, they emphasize meanings and values held by large groups of people. Both are focused on obtaining either, in a qualitative sense, a kind of consensus of meanings through an *emic* or insider perspective or, in a quantitative sense, generalizability to a larger population. What is missing from both of these approaches, however, is a focus on the individual's interaction with and perception of the older built environment and cultural landscapes. While a significant amount of rhetoric around the preservation/conservation of historic places uses language like "sense of place" and the way people connect to their environment (e.g., Benson & Klein, 2008; Hayden, 1995; Waters, 1983), few scholars have actually empirically investigated sense of place or people's affective attachment to old places through a methodologically rigorous process. This is very much in the realm of individual perception and behavior, and as such, relates most strongly to environmental psychology. Yet, few scholars have chosen to research in this area. (I expand on this discussion in chapter 5.)

Since 2008, the Environmental Design Research Association (EDRA) has had a Historic Environment Knowledge Network (which I helped found) that is one of the only forums that specifically encourages an environmental psychology approach to built heritage conservation. In 2012, the network released a guiding document for integrating environmental design and behavior research into built heritage conservation practice (EDRA Historic Environment Knowledge Network, 2018). The network also hosted a daylong intensive on human-centered heritage conservation that has since been published as the book, *Human-Centered Built Environment Heritage Preservation* (Wells & Stiefel, 2019). To date, this is the only forum where people who are engaged in environmental psychology or environment/behavior research gather to discuss issues related to the historic environment. Other organizations, however, have been engaged in broader social science approaches, if not specifically environmental psychology.

For instance, a number of NGOs have also adopted a people-centered approach in their work, such as the US-based National Trust for Historic Preservation's "Preservation for the People" that recognizes the importance of intangible heritage, diversity and inclusion, social justice, and the relationship between the historic environment and overall psychological health and well-being (National Trust, 2017). The International Centre for the Study of the Preservation and Restoration of Cultural Property (ICCROM) in Italy conducted research on "people-centred approaches to the conservation of cultural heritage." Although focused more on intangible or "living heritage" than the built environment, it is important because of its emphasis on better ways to engage with communities. Unlike the National Trust's approach, however, there is no specific emphasis on environmental psychology, psychological health, or the relationship people have with older places (Court, 2015). Implicit in the way these organizations are addressing their activities is an emphasis on the plural, "people," which makes sense given the strong desire to more effectively engage with communities. To be sure, however, this emphasis is in deference to "human" centered conservation, which implies the way the individual interacts with, perceives, and behaves in environments associated with cultural heritage, or a perspective more rooted in psychology. This assessment is not to say that one approach—cultural or psychological—is better than another, but even in the realm of NGOs, there is an overemphasis on the cultural elements of built heritage and a de-emphasis on environmental psychology.

ARTICULATING THE BARRIERS TO HUMAN-CENTERED CONSERVATION

As of the start of the third decade of the twenty-first century, we have reached a state where discussions of values-centered, people-centered, and human-centered built heritage conservation in context with critical approaches are increasingly commonplace as a way to ostensibly balance the traditional emphasis on fabric that the field has held since its inception. One could logically assume that conservation/preservation practice has followed suit, especially considering the nearly two decades of comprehensive soul-searching that the field has undergone. Arguably, this has been the case in some areas of conservation/preservation planning and the revitalization/regeneration of historic urban centers, but again, there have been no substantial changes to policy in reflection of this work.

A good planning example is the "How Should Heritage Decisions Be Made?" project at the University of Leeds (U.K.) that used community-based participatory processes to help understand how to make heritage conservation planning more inclusive, efficient, and useful (Bashforth et al., 2015). Although mostly focused on museum settings, its findings and recommendations are applicable to built heritage conservation as well, especially historic cities, as one of its cases addressed the city of York (U.K.). The key focus of this work was "talking *with* people not *about* people" in the process of "democratising decision-making" (Bashforth et al., 2015, p. 22). In the case of York, the participants in the study helped in "mapping" decision-making systems used in heritage conservation for the city (Bashforth et al., 2015, p. 46). Perhaps most interesting about the work in York was that the participants conducting the research encountered "a number of people in decision-making roles who just didn't believe in participation"; these experts would rather just leave all conservation decisions to themselves because the perception was that engaging the public was a waste of time and effort (Bashforth et al., 2015, p. 47). In recognizing these limitations, the study's participants devised ways to engage the experts collaboratively with laypeople in an environment that "humanized" the experts and encouraged laypeople to engage more in "arguments" with the experts rather than simply sharing their opinions (Bashforth et al., 2015, p. 47-48).

In 2013, Ballarat, Australia, became the first city to adopt UNESCO's Historic Urban Landscape (HUL) approach (UNESCO, 2016, 20-25) to create a small area plan for Ballarat East. The HUL approach emphasizes the need to collaboratively engage with local stakeholders, which the organizers in Ballarat attempted to implement though a series of community workshops and a strong online presence, including a "time capsule" tool, surveys, social media engagement, and a Ballarat East Network website. The website for this plan[2] exhibits maps made by community members, interactive comparisons of historical and contemporary photos of the same location, word maps, and a discussion paper. There is also a "Visualizing Ballarat" GIS tool for the public to use in their discussions and feedback to the city on the plan. What makes Ballarat's efforts unique is the extent to which the city has tried to engage as many layers of the community as possible both through in-person discussion (e.g., workshops) and through a vibrant and engaging social media presence and historical data. While there are similar examples, such as the SurveyLA project that was conducted as a partnership between the City of Los Angeles (USA) and the Getty (an NGO also located in Los Angeles), SurveyLA relied much more on traditional categories of art/historical facts to guide what was, and was not, significant about Los Angeles (Bernstein & Hansen, 2016); rather than changing practice, SurveyLA helped reinforce traditional survey systems already long used in the field. In Ballarat, the types of meanings that were acceptable for the planning process were much broader and included community stories and needs that did not necessarily have an empirical grounding in the factual history of the community. None the less, because the members of the community thought a particular aspect of their neighborhood was important, the organizers of the project listened and tried to include the information in the plan.

---

2. See http://www.hulballarat.org.au/.

Case Study: Ballarat and the Historic Urban Landscape (HUL) Approach: Putting People at the Center of Built Heritage

Built heritage professionals in the United States, throughout the twentieth century until the early 1980s, were highly influenced by their peers in Europe. The legislation that became the US National Historic Preservation Act of 1966 was largely derivative of European practice (especially in the United Kingdom) and US professionals were fundamentally involved in creating the World Heritage Convention, in collaboration with European colleagues, in the early 1970s (see Jokilehto, 1999; Rains & Henderson, 1966). The US Secretary of the Interior's Standards, first written in 1974, is a foundational public policy document, which was a direct translation of the international Venice Charter of 1964 (a doctrine largely created by Europeans). But, starting in the 1980s, as US historic preservation policy solidified, US heritage professionals disengaged with European practice and stopped following and adopting international heritage charters, especially in public policy. For all purposes and intents, since 1980, US built heritage policy has become increasingly insular, ignoring international developments and practice.

While US historic preservation policy has preserved its original mid-century fabric-based focus, since the 1980s, European countries, and in the past several decades, countries in Asia and the global south, have continually expanded on a more people-centric focus on built heritage and practice. This divergent path, epitomized by the 1994 Nara Document on Authenticity (ICOMOS, 1994), which radically redefined "authenticity" in nonmaterial terms, has resulted in slow but incremental policy reforms in the public sector, internationally, but have had essentially no effect in the United States where preservation experts and policy leaders remain largely oblivious to these discussions.

A useful example of a recent innovation in international built heritage policy, which has mostly been ignored in the United States, is UNESCO's Historic Urban Landscape (HUL) approach. Since the early 1990s, members of ICOMOS from Asia and the Global South began to criticize the dominance of fabric-based, Western heritage philosophies and the lack of interest in intangible heritage in public policy. They called upon the creation of international charters to, as Bandarin and van Oers (2012, p. 201) explain, "balance the pluralistic and sometimes divergent viewpoints emanating from the sheer diversity of cultures." This dialog eventually led to an international convening of heritage experts in May of 2011 at the UNESCO headquarters to discuss "Historic Urban Landscapes." At this meeting, a final draft of recommendations on this topic was presented to UNESCO members; it was adopted by UNESCO at its 36th session later that year (Bandarin & van Oers, 2012).

Section III in the HUL text, officially titled "Recommendation on the Historic Urban Landscape," advocates for policy reform, especially in the assessment of community values and the grassroots engagement of identified communities in the conservation of urban heritage (UNESCO, 2011). The HUL text also attempts to balance the need for the conservation of both tangible *and* intangible heritage through this revised policy framework, including recommendations that regulations need to be developed to protect and sustain intangible heritage. The "landscape" approach in the HUL text emphasizes the need for all conservation/preservation activities to embrace and capitalize on the holistic and interconnected nature of social, governmental, climate, and economic systems. In sum, the HUL text elevates the importance of intangible heritage to a level equal with tangible heritage and, in doing so, advocates for heritage professionals to adopt a more holistic, people-centric approach to the public policies that support built heritage conservation.

In 2013, the City of Ballarat (Australia), in partnership with UNESCO, became one of the first municipalities to commit to the HUL approach. As part of its community vision (i.e., what is essentially known as a comprehensive plan in the United States) for 2040, which was adopted in 2015, the HUL approach informed Ballarat's policy-based changes to its heritage conservation program. For Ballarat, the following key tasks were part of the implementation of HUL (City of Ballarat, n.d.):

- Asking the community "what is important to them";
- Relying less on architectural and social history experts to establish significance and instead "accept[ing] that things are valuable because the community values them";
- Accepting that change is not only inevitable, but desirable;
- Focusing less on preservation as a treatment and emphasizing the dynamic nature of conservation which "requires creative and innovative solutions to enable sustainable and equitable change in a historic city."

Starting in 2013, the city used the Internet (e.g., Twitter, Facebook, websites), events, markets, shops, and community meetings to gather input from residents and business owners on the values and historical significance of Ballarat. Policy changes began in 2015, culminating in the adoption of a HUL-based heritage plan by the city in 2017.

In embarking in its vision for 2040, the City of Ballarat was explicit in setting in motion a change from "a regulatory-focussed preservation model" to "a holistic and sustainable conservation model" in which "people-centred approaches" were essential (City of Ballarat, 2016, p. 12). The reason why the city chose the HUL approach was because of its focus on grassroots community engagement, participatory democracy, and measurable performance standards (City of Ballarat, 2016, p. 12). The city divided its efforts into "community engagement tools" (participation by local residents and business owners), "planning and knowledge tools" (collection of data, data transparency and online availability, best practices), "regulatory tools" (creation of new rules and regulations), and "financial tools" (grants, loans, public/private partnerships; City of Ballarat, 2016, p. 14).

In implementing the HUL approach, the city created Ballarat Imagine—the largest city-led effort for community engagement ever undertaken—in which residents consistently valued the mining heritage of their city; this process also collected additional meanings that connected the history of the community with residents' everyday lives. The sense of place and stories associated with the older part of Ballarat were of the highest value because of the way in which they contributed to quality of life; participants largely did not ascribe intrinsic value directly to historic buildings independently of what these assets brought to their own lives (City of Ballarat, 2016, p. 12). The primary themes, from community engagement work, were how people used specific places and how places catalyzed people's emotional bonds with specific assets. In exploring financial incentives and public/private partnerships to build on these themes, Ballarat's plan is similar to the comprehensive approach to downtown revitalization long used by the National Trust for Historic Preservation's "Main Street" program in the United States. Indeed, a case study on the Main Street program was included in Ballarat's plan (City of Ballarat, 2016, p. 41).

Ballarat's heritage plan is also exemplified by its recommendations to better integrate best practices in urban and regional planning with heritage planning, including the concept of "cultural mapping," in which sociocultural meanings are interrelated with tangible and intangible heritage assets (City of Ballarat, 2016, p. 49). The plan calls for new regulations that help to sustain place-based planning, human-scaled development, and mixed use (City of Ballarat, 2016, 49–62), which are commonly found in comprehensive plans but absent from traditional historic preservation plans. Intriguingly, Ballarat's heritage plan suggests codifying requirements to collect residents' place-based stories and memories, including experiences with place-based smells and sounds (City of Ballarat, 2016, p. 51).

In sum, Ballarat's HUL-based heritage plan broadens its heritage policies to consider a much wider range of meanings and values that its residents and business owners associate with "heritage" than has been commonly accepted in public preservation policy in the United States. While still embracing traditional statutory controls to protect tangible heritage, the city's heritage plan attempts to meld comprehensive people-centered policy recommendations with traditional heritage policies. But, perhaps most critically, Ballarat's heritage plan makes it clear that the primary beneficiary of protecting and conserving the older built environment is its people, which is different than traditional built heritage conservation/preservation policy which tacitly assumes that the primary beneficiary of heritage policy are historic assets.

In the United States, the "Main Street" approach, which was originally created by the US-based National Trust for Historic Preservation, is a community-led process for helping residents and business owners conserve the historic urban center of their community and use this place as a key asset for economic growth and revitalization (Wells, 2017). It was conceived as a tool for built heritage conservation in the late 1970s and retains this emphasis today. What makes the Main Street approach unique, however, is that it is nearly entirely managed by volunteer stakeholders within the framework of an NGO. The only paid staff person in a typical Main Street program is an executive director with tens, and sometimes hundreds, of volunteers who actually do most of the work. While Main Street programs collaborate with governmental and other NGO entities, the conservation work that guides the revitalization of the urban center is controlled by volunteers. For

FIGURE 1.5. The Town Hall in Ballarat, Australia. One of many mid-nineteenth century buildings in this historic mining town (sketch by author)

this reason, it is one of the few examples of a ground-up approach to built heritage conservation that has worked for many decades. The Main Street program has been particularly effective in this regard with the control of the design of historic urban centers (Wells, 2017).

As can be seen by these examples, built heritage conservation planning activities that incorporate values-centered, people-centered, and/or human-centered approaches are usually focused on ways to locate, solicit, and engage the participation of a greater number of local stakeholders, who are often residents, in existing planning frameworks. With the exception of Main Street programs, these planning efforts are typically led by conventional experts, who, in the best of circumstances, play the role of facilitator rather than director. None of these approaches, however, are human-centered to any significant degree, being more properly called people-centered, although this outcome is understandable given the sociocultural goals of these programs and activities.

Yet, the largest area of practice in built heritage conservation is driven by public policy, not by the kinds of planning activities presented here. Known by various names, the work of practitioners in this area is primarily driven by requirements dictated by laws, regulations, and guidelines, especially in the United States. Even without such data from other Western countries, it is clear that the regulatory environment is responsible for most of the jobs in the fields of historic preservation, heritage buildings preservation, and built heritage conservation on a global scale.

With this evidence that most practice in built heritage conservation exists for regulatory compliance, I will return to the original question at the beginning of this chapter that asks if we are, indeed, moving toward a more human-centered, or at least people-centered, practice. For the majority of practice in built heritage conservation, the answer is a clear "no" (Avrami, 2020; Lixinski, 2015; Wells & Lixinski, 2016, 2017; Wells & Stiefel, 2019). There is little evidence that practice catalyzed by policy has changed. The reason for this situation is deceptively simple: changing built heritage conservation policy requires *changing the laws, regulations, and guidelines* of built heritage recognition, protection, and conservation, which is a political process. But, there is a deeper answer to this question as well. Because of the demands of finality in administrative law and the lack of any existing examples of adaptive regulatory systems *anywhere* in the world (Wells & Lixinski, 2017), this situation will not change anytime soon. But what, exactly, are the laws, rules, and regulations that drive built heritage conservation practice on a global scale? They are the designation of historic buildings, design review, and environmental review. The following assessment will emphasize the United States, the United Kingdom, Australia, and Canada for the sake of brevity with a briefer assessment of other countries provided for comparison.

DESIGNATION/LISTING/RECORDING OF HISTORIC BUILDINGS

In the United States, a federal regulation (36 CFR 60) dictates that in order for a building to be recognized as "historic" it must meet one or more of the following criteria: a) association with historical events; b) association with a person or people in the past; c) representative of a significant architectural style or technique; and d) ability to provide information in the future. Registries of historic buildings and places are also possible at the state and local levels; in the vast majority of cases, the criteria for state and local listings either duplicate or mirror the criteria used in the National Register. Even though anyone can submit a nomination, the process is rigorous, time consuming, and requires knowledge of local history and archival research techniques. This process has led to a thriving consultancy in the United States based on paying experts to write National Register nominations, which are then submitted to state historic preservation offices for vetting and possible approval. Government employees will not participate in writing the nomination, although they will offer significant feedback to the submitter. A significant financial incentive, the federal Historic Rehabilitation Tax Credit (36 CFR 67), drives the need for many nominations because a building must be listed on the National Register prior to any rehabilitation work; in addition, the Secretary of the Interior's Standards (36 CFR 68) are used to "certify" the rehabilitation.

In the United Kingdom, the Listed Building Act of 1990 (Part 1, Chapter 1, Section [4]) explains that in order for a historic building to be listed, it must be of "special architectural or historical interest." Unlike the system used in the United States, there are no specific criteria that are part of the statute although policy documents suggest that age and rarity, aesthetic qualities, selectivity, national interest, and state of repair should be considered (DCMS, 2010). Although anyone can nominate a building for listing with minimal effort, the process of listing and fully documenting buildings is performed by government staff, although individuals from the private sector are sometimes involved. The final information included in the listing can be substantially altered and edited by government staff.

According to the Environment Protection and Biodiversity Conservation Act of 1999, listing a building or historic place in the National Heritage list in Australia requires that it meet at least one of the following nine criteria:

- The place has outstanding heritage value to the nation because of the place's importance in the course, or pattern, of Australia's natural or cultural history;
- Possession of uncommon, rare, or endangered aspects of Australia's natural or cultural history;
- Potential to yield information that will contribute to an understanding of Australia's natural or cultural history;

- Importance in demonstrating the principal characteristics of (i) a class of Australia's natural or cultural places or (ii) a class of Australia's natural or cultural environments;
- Importance in exhibiting particular aesthetic characteristics valued by a community or cultural group;
- Importance in demonstrating a high degree of creative or technical achievement at a particular period;
- Strong or special association with a particular community or cultural group for social, cultural, or spiritual reasons;
- Special association with the life or works of a person, or group of persons, of importance in Australia's natural or cultural history; or
- Importance as part of Indigenous tradition.

States also maintain their own historical registries and enable local governments to create their own local lists. The criteria are highly derivative of the National Heritage list. Anyone, with minimal effort, can nominate a building or place to the national, state, and local heritage lists maintained by the appropriate authorities; in some cases, there is an open call for nominations and fixed windows of time for submission. Government agencies also initiate their own nominations. Like the United Kingdom, the relevant governmental agency either does the historical/background research to substantiate the nomination and/or directly hires consultants to assist with the work. The final information included in the listing can be substantially altered and edited by government staff.

Of note is that listing buildings and places in Australia, unlike in the United States and the United Kingdom, can make a direct appeal to cultural values and meanings. In practice, however, this kind of argument is usually only used in context with Indigenous groups. Even in this case, the argument must be based on cultural *history* and not the contemporary sociocultural or experiential values held by a group of people today (Environment Protection and Heritage Council, 2008; Australian Heritage Council, 2009). In other words, unless the cultural values being expressed have an unbroken continuity with contemporary cultural meanings and values, these latter meanings and values cannot be used independently.

While the Canadian government has a national list of historic places, it simply aggregates listings performed by governments at the provincial, territorial, and local levels rather than implementing its own rule for the listing of historic buildings and places. Unlike the United States and its relationship with states, there are significant variations in how historical significance is defined across provinces, which led to the publication, in 2003, of guidance from Parks Canada that attempted a "pan-Canadian" definition of "heritage values" (see Table 1.1 entry for "Saskatchewan" for the full definition). While the provinces of Saskatchewan and Nova Scotia have implemented listing rules based on these national recommendations, the remaining provinces and one territory have their own variations, and the Northwest Territories and Nunavut have no specific regulation that addresses listing historic buildings and places. (See Table 1.1 for a full listing of significance criteria used in Canadian providences and territories.) Historically, provincial governments did most of the work in researching and listing historic buildings and places, although more recently a system has been adopted to encourage the submission of fully completed nominations by any interested individual, which more or less mirrors the system used in the United States (Dawson, 2005); but this is by no means universal throughout the country. There is an even greater variation at the level of local municipalities in Canada, which have either adopted their province's standard for historical significance, the national heritage values standard, or their own criteria to assist in the listing of historical buildings and places.

None of the providences or territories, other than Saskatchewan, Nova Scotia, and Quebec, allow arguments based on cultural significance. Based on instructional material for prospective nominators and extant nominations in these three provinces, however, cultural arguments for significance must reference past cultural practices and not contemporary sociocultural or experiential values held by people today unless the cultural group is associated with the First Nations. Regardless, even with Indigenous Peoples, cultural arguments for significance must establish that these values represent a continuity between past and present practices. In this way, much like Australia, these so-called "cultural" arguments for significance are really little different than arguments based on historical facts.

The key takeaway in terms of the values used for listing historic buildings and places in the United States, United Kingdom, Australia, and Canada is that the process is controlled by government staff trained in architecture, architectural history, and/or archaeology. Nominations, which are the basis for listing, are usually prepared by these same experts or hired experts with similar qualifications from the private sector, even though in the United States and Canada, it is possible for any citizen to submit a fully completed nomination to government officials. The United States and the United Kingdom have no ready way to accommodate contemporary sociocultural (group) or experiential (individual) values and meanings in nominations while both Canada (in some provinces) and Australia allow for the use of cultural values in defining historical significance, but these values must have continuity with the past. Contemporary cultural values and meanings of recent origin cannot be used to justify why a place is significant. In neither case are experiential meanings (i.e., from an individual, psychological perspective) normally allowed to be used for defining significance.

DESIGN REVIEW/HERITAGE IMPACT ASSESSMENTS

In general, there are two reasons to designate or list a historic building or place: 1) to officially recognize its historicity, as an honor; and 2) to protect the historical authenticity of the building or place. In the latter case, national, state, and local governments pass specific rules and regulations that control what property owners can and cannot do to these resources in terms of physical changes. Known by various names, such as "design review," "listed building consent," or a "heritage impact assessment," these laws specify a specific process under which the changes being proposed are reviewed by some kind of body of authority and then approved or denied before the changes are implemented. If the property owner makes these changes before receiving approval, they can be subject to legal prosecution, which can include fines, and in some cases, imprisonment. While there is great variation in this process from country to country, in general, this description holds true internationally. For the purposes of this analysis, I will use the phrase "design review" to refer to these activities.

The Venice Charter is the foundational document used in the United States, the United Kingdom, Australia, and Canada to create rules, regulations, and guidelines in legally mandated processes that control changes to designated historic buildings. Examples of rules and guidelines that control design review include the Secretary of the Interior's Standards (36 CFR 68) in the United States, Principles of Repair (English Heritage, 1993) and Guide to the Principles of the Conservation of Historic Buildings (British Standards Institution, 2013) in the United Kingdom, and Standards and Guidelines for the Conservation of Historic Places in Canada (Parks Canada, 2003), and in Australia, state heritage offices use the Burra Charter

TABLE 1.1. Canadian provinces and rules for listing historical buildings and places

Province	Definition of historical significance relevant to listing historic buildings and places	Implementing act
Saskatchewan	"Heritage values" definition from Parks Canada (2003, p. 2): "the aesthetic, historic, scientific, cultural, social or spiritual importance or significance for past, present or future generations. The heritage value of a historic place is embodied in its character-defining materials, forms, location, spatial configurations, uses and cultural associations or meanings"	Heritage Property Act of 1980
Nova Scotia	"Heritage values" definition from Parks Canada (2003); see above.	Heritage Property Act revised in 1989
Ontario	"1. The property has design value or physical value because it, i. is a rare, unique, representative or early example of a style, type, expression, material or construction method, ii. displays a high degree of craftsmanship or artistic merit, or iii. demonstrates a high degree of technical or scientific achievement. 2. The property has historical value or associative value because it, i. has direct associations with a theme, event, belief, person, activity, organization or institution that is significant to a community, ii. yields, or has the potential to yield, information that contributes to an understanding of a community or culture, or iii. demonstrates or reflects the work or ideas of an architect, artist, builder, designer or theorist who is significant to a community. 3. The property has contextual value because it, i. is important in defining, maintaining or supporting the character of an area, ii. is physically, functionally, visually or historically linked to its surroundings, or iii. is a landmark."	Ontario Heritage Act of 1990
Quebec	"Any immovable property that is of interest for its archaeological, architectural, artistic, emblematic, ethnological, historical, landscape, scientific or technological value, in particular a building, structure, remains or land."	Cultural Heritage Act
British Columbia	"Heritage value" defined as "the historical, cultural, aesthetic, scientific or educational worth or usefulness of a site or object."	Heritage Conservation Act of 1996
Manitoba	"The minister may, in accordance with this Part, designate any site as a heritage site … where … the site represents … an important feature of (a) the historic or pre-historic development of the province or a specific locality within the province, or of the peoples of the province or locality and their respective cultures; or (b) the natural history of the province or a specific locality within the province; as the case may be, and has by virtue thereof sufficient heritage significance to be so designated."	Heritage Resources Act of 1983

Province	Definition of historical significance relevant to listing historic buildings and places	Implementing act
New Brunswick	"(a) is associated with a person, organization, event or theme that (i) had a significant impact on provincial heritage, or (ii) illustrates an important aspect of human history in the Province; (b) has political, social, cultural, scientific or political significance at an international, national or provincial level; (c) exhibits excellence in architecture, engineering, functional design, construction or craftsmanship for a particular period; (d) exhibits or represents rare, unique, representative or early examples of style, type, expression, material or construction method; (e) yields or has the potential to yield information that significantly contributes to the understanding of provincial history and heritage; (f) is of aesthetic, visual or contextual importance at a provincial level; (g) is a landmark of provincial significance; (h) by itself, or with other places, represents a district or cultural landscape that is significant to human history in the Province; or (i) by itself, or with other places, represents an important phase, pattern or aspect of settlement in or development of the Province."	Heritage Conservation Act of 2010
Prince Edward Island	Rule directs that Heritage Board can independently define criteria for designation; nothing specific is stated in the rule itself. The national "heritage value" (Parks Canada 2003, p. 2) definition is often used as a reference; see above.	Heritage Places Protection Act
Alberta	Minister can designate anything that is a "historic resource," which is defined as "any work of nature or of humans that is primarily of value for its palaeontological, archaeological, prehistoric, historic, cultural, natural, scientific or esthetic interest including, but not limited to, a palaeontological, archaeological, prehistoric, historic or natural site, structure or object."	Alberta Historical Resources Act of 2000
Newfoundland and Labrador	"Historic resources" can be listed as long as they meet the definition of "a work of nature or of humans that is primarily of value for its archaeological, prehistoric, historic, cultural, natural, scientific or aesthetic interest, including an archaeological, prehistoric, historic or natural site, structure or object."	Historic Resources Act of 1990
Yukon	Minister can list a "historic resource" as long as it is "an important illustration of (a) the historic or pre-historic development of the Yukon or a specific locality in the Yukon, or of the peoples of the Yukon or locality and their respective cultures; or (b) the natural history of the Yukon or a specific locality in the Yukon, and has sufficient historic significance to be so designated."	Historic Resources Act of 2002
Northwest Territories and Nunavut	—	None

(Australia ICOMOS, 1999). All of these documents are, in turn, fundamentally based on the Venice Charter. The ramification of this origin is that changes to buildings are reviewed using a fabric-centered, positivistic approach that is neither people- nor human-centered. In addition, design review systems used in these countries do not allow for the use of human-based evidence to guide decisions, which can be found in similar kinds of design guidelines based in environmental design and behavior research (see Stamps, 2000). While, arguably, because of the Burra Charter, Australia does allow for the possibility of culturally influenced changes to buildings and places in order to maintain authenticity, decision-making is not informed by any kind of social-science-based evidence.

ENVIRONMENTAL ASSESSMENTS/REVIEW

The last category of laws, rules, and regulations that impact built heritage is what I will generically refer to as "environmental assessments," which is usually associated with environmental impact assessments and social impact assessments, or, in the United States, environmental review. It addresses how changes made to both natural and cultural environments impact people and other living things along with ecosystems. The scope of its activities is therefore much larger than just historic buildings and places. Unique to the United States is the conflation of the review of historic buildings and places with environmental assessments.

In the United States, environmental assessments are associated with two laws: Section 106 of the National Historic Preservation Act of 1966 (implementing rule, 36 CFR 800) and the National Environmental Policy Act of 1969 (40 CFR 1500–1508). Section 106 uses the National Register of Historic Places criteria to establish historical significance as well as the Secretary of the Interior's Standards (where applicable). The United Kingdom also uses environmental impact assessments (part of the Town and Country Planning Regulations) which, in regulation 2(1), are required to pay special attention to World Heritage sites and scheduled monuments. In Australia, the applicable law requiring environmental impact assessments is the Environment Protection and Biodiversity Conservation Act 1999, under which impacts to World Heritage properties and national heritage places must be considered. Lastly, the Canadian Environmental Assessment Act of 2012 addresses environmental assessments for all projects under federal authority; section 5(1)(c)

(ii) requires that impacts to cultural heritage must be considered. Different provinces and territories in Canada also implement their own versions of environmental assessments, although by federal law, the federal process should be coordinated with the provincial or territorial processes, when possible.

Even though environmental assessments are supposed to address social impacts, the process of creating environmental impact assessments has been critiqued across many countries, including the ones under review here, for failing to incorporate either social science perspectives or actual social scientists, such as anthropologists, sociologists, or psychologists (Freudenburg, 1989; Glasson & Bellanger, 2003; Stoffle & Minnis, 2013; Taylor, Dale, & Lane, 2001; Vanclay, 2006). According to Reser and Bentrupperbäumer (2001, p. 106), social aspects of environmental assessments often fail to gather any data directly from affected stakeholders and instead consist of "a type of socio-economic and market research-based cost/benefits analysis and forecasting" using existing data, a contention that is also supported by Thomas King (2010). This omission is even more significant considering that the laws of these countries specifically describe the importance of understanding the social, cultural, and/or psychological impacts of development.

The takeaway in terms of environmental assessments is that they are ostensibly designed to help authorities make better informed decisions about whether changes to built heritage will have negative impacts on contemporary peoples. This method of assessment is supposed to take advantage of social science methods conducted by social scientists. In reality, there are often no social scientists involved at all in environmental assessments, much less assessments that specifically address heritage resources. Therefore, even though changes to built heritage may have significant social, cultural, and psychological impacts on people, authorities often do not take the time or consideration to make sure that appropriately trained people are conducting this work using relevant methods to gather essential data used in decision-making processes. The end result is often poor decision making that favors developers and disempowers and disaffects the majority of stakeholders.

CONCLUSION

In reviewing the practice of built heritage conservation, it is clear that it is a system that favors architects, architectural historians, archaeologists, and developers while disempowering, if not entirely sidelining, the majority of stakeholders and their values and priorities. This system privileges scientism and objectivity while its associated policies require that the meanings and values held by members of various communities be ignored. While there are planning activities outside of the direct influence of public policy, these activities constitute a minority of built heritage conservation practice. At a distance, built heritage conservation looks much more like building code enforcement than it does planning. To be sure, it lacks a central focus on understanding and acting on heritage meanings, or, indeed, benefiting the public. It is a system designed for a few, promulgated by a few, and protected against outsider influence.

While there is promise that built heritage conservation could become more people-centered, by working *with* people and adopting social science perspectives and methods from anthropology and sociology, and more human-centered, by adopting methods and perspectives from environmental psychology, overcoming orthodox policy barriers is a formidable challenge. The fact that the orthodox doctrines (and associated ontological and epistemological perspectives) for much of built heritage conservation have remained unchanged since the mid-1960s serves as a reminder that once laws are created to enforce a system, the laws become mechanisms to preserve the system itself. Many scholars and practitioners argue that built heritage conservation seems to exist to preserve itself, and, in the process has become ossified, rigid, and unyielding to changes in culture, values, and social justice (Breglia, 2006, p. 3; Kaufman, 2009, p. 8; Kelbaugh, 2017, p. 64; Meeks & Murphy, 2016, p. 259). This is why we need a fundamental reexamination of the relationship people have with historic places, which is what I will explore next.

Works Cited
Akagawa, N. (2015). *Heritage conservation and Japan's cultural diplomacy: Heritage, national identity and national interest*. Routledge.
The anti-restoration movement. (1878, July 13). *The Architect*, 17-18.
Antons, C. (Ed.). (2017). *Routledge handbook of Asian law*. Routledge.
Association for Conservation of National Treasures (ACNT). (n.d.). https://www.kokuhoshuri.or.jp.
Australia International Council on Monuments and Sites (ICOMOS). (1999). *The Burra Charter*. https://australia.icomos.org/wp-content/uploads/The-Burra-Charter-2013-Adopted-31.10.2013.pdf.
Australian Heritage Council. (2009). *Guidelines for the assessment of places for the National Heritage List*. Commonwealth of Australia.

Avrami, E. (Ed.). (2020). *Preservation and social inclusion*. Columbia University Press.

Avrami, E., Mason, R., & Torre, M. (2000). *Values and heritage conservation*. Getty Conservation Institute.

Aygen, Z. (2014). *International heritage and historic building conservation: Saving the world's past*. Routledge.

Bandarin, F., & van Oers, R. (2012). *The Historic Urban Landscape: Managing heritage in an urban century*. Wiley-Blackwell.

Bashforth, M., Benson, M., Boon, T., Brigham, L., Brigham, R., Brookfield, K., Brown, P., Callaghan, D., Calvin, J.-P., Courtney, R., Cremin, K., Furness, P., Graham, H., Hale, A., Hodgkiss, P., Lawson, J., Madgin, R., Manners, P., Robinson, D., . . . Turner, R. (2015). *How Should Heritage Decisions be Made? Increasing Participation From Where You Are*. Project Report. Connected Communities: Arts & Humanities Research Council. http://heritagedecisions.leeds.ac.uk/publications/.

Benson, V. O., & Klein, R. (2008). *Historic preservation for professionals*. Kent State University Press.

Bernstein, K., & Hansen, J. (2016). SurveyLA: Linking historic resources surveys to local planning. *Journal of the American Planning Association, 82*(2), 88–91.

Bonnici, U. M. (2008). *An introduction to cultural heritage law*. Midsea Books.

Breglia, L. (2006). *Monumental ambivalence: The politics of heritage*. University of Texas Press.

British Standards Institution. (2013). *Guide to the principles of the conservation of historic buildings; BS 7913: 2013*. British Standards Institution.

Brownlee, J. S. (1997). *Japanese historians and the national myths, 1600–1945: The age of the gods and Emperor Jimmu*. University of British Columbia Press.

Byrne, D. (2012). Anti-superstition: Campaigns against popular religion and its heritage in Asia. In P. Daly & T. Winter (Eds.), *Routledge handbook of heritage in Asia* (pp. 295–310). Routledge.

Carman, J., & Sørensen, M. L. S. (2009). Heritage studies: An outline. In M. L. S. Sørensen & J. Carman (Eds.), *Heritage studies: Methods and approaches* (pp. 11–28). Routledge.

Chen, X. (2016). Academic origins and characteristics of the Chinese stylistic restoration. *Frontiers of Architectural Research, 5*, 353–359.

Chung, S. (2005). East Asian values in historic conservation. *Journal of Architectural Conservation, 11*(1), 55–70.

City of Ballarat. (n.d.). Historic Urban Landscape Ballarat. https://www.hulballarat.org.au.

City of Ballarat. (2016). *Our people, culture & place: A new heritage plan for Ballarat 2016–2030*. City of Ballarat. https://maynard.cerdi.edu.au/view_resource.php?resource_id=4403&account=9642f46e025f0b9d3a7c15ce1c911a47.

Congress in Athens. (1931). *The Athens Charter*. First International Congress of Architects and Technicians of Historic Monuments. https://www.icomos.org/en/167-the-athens-charter-for-the-restoration-of-historic-monuments.

Court, S. (2015). *People-centred approaches to the conservation of cultural heritage: Living heritage*. ICCROM.

Daly, P., Chan, B. (2015). "Putting broken pieces back together": Reconciliation, justice, and heritage in post-conflict situations. In Logan. W., Craith, M. C., Kockel, U., *A companion to heritage studies* (pp. 491–506). Wiley-Blackwell.

Dawson, B. (2005). "Why are you protecting this crap?": Perceptions of value for an invented heritage—a Saskatchewan perspective. In *Value-based decision-making for conservation: Canadian studies heritage conservation programme symposium, November 18, 2005, Ottawa*. School of Canadian Studies Heritage Conservation Programme, Carleton University.

Department for Culture, Media and Sport (DCMS). (2010). *Principles of selection for listing buildings*.

Editor. (1908). The preservation of ancient buildings. *The Burlington Magazine for Connoisseurs*, *13*(65), 251-252.

Edwin O. R. (1965). The dynastic cycle. In J. Meskill (Ed.), *The pattern of Chinese history* (pp. 31-33). D. C. Heath and Company.

Elliott, J. (2019). The mystery of history and place: Radical preservation revisited. In J. C. Wells & B. Stiefel (Eds.), *Human-centered built environment heritage preservation: Theory and evidence-based practice*. Routledge.

Emerick, K. (2014). *Conserving and managing ancient monuments: Heritage, democracy, and inclusion*. Boydell & Brewer.

Engelstad, E. (1991). Images of power and contradiction: Feminist theory and post-processual archaeology. *Antiquity*, *65*(248), 502-514.

English Heritage. (1993). *Principles of repair*. English Heritage.

English Heritage. (2008). *Conservation principles: Policies and guidance for the sustainable management of the historic environment*.

Environmental Design Research Association (EDRA) Historic Environment Knowledge Network. (2018). Appendix A: The Palmer House Charter: Principles for integrating environmental design and behavior research into built heritage conservation practice. In J. C. Wells & B. Stiefel (Eds.), *Human-centered built environment heritage preservation: Theory and evidence-based practice*. Routledge.

Environment Protection and Heritage Council. (2008). *A guide to heritage listing in Australia*. Department of the Environment, Water, Heritage and the Arts.

Erder, C. (1994) The Venice Charter under review. In *ICOMOS Scientific Journal, The Venice Charter—La Charte de Venise 1964-1994* (pp. 24-31). ICOMOS. (Original work published 1977).

Fisch, S. (Ed.). (2008). *National approaches to the governance of historical heritage over time: A comparative report*. IOS Press.

Fredheim, L.H., & Khalaf, M. (2016). The significance of values: Heritage value typologies re-examined. *International Journal of Heritage Studies*, *22*(6), 466-481.

Freudenburg, W. R. (1989). Social scientists' contributions to environmental management. *Journal of Social Issues*, *45*(1), 133-152.

Future for Religious Heritage (FRH). (n.d.). *Canada: 600 participants attended the conference "What does heritage change?"* The European Network for Historic Places of Worship. https://www.frh-europe.org/canada-600-participants-attended-the-conference-what-does-heritage-change/.

Gibson, L., & Pendlebury, J. (Eds.). (2009). *Valuing historic environments*. Ashgate Publishing.

Glasson, J., & Bellanger, C. (2003). Divergent practice in a converging system? The case of EIA in France and the UK. *Environmental Impact Assessment Review*, *23*(5), 605-624.

Hardy, M. (Ed.). (2008). *The Venice Charter revisited: Modernism, conservation and tradition in the 21st century*. Cambridge Scholars.

Harrison, R. (2013). *Heritage: Critical approaches.* Routledge.

Hayden, D. (1995). *The power of place.* MIT Press.

Ho, P., Lo, K. Y., Ho, S. Y., Ng, W. Y., & Yuen, M. S. (2014). *Consultancy study on the heritage conservation regimes in other jurisdictions.* Development Bureau, The Government of Hong Kong Special Administrative Region.

Hodder, I. & Hutson, S. (2003). *Reading the past: Current approaches to interpretation in archaeology.* Cambridge University Press.

Hudgins, C. (2012). *Transcription of W. Morton Brown III, Hon. AIA, interview.* Clemson/College of Charleston Historic Preservation Graduate Program.

Institute for Historic Building Conservation (IHBC). (2008). *Membership standards, criteria & guidelines.*

International Council on Monuments and Sites (ICOMOS). (1964). *The Venice Charter.* https://www.icomos.org/en/participer/179-articles-en-francais/ressources/charters-and-standards/157-thevenice-charter.

International Council on Monuments and Sites (ICOMOS). (1994). *Nara document on authenticity.* https://www.icomos.org/en/participer/179-articles-en-francais/ressources/charters-and-standards/157-thevenice-charter

International Council on Monuments and Sites–China (ICOMOS–China). (2004). *Principles for the conservation of heritage sites in China.* Getty Conservation Institute.

Japanese Association for Conservation of Architectural Monuments (JACAM). (n.d.). https://www.bunkenkyo.or.jp/en/

Jokilehto, J. (1999). *A history of architectural conservation.* Butterworth Heinemann.

Kaufman, N. (2009). *Place, race, and story: Essays on the past and future of historic preservation.* Routledge.

Kelbaugh, D. (2017). *Repairing the American metropolis: Common place revisited.* University of Washington Press.

King, T. (2010). Estudo de impacto ambiental, gestão de patrimônio cultural e bens históricos. Aprendendo com os erros dos Estados Unidos da América. *Cadernos de Ciências Humanas 11 e 12, Números 20 e 21, 2008-2009.* Universidade Estadual de Santa Cruz.

Krishna, A. (2014). The care and management of historic Hindu temples in India: An examination of preservation policies influenced by the Venice Charter in non-Judeo-Christian contexts. *Change Over Time: International Journal of Conservation and the Built Environment, 4*(2), 358-386.

Lagae, J. (2008). From "patrimoine partagé" to "whose heritage"? Critical reflections on colonial built heritage in the city of Lubumbashi, Democratic Republic of the Congo. *Afrika Focus, 21*(1), 11-30.

Larsen, K. E. (1994). Preservation of historic buildings in Japan: Principles and practices in an international perspective. In *Kyoto conference on Japanese studies 1994,* (vol. III, pp. 61-65). International Research Center for Japanese Studies.

Lipe, W. D. (1984). Value and meaning in cultural resources. In H. Cleere (Ed.), *Approaches to the archaeological heritage* (pp. 1-11). Cambridge University Press.

Listed Building Act. (1990). Planning (Listed Buildings and Conservation Areas) Act 1990 (U.K.).

Little, B. (2014). Values-based preservation, civic engagement, and the US National Park Service. *APT Bulletin: The Journal of Preservation Technology, 45*(2/3), 49-56.

Lixinski, L. (2015). Between orthodoxy and heterodoxy: The troubled relationships between heritage studies and heritage law. *International Journal of Heritage Studies*, *21*(3), 203-214.

Low, S. M. (2003). Social sustainability: People, history, and values. In *Managing change: Sustainable approaches to the conservation of the built environment* (pp. 47-64). Getty Conservation Institute.

Lowenthal, D. (1985). *The past is a foreign country*. Cambridge University Press.

Meeks, S., & Murphy, C. (2016). *The past and future city: How historic preservation is reviving America's communities*. Island Press.

Muñoz Viñas, S. (2005). *Contemporary theory of conservation*. Elsevier.

Murray, N. (2005). Cape Town's Tana Baru burial ground: Wasteland or prime property? *Journal for Islamic Studies*, *25*, 55-77.

Nanda, R., Burke, F., Burman, P. A. T. I., Kohler, N., Mileti, D. S., Roemich, H., Snickars, F., & Sörlin, S. (2001). Group report: Values and society. In N. S. Baer & F. Snickars (Eds.), *Rational decision-making in the preservation of cultural property* (pp. 61-80). Dahlem University Press.

National Trust for Historic Preservation. (2017). *Preservation for people: A vision for the future*.

Obafemi, O. (2017). Against the reception of Eurocentric heritage theories on non-Western cultures: A case of pre/post colonisation in Nigeria. In J. Rodrigues dos Santos (Ed.), *Preserving transcultural heritage: Your way or my way?* (pp. 953-963). Caleidoscópio.

Ohba, G. (2017). Two approvals from the 1931 Athens conference: Anastylosis and international collaboration for architectural conservation: New evidence. *Conservation and Management of Archaeological Sites*, *19*(2) 99-105.

Organization of World Heritage Cities–Asia Pacific (OWHC-AP). (2014). *First OWHC Asia-Pacific regional meeting for World Heritage cities* (program). OWHC Asia Pacific Regional Secretariat, Korean National Commission for UNESCO, UNESCO Bangkok Office.

Parks Canada. (2003). *Standards and guidelines for the conservation of historic places in Canada*.

Pickard, R. (2012). *Policy and law in heritage conservation*. Spon Press; Taylor and Francis.

Rains, A., & Henderson, L. G. (1966). *With heritage so rich*. Random House.

Reser, J. P., & Bentrupperbäumer, J. M. (2001). Reframing the nature and scope of social impact assessment: A modest proposal relating to psychological and social (psychosocial) impacts. In A. Dale, N. Taylor, & M. Lane (Eds.), *Social assessment in natural resource management institutions* (pp. 106-122). CSIRO Publications.

Restoration of the Paul Revere House, Boston. (1914, July). *The Architectural Record*, *36*, 80.

The restoration of Westminster Hall. (1885, March 28). *The Athenaeum*, *2996*, 414.

The restoration of the White House. (1903, February 29). *The American Architect and Building News*, *79*, 67.

Rodenberg, J., & Wagenaar, P. (2023). Understanding the governance of heritage: A plea for using public administration theories in heritage studies. In J. Rosenberg, P. Wagenaar, & G. J. L. M. Burgers (Eds.), *Calling on the community: Understanding participation in the heritage sector, an interactive governance perspective* (pp. 7-27). Berghahn Books.

Rouse, W. B. (2007). *People and organizations: Explorations of human-centered design*. John Wiley & Sons.

Rwanda Parliament. (2016). Law on the Preservation of Cultural Heritage and Traditional Knowledge. https://rwandalii.org/akn/rw/act/law/2016/28/eng@2016-08-15.

Sauvegrain, A. (2001). Dialogues of architectural preservation in modern Vietnam: The 36 Streets commercial quarter of Hanoi. *Traditional Dwelling and Settlements Review*, *13*(1), 23-31.

Semes, S. W. (2009). *The future of the past: A conservation ethic for architecture, urbanism, and historic preservation*. W. W. Norton & Company.

Silberman, N., & Puser, M. (2012). Collective memory as affirmation: People-centered cultural heritage in a digital age. In E. Giaccardi (Ed.), *Heritage and social media: Understanding heritage in a participatory culture* (pp. 13-29). Routledge.

Silliman, S. W. (2008). Collaborative Indigenous archaeology: Troweling at the edges, eying the center. In S. W. Silliman (Ed.), *Collaborating at the trowel's edge: teaching and learning in Indigenous archaeology* (pp. 1-24). University of Arizona Press.

Silva, R. (1994). The significance of the Venice International Charter for the conservation and restoration of monuments and sites, with special reference to eastern countries. In *ICOMOS Scientific Journal, The Venice Charter – La Charte de Venise 1964-1994* (pp. 40-44). ICOMOS. (Original work published 1983)

Smith, G. S., Messenger, P. M., & Soderland, H. A. (Eds.). (2010). *Heritage values in contemporary society*. Left Coast Press.

Smith, L. (2006). *Uses of heritage*. Routledge.

———. (2012). Editorial: A critical heritage studies? *International Journal of Heritage Studies*, *18*(6), 533-540.

Smith, L., Shackel, P., Campbell, G. (2011). Introduction: Class still matters. In L. Smith, P. Shackel, G. Campbell (eds.), *Heritage, Labour and the Working Classes* (pp. 1-16). Routledge.

Sprinkle, J. H. (2014). *Crafting preservation criteria: The National Register of Historic Places and American historic preservation*. Routledge.

Stamps, A. E. (2000). *Psychology and the aesthetics of the built environment*. Kluwer Academic.

Starn, R. (2002). Authenticity and historic preservation: Toward an authentic history. *History of the Human Sciences*, *15*(1), 1-16.

Stenmark, M. (2017). *Scientism: Science, ethics, and religion*. Routledge.

Stipe, R. E. (ed.) (2003). *A richer heritage: Historic preservation in the twenty-first century*. University of North Carolina Press.

Stoffle, R., & Minnis, J. (2013). Resilience at risk: Epistemological and social construction barriers to risk communication. In A. Boholm (Ed.), *New perspectives on risk communication: Uncertainty in a complex society* (pp. 55-68). Taylor and Francis.

Swenson, A. (2013). *The rise of heritage: Preserving the past in France, Germany and England, 1789-1914*. Cambridge University Press.

Taylor, N., Dale, A., & Lane, M. (2001). Conclusions: The way forward. In A. Dale, N. Taylor, & M. Lane (Eds.), *Social assessment in natural resource management institutions* (pp. 283-298). CSIRO Publishing.

Tuan, Y.-F. (1974). *Topophilia: A study of environmental perception, attitudes, and values*. Prentice-Hall.

Tunbridge, J. E., Ashworth, G. J. (1996). *Dissonant heritage: the management of the past as a resource in conflict*. J. Wiley.

Tyler, N., Ligibel, T. J., & Tyler, I. R. (2009). *Historic preservation: An introduction to its history, principles, and practice*. W. W. Norton & Co.

United Nations Educational, Scientific and Cultural Organization (UNESCO). (2011). *Recommendation on the Historic Urban Landscape*. https://whc.unesco.org/uploads/activities/documents/activity-638-98.pdf.

United Nations Educational, Scientific and Cultural Organization (UNESCO). (2016). *The HUL guidebook: Managing heritage in dynamic and constantly changing urban environments.*

Vanclay, F. (2006). Principles for social impact assessment: A critical comparison between the international and US documents. *Environmental Impact Assessment Review*, 26(1), 3-14.

Walter, N. (2014). From values to narrative: A new foundation for the conservation of historic buildings. *International Journal of Heritage Studies*, 20(6), 634-650.

Waters, J. (1983). *Maintaining a sense of place: A citizen's guide to community preservation*. Institute of Community and Area Development, University of Georgia.

Waterton, E., Watson, S., Silverman, H. (2017). An introduction to heritage in action. In H. Silverman, E. Waterton, S. Watson (eds.), *Heritage in action* (pp. 3-16). Springer.

Weeks, K. D., & Jandl, H. W. (1996). The Secretary of the Interior's Standards for the Treatment of Historical Properties: A philosophical and ethical framework for making treatment decisions. In S. J. Kelley (Ed.), *Standards for preservation and rehabilitation* (pp. 7-23). ASTM.

Wells, J. C. (2007). The plurality of truth in culture, context, and heritage: A (mostly) post-structuralist analysis of urban conservation charters. *City and Time*, 3(2:1), 1-13.

———. (2015). In stakeholders we trust: Changing the ontological and epistemological orientation of built heritage assessment through participatory action research. In B. Szmygin (Ed.), *How to assess built heritage? Assumptions, methodologies, examples of heritage assessment systems* (pp. 249-265). ICOMOS International Scientific Committee for Theory and Philosophy of Conservation and Restoration; Romualdo Del Bianco Foundatione; Lublin University of Technology.

———. (2016). Can critical heritage studies provide a workable theory for the future of conservation? In B. Szmygin (Ed.), Heritage in transformation: Cultural heritage protection in XXI century—problems, challenges, predictions (pp. 209-226). ICOMOS-Poland; Romualdo Del Bianco Foundatione; Lublin University of Technology.

———. (2017). The Main Street approach to community design. In K. Melcher, B. Stiefel, & K. Faurest (Eds.), *Community-built: Art, construction, preservation, and place* (pp. 172-189). Routledge.

———. (2021). Does intra-disciplinary historic preservation scholarship address the exigent issues of practice? Exploring the character and impact of preservation knowledge production in relation to critical heritage studies, equity, and social justice. *International Journal of Heritage Studies*, 27(5), 449-469.

Wells, J. C., & Lixinski, L. (2016). Heritage values and legal rules: Identification and treatment of the historic environment via an adaptive regulatory framework (part 1). *Journal of Cultural Heritage Management and Sustainable Development*, 6(3), 345-364.

———. (2017). Heritage values and legal rules: Identification and treatment of the historic environment via an adaptive regulatory framework (part 2). *Journal of Cultural Heritage Management and Sustainable Development*, 7(3), 345-363.

Wells, J. C., & Stiefel, B. (Eds.). (2019). *Human-centered built environment heritage preservation: Theory and evidence-based practice*. Routledge.

Wills, J. E. (1994). *Mountain of fame: Portraits in Chinese history*. Princeton University Press.

Wilson, M. (2017, January 18). What Apple, Google, and Tesla get wrong. *Co.Design/Fast Company*. https://www.fastcodesign.com/3067277/don-norman-on-what-apple-google-and-tesla-get-wrong

Winter, T. (2013). Clarifying the critical in critical heritage studies. *International Journal of Heritage Studies*, *19*(6), 532–545.

Witcomb, A., Buckley K. (2013). Engaging with the future of "critical heritage studies": looking back in order to look forward. *International Journal of Heritage Studies, 19*(6), 562–578.

Worthing, D., & Bond, S. (2008). *Managing built heritage: The role of cultural significance*. Blackwell Publishing.

Yang, Z. (2021). The City Destructive reconstruction in China: Interpreting authenticity in the Shuidong Reconstruction Project, Huizhou, Guangdong Province. *Built Heritage*, *5*(15), 1–14.

Zhao, L. (2006). 遗产保护与避暑山庄 (Heritage protection and the mountain resort). 辽宁民族出版社 (Shenyang Shi: Liaoning min zu chu ban she).

CHAPTER 2

Being Affected by Old Places and the Person–Patina Relationship

> What is the role of bodies, emotions, the senses [in heritage management]? (Ireland, Brown, & Schofield 2020, p. 827)

> Despite the attention paid to emotional qualities and phenomenological experiences of places in assessments of significance there remains a hierarchy of knowledges that privileges the apparently—the factual, the descriptive, and the materiality, rather than the human meaning and felt experience. (Hoskins, 2014, p. 23)

INTRODUCTION

City planners often uncritically tout the importance of built heritage conservation in retaining an area's "sense of place." The reality is that there has been little research into the essential elements that define sense of place in relation to historic environments, especially from a phenomenological perspective, or a perspective that understands the psychological relationship between an individual and a particular environment. What this chapter will reveal is the unique role that environmental patina plays in "Being Affected by Old Places" (BAOP), or the relationship between patina—a key characteristic of physical age in an environment—and emotional affect. I will begin with a brief overview of the history of research into the emotional affect that the historic environment has on individuals and the role that the physical age of places, as manifested through decay or patina, plays in the lifeworld, which is a concept fundamental to phenomenology. Lastly, I will introduce the concept of a "spontaneous fantasy" along with the proposition that this phenomenon is essential for the emotional attachment to historic places.

Although it is not the purpose of this chapter to define the nature of phenomenologies and phenomenological reductions, as this has been done in great detail elsewhere (see Merleau-Ponty, 1962; Moustakas, 1994; Ray, 1994; van Manen, 1990; von Eckartsberg, 1998), it is useful to provide a brief overview of these topics in order to orient the reader who may be unfamiliar with these terms. In general, a phenomenology is a methodology used to understand the embedded experience of being in the world and is based on the philosophical work of Martin Heidegger (1927/1962). This chapter, in particular, focuses on what is known as existential phenomenology, which was first explored by Merleau-Ponty (1962). The assumption is that it is impossible for a human being to exist independently of place or a particular environment. We therefore experience reality through our bodies—hence, the emphasis on the embodied experience. In other words, we cannot experience the world independently of how our bodies interface with the environment. Phenomenologies are very interested in exploring this interface between body and environment, especially how it manifests in a precognitive fashion. For this reason, phenomenologies are frequently used in research that explores the nature of emotions and feelings. This characteristic is a primary reason why phenomenologies are frequently used in nursing research to understand pain as experienced by medical patients. Phenomenologies also feature prominently in the work of humanistic geographers who wish to explore the subjective experiences of place (e.g., Relph, 1976; Seamon, 1979; Tuan, 1974). A phenomenological reduction is a way of bracketing the world so that the focus is on the precognitive experience of being in the world and is used to understand the affective quality of places. Critically, phenomenologies also have much in common with the gestalt psychological methods upon which the authors of built heritage conservation doctrine based their theories (see chapter 3), yet this has been largely forgotten by the field.

A BRIEF HISTORY OF EXPLORATIONS INTO THE EMOTIONAL AFFECT OF THE HISTORIC ENVIRONMENT

In the early part of the nineteenth century, John Ruskin, an eccentric English art critic widely credited with developing the foundation for architectural conservation theory, became fascinated with ancient buildings, and especially Gothic cathedrals. He spent a great deal of time absorbing, sketching, and then writing about his experience of being in these ancient places in *Seven Lamps of Architecture* (1849) and the *Stones of Venice* (1851; 1853a; 1853b). While it would not be technically correct to assign Ruskin's work a phenomenological label, his writings often focused on the subjective experience of being in certain places. In particular, he focused on the aesthetic character of Gothic buildings, extolling their superior and honest nature of craftsmanship compared to contemporary construction and how these characteristics made him feel, especially as expressed through their age. It was this exploration of the effect that the physical age of these places had on his emotional state that was most profound. For Ruskin, the decayed state of ancient buildings was essential in catalyzing a "feeling of mixed melancholy" when he experienced them (Ruskin, 1877, p. 74). He described how this aged appearance of buildings manifested as a "deep sense of voicefulness, of stern watching, of mysterious sympathy" and how the decayed patina of surfaces literally absorbed the essence of the "passing waves of humanity" that the building had experienced over time (Ruskin, 1849, p. 249). In his writings, Ruskin demonstrated what might accurately be called an obsession with trying to understand the emotions that this "golden stain of time" (Ruskin, 1849, p. 249) instilled in his being, often comparing the decay of nature with the decay of buildings (Ruskin, 1877, p. 73). In this sense, Ruskin undertook one of the first methodical explorations of how an individual's emotional state is affected by aged surfaces in a historic environment.

There are many other examples of nineteenth century literature that discuss the effect of the physical age upon the viewer, linking the experience with the sublime and altered emotional states; it was this experience that drove the Romantic era's fascination for architectural ruins (Crane, 2000, pp. 19-34). By the turn of the twentieth century, however, professional attitudes toward historic preservation took a decidedly positivistic turn, while laypeople continued to extoll the emotional virtues of the physical age of ancient places; for example, Mildred Cram (1917) describes the old part of Charleston, South Carolina, as having a "rare and very personal quality, a patina, of inimitable luster" that is "two-thirds atmospheric and one-third physical" in recognition of the emotional affect that this area had upon her (Cram, 1917, pp. 114-115). In this era, the practice of history, and especially archaeology, assumed a "spirit of scientific accuracy and impartiality" as Henry Smith Williams (1904, p. 4) relates in his essay on the best practices of the period. Alois Riegl (1903/1996), an Austrian art historian, understood the growing dichotomy between the subjectivism epitomized by Ruskin's work and this rise of scientism when he created the concept of "age value," which "addresses the emotions directly" as opposed to "historical value" that "rests on a scientific basis" (Riegl, 1903/1996, p. 74) in how one either experiences or objectively describes historic places, respectively. Through these concepts, Riegl helped cement the importance of decay and patina in architectural conservation theory, but unfortunately, over the next century, conservation practice paid little attention to the experiential qualities of decay.

By the time of Colonial Williamsburg's restoration in the 1930s, a foundational activity for heritage conservation in the United States, the practice of built heritage conservation had effectively abandoned the importance of the personal, subjective experience of the older built environment and the effect that the age of building materials had on one's emotional state. Practitioners instead placed an extreme emphasis on the scientific method to define their activities (Kimball, 1935). In the twentieth century, the Athens Charter (Congress in Athens, 1931) and the Venice Charter (ICOMOS, 1964) solidified this positivistic approach adopted by preservation experts that continues to be promulgated to the present (Wells, 2007). The first half of the twentieth century was therefore remarkable in its effectiveness in reinforcing positivistic approaches to exploring the values of the historic environment and, in effect, denying even the possibility that a person's fundamental reaction to historic buildings and places could be emotional, rather than objective.

Maurice Merleau-Ponty is credited with developing existential phenomenology (e.g., Priest, 1998; Seamon, 1982), and while he did not focus on historic environments, he established the place of historical significance as residing not only in the present, but also within himself (Merleau-Ponty, 1962, p. 413) in contradiction to contemporary preservation practice's insistence that significance is in the past and somehow physically embodied in building fabric (Waterton, Smith, & Campbell, 2006, p. 349). It was not until the 1970s that Yi-Fu Tuan (1974, 1977) renewed the scholarly investigation of the subjective experience of historic places through a phenomenological approach to a limited extent, as it was not his primary focus. Other researchers (Dovey, 1985; Relph, 1976) use a phenomenological perspective to understand what makes a place "authentic," which is related to its perceived history. This approach holds the promise to greatly inform the concept of historical authenticity by moving beyond purely objective and factual ways to visually describe buildings and places and instead focusing on emotional affect, being, and experience. Dovey (1985), in particular, emphasized that the use of space had much more to do with experienced authenticity than anything objectively visual; this kind of use generates emotional attachment to places.

While the 1970s and 80s were clearly the height of scholarly interest in the use of phenomenologies to understand the person–place relationship, a number of researchers continue this work into the present (Casey, 1993, 1997, 2007; Malpas, 1999, 2006; Mugerauer, 1994, 1995; Seamon, 1979, 1984, 1993). A thread through all this work is the centrality of place to human existence, and especially human memory. Indeed, memory independent of place is probably a fallacy: psychologists have long established that if a person wants to remember a sequence of facts, recall is more reliable if the facts are embedded within an imagined physical environment (Wingfield & Byrnes, 2014, pp. 349–350). Malpas (1999, p. 186) reinforces this relationship between memory and a physical place in explaining that the "pathways, monuments and sites" in an environment are useful mnemonic devices to access "cultural memory and [a] storehouse of ideas." A theme long established in phenomenologies, however, is that memory accessed in this way is often fabricated, or in a more positive sense, creatively imagined such that a place can create illusions in the mind of the observer (Merleau-Ponty, 1962, p. 242; Malpas, 1999, p. 86). In the absence of objective facts about a place, it is even more likely that people will imagine memories about a specific place, developing a sense of nostalgia for something that actually probably never existed (Casey, 1987).

Jack Elliott, Jr. (2002, p. 54) argues that phenomenologies should be used more frequently when trying to understand why a "historic" place is significant or meaningful to people—especially members of the public who may not be trained in the art/historical associations of heritage experts. Yet, researchers have not had much interest in using phenomenologies in this way, beyond a few examples (Byrne, 2013; Farmer & Knapp, 2008; Greenspan, 2005; Stefanovic, 1998). A possible reason for this situation might simply be that as a research methodology, phenomenology is no longer as "popular" as it was during its geographical heyday in the 1970s and 1980s. While the approach has remained in strong use in nursing research, for instance, researchers in the built environment have moved on to other methodologies or simply rejected the use of empirical evidence in informing either historical significance or design, instead relying on rationalistic arguments for theory and practice.

In addition, with the exception of my own research (e.g., Wells & Baldwin, 2012), there does not appear to be any published phenomenological studies that specifically address how the physical age of places manifested through patina affects people, which is surprising considering the early genesis of some of these ideas in Ruskin's work. This may be explained, in part, by the dominance of heritage conservation doctrine and rules, laws, and regulations that, by design, deprecate investigations into the subjective, emotional experience of the historic environment (Wells, 2007; Wells & Lixinski, 2016, 2017). In my study, I did a comparative analysis of I'On, a new urbanist community, with the location of the United States' first historic district in Charleston, South Carolina, which represented a "new" versus an "old" place, respectively. The physical designs of both places were remarkably similar in terms of architectural styles, density, the street network, street widths, buildings setbacks, and materials. The most significant difference was age: I'On did not exist before about 1998, while historic Charleston existed before 1860. By conducting a third-person phenomenology on each of these places, I was able to understand how the experience of these places differed and then attributed this difference to the appearance of physical age through environmental patina (Wells & Baldwin, 2012).

THE EXPERIENCE OF AGE THROUGH ENVIRONMENTAL PATINA

Age is the physical description of an object's or an environment's inevitable decay over time. People experience the physical age of places at the point where perception merges into feelings that result from being in and experiencing the historic environment. This perception of physical age is "the province of biology—of animal sense perception—not of physics" (Lanza, 2007, p. 22) and as such defies simple quantification and objective descriptions. The experience of age is therefore part of the lifeworld as Jack Elliott (2002) describes where the "physical character and matrices of historical, mythical, and social associations can and do evoke experiences of awe, wonder, beauty, and identity, among others" (Elliott, 2002, p. 54). "Age value" adds an experiential dimension to the purely objective description of the way building materials naturally change and degrade over time. Barbara Appelbaum (2007, p. 104) succinctly indicates that "an object has age value when it *is* old, it *looks* old, and we *like* that it looks old" (original author's emphasis). Moreover, age value is related to authenticity and to the ideal of telling the "truth" about objects because for "objects that are no longer new, the look of newness can be unsettling. . . . An unpleasant air of false newness is often caused by overly shiny surfaces, perhaps because of an incongruity between an object's sign of age and the newness that the shine implies" (Appelbaum, 2007, p. 109). Riegl (1903/1996, p. 73) refers to age value visually with direct references to the deteriorated state of surfaces, such as an "imperfection, a lack of completeness, a tendency to dissolve shape and color" and "decay and disintegration."

Humans seem to have an innate ability to assess the age of an environment (Tuan, 1977, p. 125; Wells, 2020) and can accurately judge the authenticity of a new place from an old place, even if the design of both environments are extremely similar. The degradation of building and landscape materials as well as art-historical changes in taste and design guide one's perception of age. Authenticity is in part evinced from the presence of a sufficient degree and character of decay in a particular environment; the lack of decay bespeaks of insufficient authenticity (Wells, 2020). In this sense, old buildings have "history written on their faces" and can "proclaim [their] age" (Architectural Review quoted in Lowenthal, 1985, p. 151). Certain places are known specifically for the overt signs of decay and its associated verisimilitude, such as ghost towns where "artifacts are expected to show signs of wear, and it is in large part this antiqued patina that lends a ghost town its authenticity" (DeLyser, 1999, p. 614).

In order to understand how patina affects people, it is useful to define the physical manifestation of decay in relation to perception through the use of a scale (see Figure 2.1). On the left side of the scale there is no evidence of decay at all; the materials or landscape appears to be "new." On the opposite end of the scale is complete dissolution of form to the point where it is impossible to deduce original appearances. Although bricks from a building are used in the example, complete landscapes could also be assessed in a similar way. This device should make clear the relationship between perceived age, decay, authenticity, and complexity. As materials and landscapes age, both undergo a change in perception toward increased authenticity and complexity.

Physical decay and perception		
No decay	**Some decay**	**Complete decay**
New	Old	Very old
Readable	Mostly readable	Illegible
Ordered	Semi-ordered	Chaos
Simplicity	Complexity	Extreme complexity
Questionable authenticity	Authentic	Cannot assess authenticity

FIGURE 2.1. Physical decay and perception scale (photos by author)

Ruskin (1849, p. 249) described building material decay as the "golden stain of time." The idea of a stain is appropriate because "patina" refers to the surface of objects and, in a metaphorical sense, the surface of landscapes. Patina is loaded with meanings of authenticity and value as Bernard Feilden (1994) relates: "Patina is acquired by the materials of an historic building through age, by weathering or oxidation and by use. It is something which cannot be produced artificially, for the artificial aging which forgers and commercial restorers apply will always look false after a short time.... Patina is precious because it can only be acquired by time" (Feilden, 1994. pp. 247-248). The value associated with patina makes it easy to imbue it with a heightened artistic quality; the brush of nature improves humankind's work through the "festoons of ornamentation comprising bubbles, cracks, peelings, emergent mould, random discolourings, and the residues deposited by water" (Edensor, 2005, p. 72).

Decay generally has negative connotations, such as when referring to "rust or mildew," while pleasing decay is referred to as "patina." But not all materials receive equal treatment in terms of whether they can acquire decay or patina through time. Materials long used by builders, such as stone, brick, and bronze, most certainly acquire patina, but materials that gained widespread use in the twentieth century, such as concrete, aluminum, or steel,

FIGURE 2.2. Decay or patina? The answer depends on bodily experience (photo by author)

are usually understood to simply decay, rust, or corrode (Dekkers, 2000, p. 51). The key concept at hand is that determining whether something is decay or patina is influenced not only by individual perception, but also by cultural contexts. Someone may think dirt adds a pleasant surface to stone, while someone else may react with revulsion and an innate desire to clean the surface (Muñoz Viñas, 2005, p. 104; see Figure 2.2). Figure 2.3 presents a flowchart of how this process may occur.

According to Phoebe Weil (1976/1996, pp. 398-399), the term "patina" first came into use in the seventeenth century to describe a dark surface finish "which time causes to appear on paintings, that can occasionally be flattering to them." The application of this finish is known as "patination"—the same term often applied to the antiquing process of certain metals. Only humans engage in patination while nature simply creates a patina (i.e., patination is the exclusive domain of people, not nature). The architectural and art conservator Paul Philippot (1996, p. 373) defines patina as the "relationship between the original state and the present state of the original materials" of a historical object. This relationship is not simply a physical description, but one that requires deliberation and interpretation. For Philippot, patina "is not physical or chemical, but a critical concept" (Philippot, 1996, p. 373). Patina is therefore created by acts of nature and humans: when the change

FIGURE 2.3. Process of the perception of patina, decay, or forgery

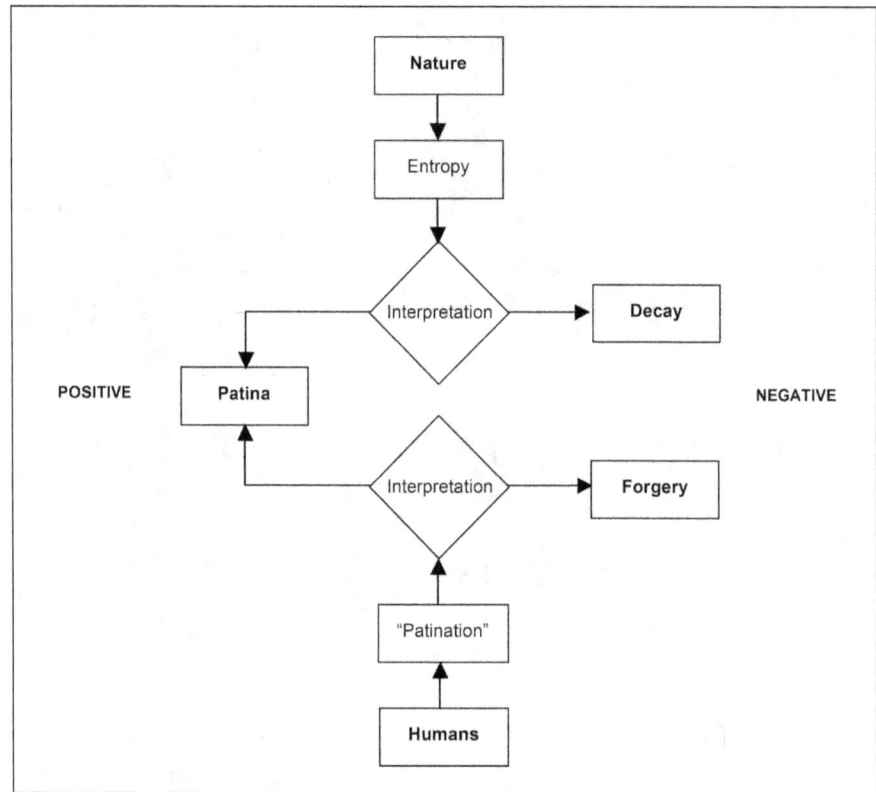

is of natural origins, it tends to be used synonymously with decay or degradation; when the change is artificial through the process of patination it is either artistic embellishment or an attempt at forgery. Decay and artifice become patina when they acquire positive connotations for the interpreter of the historical object.

While age can add positive value to a place—e.g., through patina—it can also be perceived negatively depending on context. For instance, we think decay in animals is ugly while decay in vegetation is generally beautiful, but even in this context, too much deterioration of plant material can be unsettling—a landscape too closely associated with death is undesirable (Lowenthal, 1985, p. 135). But even the products of death can be construed in a positive light, as David Lowenthal (1994, p. 41) explains:

> Viewed without prejudice, products of plant decay can be seen to have a charm of their own. Slime molds congeal into a mass of powdery grey or sulfur and crimson spores that enliven lawns. The intricacy of bird's nest fungus is a fascinating adjunct of stem decay. When bacterial fasciation

infects forsythia, flower-fanciers generally cut off the clusters of distorted leaves that tip the plank-like shoots. Yet their oddity would add varietal interest to any garden.

The idea is that decay in itself can add value to landscapes that would otherwise be feared or abhorred. Ruins are an example of this phenomenon—places that may have strongly negative associations yet have become revered places for their melancholia. The Romantic Period of the nineteenth century ushered in the passion for ruins—typically Classical or Medieval variations—to the degree that wealthy individuals had "new" ruins created that attempted to mimic the decay of the authentic objects (Roth, Lyons & Merewether, 1997, p. 79) so that the same feeling could be engendered.

Can modern monuments, such as old warehouses, skyscrapers, prisons, and modern-era landscapes also be imbued with positive connotations due to their age? James Dickinson (2001, p. 55), a sociologist, believes that this possibility is indeed plausible: "Obsolete industrial structures constitute an important stock of potential symbolic architecture and thus are prime candidates for transformation into historical monuments." These monuments become increasingly valuable as they "gradually acquire the worn patina and fragmented, eroded structure that give familiar survivals of the past, such as castles, temples, and pyramids their distinctive allure" (Dickinson, 2001, p. 58).

Since the 1960s, artists have increasingly depicted and photographed industrial areas and "ordinary" modern landscapes that exhibit signs of decay. The end result of their work is a new definition of beauty in which modern decay is transformed into art. Ruins have even spawned coffee table books such as American Ruins by Camilo Vergara (1999, p. 11), a work that explores the "peculiar beauty" of the ruined inner cities of New York, Camden, Newark, Philadelphia, Baltimore, Chicago, Gary, Los Angeles, and Detroit. These are places universally perceived as dangerous and forbidding, yet they have an allure of mystery and an aesthetic appeal unique to these landscapes. Ruins are poetic, magical places, "a fantasy that dances in the moonlight. Ruinmood excites wonder. Enthralled, we are captivated by inchoate feelings that come to light like moonbeams and then sink behind the shadows of primitive walls. Shudder with delight" (Ginsberg, 2004, p. 317).

Ruins obtain their value in part through the "intersection of culture and nature" (Dickinson, 2001, p. 60), much in the way that Ruskin perceived his

FIGURE 2.4. Al Capone's cell at Eastern State Penitentiary, Philadelphia, rendered more authentic and vicarious because of extensive decay (photo by author)

"golden stain of time" to evolve. Normally through regular maintenance, plants, lichens, and mildew are not allowed to begin to digest and slowly dissolve structures. With ruins, however, nature has free abandon and adds to the patina of place, adding an extra aesthetic layer of appreciation. In the extreme, it becomes difficult to determine where culture ends and nature begins as both blur into the experience.

Eastern State Penitentiary (see Figures 2.4 and 2.5), located in Philadelphia, Pennsylvania, is revered around the world specifically for its melancholy decay. This place has housed the worst examples of human behavior since its construction in the early part of the nineteenth century. Abandoned in the 1970s, it was left to molder but was resurrected as a monument in the 1990s. It is now open for tours; the Halloween tours are one of the most popular events at the site, capitalizing on the mystery and intrigue of the decayed surroundings. (The author used to be employed at this site and has participated in the Halloween tour.)

In summary, while decay in built environments can be interpreted in a negative light, it is often just the opposite. When decay becomes patina, it is a revered, precious commodity that lends authenticity to place and allows us to use our imagination to connect with the past. Patina, therefore, opens the

FIGURE 2.5.
Eastern State Penitentiary Historic Site, Philadelphia (photo by author)

door to spontaneous fantasies—stories rooted in particular places catalyzed by the physical appearance of objects in landscapes.

THE ROLE OF SPONTANEOUS FANTASY IN THE EMOTIONAL ATTACHMENT TO HISTORIC ENVIRONMENTS

Many people enjoy historic urban places because of their ability to catalyze our imagination; sitting in a street cafe in Paris, for instance, it is hard to not have one's mind drift to Paris as Vincent Van Gogh experienced it in the nineteenth century. The key to this experience is that the images in our mind only have a tangential connection with a real or genuine past. This phenomenon is the difference between what David Lowenthal (1998) refers to as history (the objective past) and heritage (the subjective and revisioned past that most of us experience). Knowing the "real" history of a place and whether the buildings are authentic or not is not necessary in order to become attached to it. In fact, knowing too much about the objective history of a place can ruin the sense of discovering it for the first time (Bell, 1999, p. 93).

Guided by heritage conservation doctrine, the professional and academic practice of historic preservation focuses on the objectification of history, while tangentially addressing the role of heritage in defining historical significance. The more objective the history, the higher the degree of supposed historical significance. This practice, unfortunately, ignores the role of the lifeworld in the experience of place, as Jack Elliott (2002, p. 54) describes. Fundamentally, people experience place in a subjective fashion and knowing or revealing an objective or "true" history does not necessarily correspond to an increase in the overall affective experience, nor does it necessarily relate to how important the place is to an individual or groups of people. This subjective quality of the historic built environment is fundamentally at odds with the golden rule of preservation/conservation: Do not create a "false sense of history" to prevent the "subjective" aspects of an affective experience from entering the picture (Weeks & Jandl, 1996, p. 19). Salvador Muñoz Viñas (2005, p. 93) explains that the fundamental problem with this line of reasoning is that for an object to have a false history, its existence must also therefore be false, but this cannot be as "objects cannot exist in a state of falsehood, nor can they have a false nature. If they really exist, they are inherently real."

Because of the penchant for positivism in built heritage conservation, these images held in the minds of people who experience older places have all too often been discarded as irrelevant to informing why historic places are significant. Yet, these vignettes of the past may be one of the most important reasons why older or "historic" places are important to everyday people. Beyond Robert Riley's (1997) discussion of how the "vicarious landscape" can be more important and real to people than an actual landscape, there is little in the way of literature that discusses imagined places and the emotional import on people. It is for this reason that I wanted to better understand the relationship between fantasies—manifesting as images of the past in the mind's eye of the observer—and experiences, especially emotional experiences. From my research (Wells, 2017), I have been able to establish a relationship between the experience of patina that is an intimate part of old places, spontaneous fantasies, and an increased amount of emotional attachment to specific places. Spontaneous fantasies, therefore, are related to the experience of the physical age of places.

It is, however, important to differentiate spontaneous fantasy from premeditated fantasy. In the latter, cognition and higher-order thought processes come into play when creating a narrative. In the former, however, the narrative simply appears without significant effort on the part of the affected individual. These spontaneous fantasies seem to arise unconsciously and automatically and as such it may be difficult, if not impossible, to repress the formation of these imaginative narratives about the past (Wells & Baldwin, 2012). While one could delve into the Freudian implications of the nature of these fantasies, the fact remains that they will happen, and continue to happen, regardless of cultural or societal mores. To deny these kinds of spontaneous fantasies is to deny human nature.

Because it appears that the imaginary history of a place—through the experience of spontaneous fantasy—increases personal attachment (Wells, 2017), the meanings and values derived from this experience are fundamentally at odds with both preservation/conservation practice and theory. Such subjective approaches to preservation practice are likely to be maligned as a nostalgic, "romantic vision" of the past (Cliver, 1992, p. 177). Indeed, spontaneous fantasy and the imagination are problematic concepts for all disciplines of the built environment. These words conjure pejorative images of the "Disneyfication" of landscape and the ills of nostalgia; it is the ultimate of irrational frivolity that designers should avoid at all costs.

The existence, however, of a relationship between patina and spontaneous fantasy cannot be erased by the diatribes of designers. Others, such as Rodney Harrison (2004, p. 204) recognize that "ruin and decay [evoke] the phenomenological sense of 'being-affected-by-the-past'" and foster a "creative space within which new memories can be evoked and created." Indeed, spontaneous fantasies might have a relationship with improving human flourishing. And what is the nature of this process of "being affected"? Inevitably, the answer leads to the creative act of the imagination. Robert Riley (1997, p. 207) refers to the term "vicarious" as a type of landscape experience "in which the real, observed landscape leads to an internally experienced landscape that is far richer and more personal than the 'real' landscape. Vicarious is an inadequate name for this experience, but it does dramatically mark the distinction from the 'real,' or observable, landscape experience, and it is at least as adequate as the other terms that come to my mind—fantasy

FIGURE 2.6. Ghost towns are places of magic (photo by author)

landscape or internal landscape narrative" (author's emphasis). After all, "the most perfectly preserved building or document becomes evocative, indeed, 'historical,' only through our imagination" (Lukacs, 1968/1994, p. 238).

Spontaneous fantasy, decay, and ruins are a prominent theme in the literature of many disciplines, including history and geography. The authentic appearances of objects from the past, evinced through the display of patina, "act as focal points for creatively imagining the actions of ancestors" (Harrison, 2004, p. 204). There is no better example of this phenomenon than ghost towns—places in which patina is ubiquitous (Figure 2.6). According to Dydia DeLyser (1999, p. 626), ghost towns are "a mythic West of the imagination" where "authenticity is a vehicle through which [visitors] can experience a fantasy past that may never have been, but that nevertheless holds meaning for each person who imagines it." Ghost towns typically have the appearance of ruins; as far back as the early nineteenth century, Romantic landscape painters were motivated to paint decrepitude because "ruins embodied [their] inner fantasy" (Burns, 2004, p. 25). And, as D. Fairchild Ruggles (2000, p. 136) reminds us, a ruin "allows the mind's recollection to reconstruct the place as it might have and ought to have been." Instead of creating an accurate, objective story of the past, spontaneous fantasy involves the creation of memories and meanings that never previously existed and which "haunt" our experiences.

To be sure, places that people associate with ghosts (e.g., ghost towns, old houses) are often described as both enchanting and magical, although it is uncertain if the perceived "ghosts" create the magic or vice versa (Jawer et al., 2020; Franz, 2021). Marisa Franz (2021, p. 383) relates that "haunting is an experience that draws us into a place, as if by magic, to alter something about us that is embodied and affectively powerful." Intriguingly, there is some evidence that the infrasound (very low frequencies) created by the decaying parts of old buildings may influence this perception of places being "haunted." These sounds, which are too low to hear, are still felt by the body and impact the overall, affective experience (McAndrew & Koehnke, 2016). Thus, the increasing disorder that age imposes on older buildings results in a sense of ambiguity that, in turn, instills an affective response that can make such places feel haunted (Jawer et al., 2020). It is therefore possible that this connection between the perception of haunting, magic, and spontaneous fantasies may be understood through the concept of the gestalt influences of atmosphere and ambiguity (Jawer et al., 2020).

As these and many other authors describe, the process through which spontaneous fantasy occurs is "involuntary" and, indeed, "haunts" our "foreground experiences of memory." Any attempt to rationally analyze the meanings of these spontaneous fantasies is met with failure (Edensor, 2005, p. 18) because they are not real, truthful, or accurate. They are, by definition, artificial meanings that may be entirely divorced from historical events. So why does the human mind persist in their creation, even if we mightily attempt to will them from existence through preservation doctrine? Edensor (2005) explains that we value spontaneous fantasy because it offers the transcendent experience of discovery, magic, novelty, and mystery:

> The promise of extraordinary sights and mysterious experiences is built into the popular culture of children with its myriad tales of adventures in secret gardens, magical labyrinths and dense, enchanted forests. . . . Ruins [have this] promise of the unexpected. Since the original uses of ruined buildings have passed, there are limitless possibilities for encounters

with the weird, with inscrutable legends inscribed on notice boards and signs, and with peculiar things and curious spaces which allow wide scope for imaginative interpretation, unencumbered by the assumptions which weigh heavily on highly encoded, regulated space. Bereft of these codings of the normative—the arrangement of things in place, the performance of regulated actions, the display of good lines up as commodities or for show—ruined space is ripe with transgressive and transcendent possibilities. (Edensor, 2005, pp. 3-4)

Natural landscapes are also associated with spontaneous fantasy. For instance, the Grand Canyon in the United States has been called a "geography of fantasy" where place becomes a "space of invention" (Neuman, 2002, p. 41). Thus, it is not natural nor cultural landscapes which produce spontaneous fantasy, but rather the combination of both through the manifestation of patina. Without nature, patina would not form and without culture, there would not be the interpretive acts required to invent new meanings from which to engender attachment.

Heritage values derived from the lifeworld are therefore manufactured through experience and are not, as heritage conservation doctrine, rules, laws, and regulations would dictate, based on an objective reality based on historical facts. This idea is different than the "heritage-as-artifact" or historical approach which focuses only on issues of time and authenticity—elements that are often external to the sphere of the everyday experience of place. According to Lisa Breglia (2006, p. 34), an anthropologist, heritage is "a contingent practice situated in actual time and space" and is based on individual experience which defies single, monolithic definitions (Breglia, 2006, p. 27). The context of heritage engenders specific memories, ideas which Foucault (1972, p. 100) has called meanings contingent on "material existence"—similar experiences in different contexts will alter the resulting meanings of those contexts.

CONCLUSION

While the physical age of places has a fundamental role in the practice of built heritage conservation and in its theory, preservation/conservation practitioners do not consider the lifeworld when evaluating the historical significance of places, especially through the concept of a person–patina relationship predicated on age value. More research is necessary to understand the historic environment by phenomenologists, who have not paid particular attention to specific phenomena, such as spontaneous fantasy, and how these experiences could better inform the construction of historical significance. Decay and patina give us clues to the historical authenticity of a place, but more importantly, are critical in fostering an altered emotional state that is the prerequisite for place of attachment. Much has been written about the "sense of place" engendered by historical places, but in a noncritical fashion that takes the experience at face value, without trying to understand its role in the lifeworld. Ultimately, a better understanding of the historic environment through phenomenology may lead to more effective tools for identifying and conserving historic places.

Works Cited

Appelbaum, B. (2007). *Conservation treatment methodology*. Butterworth-Heinemann.

Bell, S. (1999). *Landscape: Pattern, perception, and process*. E & FN Spon.

Breglia, L. (2006). *Monumental ambivalence: The politics of heritage*. University of Texas Press.

Burns, S. (2004). *Painting the dark side: Art and the Gothic imagination in nineteenth-century America*. University of California Press.

Byrne, D. (2013). Love & loss in the 1960s. *International Journal of Heritage Studies*, 19(6), 596-609.

Casey, E. S. (1987). The world of nostalgia. *Man and World*, 20(4), 361-384.

———. (1993). *Getting back into place: Toward a renewed understanding of the place-world*. Indiana University Press.

———. (1997). *The fate of place: A philosophical history*. University of California Press.

———. (2007). *The world at a glance*. Indiana University Press.

Cliver, E. B. (1992). Revisiting past rehabilitation projects. In A. J. Lee (Ed.), *Past meets future: Saving America's historic environments* (pp. 175-180). Preservation Press.

Congress in Athens (1931). The Athens Charter. First International Congress of Architects and Technicians of Historic Monuments. https://www.icomos.org/en/167-the-athens-charter-for-the-restoration-of-historic-monuments.

Cram, M. (1917). *Old seaport towns of the South*. Dodd, Mead & Company.

Crane, S. A. (2000). *Collecting and historical consciousness in early nineteenth-century Germany*. Cornell University Press.

Dekkers, D. M. (2000). *The way of all flesh: The romance of ruins* (S. Marx-Macdonald, Trans.). Ferrar, Straus and Giroux.

DeLyser, D. (1999). Authenticity on the ground: Engaging the past in a California ghost town. *Annals of the Association of American Geographers*, 89(4), 602-632.

Dickinson, J. (2001). Monuments of tomorrow: Industrial ruins at the millennium. *Critical Perspectives on Urban Redevelopment*, 6, 33-74.

Dovey, K. (1985). The quest for authenticity and the replication of environmental meaning. In D. Seamon, & R. Mugerauer (Eds.), *Dwelling, place and environment* (pp. 33-50). Martinus Nijhof.

Edensor, T. (2005). *Industrial ruins: Spaces, aesthetics, and materiality*. Berg.

Elliott, J. D. (2002). Radical preservation: Toward a new and more ancient paradigm. *Forum Journal, 16*(3), 50-56.

Farmer, J., & Knapp, D. (2008). Interpretation programs at a historic preservation site: A mixed methods study of long-term impact. *Journal of Mixed Methods Research, 2*(4), 340-361.

Feilden, B. M. (1994). *Conservation of historic buildings*. Architectural Press.

Foucault, M. (1972). *The archaeology of knowledge*. Partheon Books.

Franz, M. K. (2021). Haunted intimacy: Spectral and vital space within a historic house museum. *Museum & Society, 19*(3), 382-394.

Ginsberg, R. (2004). *The aesthetics of ruins*. Rodopi.

Greenspan, E. (2005). A global site of heritage? Constructing spaces of memory at the World Trade Center site. *International Journal of Heritage Studies, 11*(5), 371-384.

Harrison, R. (2004). *Shared landscapes: Archaeologies of attachment and the pastoral industry in New South Wales*. UNSW Press.

Heidegger, M. (1962). *Being and time: A translation of sein and zeit*. Blackwell Publishing. (Original work published 1927)

Hoskins, G. (2014). Locating value: Making significance in the historical built environment, a trans-Atlantic review (report for the Arts and Humanities Research Council). Aberystwyth University.

International Council on Monuments and Sites (ICOMOS). (1964). *The Venice Charter*. https://www.icomos.org/en/participer/179-articles-en-francais/ressources/charters-and-standards/157-thevenice-charter.

Ireland, T., Brown, S., & Schofield, J. (2020). Situating (in)significance. *International Journal of Heritage Studies, 26*(9), 826-844.

Jawer, M. A., Massullo, B., Laythe, B., & Houran, J. (2020). Environmental "gestalt influences" pertinent to studies of haunted houses. *Journal of the Society for Psychical Research, 84*(2), 65-92.

Kimball, F. (1935). The restoration of Colonial Williamsburg in Virginia. *The Architectural Record, 78*(6), 359.

Lanza, R. (2007). A new theory of the universe. *The American Scholar, 76*(2), 18-33.

Lowenthal, D. (1985). *The past is a foreign country*. Cambridge University Press.

———. (1994). The value of age and decay. In W. E. Krumbein, P. Brimblecombe, D. E. Cosgrove, & S. Staniforth (Eds.), *Durability and change: The science, responsibility, and cost of sustaining cultural heritage* (pp. 39-49). John Wiley.

———. (1998). *The heritage crusade and the spoils of history*. Cambridge University Press.

Lukacs, J. (1994). *Historical consciousness: The remembered past*. Transaction Publishers. (Original work published 1968)

Malpas, J. (1999). *Place and experience: A philosophical topography*. Cambridge University Press.

———. (2006). *Heidegger's topology: Being, place, world*. MIT Press.

McAndrew, F. T., & Koehnke, S. S. (2016). On the nature of creepiness. *New Ideas in Psychology, 43*, 10-15.

Merleau-Ponty, M. (1962). *Phenomenology of perception: An introduction* (C. Smith, trans.). Routledge.

Moustakas, C. E. (1994). *Phenomenological research methods*. Sage Publications.

Mugerauer, R. (1994). *Interpretations on behalf of place: Environmental displacements and alternative responses*. State University of New York Press.

———. (1995). *Interpreting environments: Tradition, deconstruction, hermeneutics*. University of Texas Press.

Muñoz Viñas, S. (2005). *Contemporary theory of conservation*. Elsevier.

Neuman, M. (2002). Making the scene: The poetics and performances of displacement at the Grand Canyon. In S. Coleman, & M. Crang (Eds.), *Tourism: Between place and performance* (pp. 38-53). Berghahn Books.

Philippot, P. (1996). The idea of patina and the cleaning of paintings. In N. Price, M. K. Talley, Jr., & A. M. Vaccaro (Eds.), *Historical and philosophical issues on the conservation of cultural heritage* (pp. 372-376). The Getty Conservation Institute. (Original work published 1966)

Priest, S. (1998). *Merleau-Ponty*. Routledge.

Ray, M. A. (1994). The richness of phenomenology: Philosophic, theoretic, and methodologic concerns. In J. M. Morse (Ed.), *Critical issues in qualitative research methods* (pp. 117-133). Sage.

Relph, E. C. (1976). *Place and placelessness*. Pion.

Riegl, A. (1996). The modern cult of monuments: Its essence and its development. In N. S. Price, M. K. Talley, Jr., & A. M. Vaccaro (Eds.), *Historical and philosophical issues on the conservation of cultural heritage* (pp. 69-83). The Getty Conservation Institute. (Original work published 1903)

Riley, R. B. (1997). The visual, the visible, and the vicarious: Questions about vision, landscape, and experience. In P. Groth & T. Bressi (Eds.), *Understanding ordinary landscapes* (pp. 200-209). Yale University Press.

Roth, M. S., Lyons, C., & Merewether, C. (1997). *Irresistible decay: Reclaiming ruins*. The Getty Research Institute.

Ruggles, D. F. (2000). *Gardens, landscape, and vision in the palaces of Islamic Spain*. Pennsylvania State University Press.

Ruskin, J. (1849). *The seven lamps of architecture*. Smith, Elder, and Co.

———. (1851). *The stones of Venice: The foundations*. John Wiley.

———. (1853a). *The stones of Venice: The fall*. Smith, Elder, and Co.

———. (1853b). *The stones of Venice: The sea-stories*. Smith, Elder, and Co.

———. (1877). *The poetry of architecture: Cottage, villa, etc.* John Wiley & Sons.

Seamon, D. (1979). *A geography of the lifeworld*. Croom Helm.

———. (1982). The phenomenological contribution to environmental psychology. *Journal of Environmental Psychology, 2*(2), 119-140.

———. (1984). Emotional experience of the environment. *American Behavioral Scientist, 27*(6), 757-770.

———. (1993). *Dwelling, seeing, and designing: Toward a phenomenological ecology*. State University of New York Press.

Stefanovic, I. L. (1998). Phenomenological encounters with place: Cavtat to Square One. *Journal of Environmental Psychology, 18*(1), 31-44.

Tuan, Y.-F. (1974). *Topophilia: a study of environmental perception, attitudes, and values*. Prentice-Hall.

———. (1977). *Space and place: The perspectives of experience*. University of Minnesota Press.

van Manen, M. (1990). *Researching the lived experience*. University of Western Ontario.

Vergara, C. (1999). *American ruins*. Monacelli Press.

von Eckartsberg, R. (1998). Introducing existential-phenomenological psychology. In R. Valle (Ed.), *Phenomenological inquiry in psychology* (pp. 3-20). Plenum Press.

Waterton, E., Smith, L., & Campbell, G. (2006). The utility of discourse analysis to heritage studies: The Burra Charter and social inclusion. *International Journal of Heritage Studies, 12*(4), 339-355.

Weeks, K. D., & Jandl, H. W. (1996). The Secretary of the Interior's Standards for the Treatment of Historical Properties: A philosophical and ethical framework for making treatment decisions. In S. J. Kelley (Ed.), *Standards for Preservation and Rehabilitation* (pp. 7-23). ASTM.

Weil, P. D. (1996). A review of the history and practice of patination. In N. S. Price, M. K. Talley, Jr., & A. M. Vaccaro (Eds.), *Historical and philosophical issues on the conservation of cultural heritage* (pp. 394-414). The Getty Conservation Institute. (Original work published 1976).

Wells, J. C. (2007). The plurality of truth in culture, context, and heritage: A (mostly) post-structuralist analysis of urban conservation charters. *City and Time, 3*(2:1), 1-13.

——— (2017). How are old places different from new places? A psychological investigation of the correlation between patina, spontaneous fantasies, and place attachment. *International Journal of Heritage Studies*, 23(5), 445-469.

———. (2020). Probing the person–patina relationship: A correlational study on the psychology of senescent environments. *Collabra: Psychology*, 6(1), 41.

Wells, J. C., & Baldwin, E. D. (2012). Historic preservation, significance, and age value: A comparative phenomenology of historic Charleston and the nearby new-urbanist community of I'On. *Journal of Environmental Psychology*, 32(4), 384-400.

Wells, J. C., & Lixinski, L. (2016). Heritage values and legal rules: Identification and treatment of the historic environment via an adaptive regulatory framework (part 1). *Journal of Cultural Heritage Management and Sustainable Development*, 6(3), 345-364.

———. (2017). Heritage values and legal rules: Identification and treatment of the historic environment via an adaptive regulatory framework (part 2). *Journal of Cultural Heritage Management and Sustainable Development*, 7(3), 345-363.

Williams, H. S. (1904). *The historians' history of the world*. The Outlook Company.

Wingfield, A., & Byrnes, D. L. (2014). *The psychology of human memory*. Elsevier Science.

CHAPTER 3

Pure and Naked Heritage
Revealing the Vulnerability of Orthodoxy

INTRODUCTION

In this chapter, I explore the ideas, meanings, and values that define the ontological and epistemological bases of orthodox built heritage conservation doctrine and policy, and in the process, reveal what has been excluded in the development of the discipline's paradigm. Thus, this is a story of "pure" heritage and the "naked" heritage that is left behind when the purity of orthodox preservation/conservation doctrine and policy is removed. My reference to naked heritage is a purposeful allusion to Hans Christian Andersen's well known story, *The Emperor's New Clothes*. In that story, the emperor's clothes were an illusion—they did not exist, yet he was firmly convinced, by others, that they were real. In the end, his insistence on the reality of the illusion made him appear foolish and out of touch with the professionals who served him. Similarly, if, as a growing body of evidence is substantiating, most people do not value heritage places based on their objective visual and art/historical facts, as has long been claimed in orthodox doctrine, then the entire premise upon which the built heritage regulatory system is based is an illusion. If one removes the false veil of objectivity from practice, there is nothing underneath upon which orthodox heritage practitioners can latch their practice. In this allegory, heritage conservation practice becomes exposed and *naked* and therefore highly vulnerable to criticism and calls for change. This chapter thus explores the discipline though this vulnerability that fundamentally challenges core, accepted notions in preservation/conservation doctrine and policy.

To be sure, it has always been difficult to accommodate the radical plurality of the affective, lived relationship that people have with heritage places into the professional, policy-driven systems that identify and protect such heritage. This observation is especially relevant considering that public policy (e.g., laws, regulations, and guidelines) drives most preservation/conservation work, especially when the implementation of public policy demands objectivity and due process. Meanings outside of orthodoxy are therefore usually excluded and sidelined because they are not sufficiently objective, simple, and predictable (Wells, 2017; Scott, 1998); the heterodox meanings and values associated with built heritage are therefore not, as Laurajane Smith (2006) describes, part of the "Authorized Heritage Discourse." But what if this heterodox perspective, based on imagined and lived heritage, which stems from "Being Affected by Old Places" (BAOP; see chapter 2), is fundamental to the layperson's experience of heritage, as a growing amount of evidence substantiates? The natural conclusion, then, is that orthodox doctrine and policies that drive most of built heritage conservation practice fail to incorporate, much less understand, a fundamental reason why people value and ascribe meaning to older places.

Disciplines, as they develop and mature, go through a process of purification in which their objects of focus, theories, and methods are narrowed in order to become more specialized and differentiated (Younès, 2006), and historic preservation was not exempt from this undertaking. Moreover, the creation of a discipline also involves placing limits on professional behavior, through a moral overlay in which a dichotomy of inclusion and exclusion drives the definitions of acceptable ontological and epistemological orientations (Foucault, 1991). As the need for specialization (and exclusion) becomes increasingly important, members of a burgeoning discipline are more likely to see themselves in an "us" versus "them" dichotomy in terms of who is, and is not, included in the discipline with which they identify (Becher, 1981). Through this context, it becomes easier to understand that, as the discipline of historic preservation developed, it acquired a strong sense of morality and a desire for purity in its practices, especially around the need for the presence of authentic building fabric and an ethical prerogative to protect this fabric from adulteration.

Through this lens, therefore, it becomes apparent that as historic preservation developed as a discipline, it succeeded in creating an increasingly purer version of an accepted heritage discourse. Thus, what emerges from this discourse are four primary characteristics that define the discipline of historic preservation: fabric purity, ontological purity, epistemological purity, and social purity. What remained were the "impure" ideas, meanings, and values of built heritage, which orthodox doctrine, and later regulations, discarded.

FABRIC PURITY

Of all the values associated with orthodox built heritage conservation, the unadulterated authenticity of historical building fabric is the most important. It is also the field's oldest value, with origins in the early nineteenth century and Victor Hugo's (1831/1888) well-known rant about the desecration of the Notre Dame Cathedral. Unless this fabric is genuine, then there is no possibility of historic preservation. Without these visible, tangible elements of the past remaining in the present, then the work done to extant buildings and places that lack this historical authenticity is outside the domain of historic preservation/built heritage conservation. Without sufficient authenticity, work on buildings and places is simply not the field's concern; it is, instead, the purview of other built environment disciplines to engage with buildings and places in this context.

In orthodox US practice, as directed by doctrine and policy, a historic preservation professional determines if a historic resource has sufficient authenticity, or "historical integrity," by determining the extent to which building or landscape fabric remains from certain periods of time; these time periods are typically defined in part through associations with past historical events or people—i.e., the fabric of place must "bear witness" to certain historical events. Therefore, as defined through the Western practice of preservation, historical significance is "communicated" through the presence of this essential fabric (NPS, 1997a, 1997b; O'Donnell, 1998). If there is insufficient fabric from defined periods of significance, then the building, structure, or place is deemed to no longer have historical integrity and therefore lacks sufficient historical significance. Such a building or place is therefore not worthy of preservation. In another sense, if a building's or place's fabric is not genuine, then it is not sufficiently historically pure to warrant attention; the fabric's purity has been adulterated with too many later changes.

A primary goal of historic preservation, therefore, is to carefully manage the changes that occur to the materials of buildings, structures, and places in order to retain their material authenticity or their historical purity. The method used to establish the binary presence of historical integrity is defined in the US federal regulation that established the National Register of Historic Places (36 CFR 60). Other countries have similar regulatory and policy-based systems, all of which are grounded in nineteenth-century preservation doctrine originally developed by elite, wealthy, northern European men associated with the Arts and Crafts movement, such as John Ruskin and William Morris (Jokilehto, 1999). The basic precepts of what defines historical integrity were first explored in the well-known "scrape" versus "anti-scrape" debates of the latter half of the nineteenth century, in which the French restoration architect Eugène Emmanuel Viollet-le-Duc was vilified by preservationists who advocated to retain as much of the extant fabric of a building as possible, even if the fabric was modified long after the building's construction (Jokilehto, 1999). To be sure, the rivalry defined as "Ruskin" versus "Viollet-le-Duc" is the foundational story in historic preservation education and the point at which the preservation ethic is developed in nascent professionals. All professional historic preservationists know this story, as learning and discussing it is a rite of passage into the field.

Historic preservation's reverence for the purity of historical fabric—which has also been referred to as the field's "material fetish"—is a fundamentally important and emotionally powerful value, as explained by the materials conservator, Salvador Muñoz Viñas (2005, p. 84): "The fact is that for many people, the authentic material has a numinous quality . . . that renders it very powerful in comparison with replicas or virtual experiences—an attitude which is not very far from that seen in the case of the Carcaixent Virgin."[1] This connection with religious experience is appropriate because the historic preservation field borrows much of its reverence for material authenticity from Christianity and the sociocultural role of relics, such as

---

1. In 1736, a fire destroyed part of a statue of the Virgin and the Child in the town of Carcaixent, Spain. While most of the statue was destroyed, the heads of the Virgin and Child survived and were placed inside of a new statue along with the remaining crushed fragments. It was thought that the original material from the statute contained a kind of essence that could then be transferred to the copy of the destroyed statue.

the bones of saints; for the devout, if such a relic is deemed authentic and pure (i.e., unadulterated), then it contains an ephemeral spirit that connects the believer to the truth of the past—be it a saint or holy deed. But, most importantly, a genuine relic emotionally conveys its significance (and power) to the viewer, much as an authentic historical building emotionally conveys its significance to the people who experience it. Adulterated relics have no such power.

In the nineteenth century, during the time in which concepts of material authenticity were being developed in historic preservation, proponents of this nascent field described buildings and places with words borrowed from religion, such as "revere," "sacred," "desecrate," "consecrate," "venerate," and "spirit." John Ruskin (1849, p. 165), a Christian fanatic who is widely acknowledged as the godfather of preservation, frequently used his religious beliefs to advocate for preservation; for instance, he described a historic building as a "temple" that if lived in, will "make us holy." Through these examples, this ontological connection of religious purity and fabric purity becomes quite apparent. But, to be sure, orthodox historic preservation doctrine and policy does not reference, nor does it appear to be embedded in, religion or mysticism, yet these origins cannot be dismissed. What, therefore, is there to be made of this relationship between historic preservation and religious belief, which is especially important given that the field's doctrine and policy are most often associated with objectivity and scientific principles? This is a question that Muñoz Viñas (2005, p. 87) ponders when describing how the "scientific theory" of materials conservation developed in the twentieth century, based on principles of psychological perception (i.e., gestalt psychology) in which there was a desire to link the authenticity of a historical object and its ability to create an "intense" emotional experience:

> It is because of this material fetishism that, for most Western people, the conservation of the material components of an object is a worthwhile endeavor, even when it is physically unnoticeable. Physical stimuli provided by replicas or reproductions may be objectively similar to those provided by the original object, but they are not perceived as being as intense and complete as those provided by *real* objects, or, to be precise, by objects whose material components are the original [or pure, unadulterated] ones. This recognition plays an important role in the implicit scientific theory of conservation that emerged between 1930 and 1950, as it mandates that

conservation should avoid, as much as possible, the elimination, alteration or concealment of original materials.

By moving historic preservation from belief and into a more objective realm, where the tangible, and often visual, elements of an historic object could be readily documented and addressed, the scientific theory of materials conservation maintained the religiously-derived primacy of material authenticity while operationalizing it within a positivistic, nonreligious frame. Thus, in its professionalization, historic preservation became what Muñoz Viñas (2005, p. 91) refers to as a "truth-enforcement" operation "to reveal and preserve an object's true nature or true condition" and, in the process, avoid the adulteration of the purity of the object's fabric.

The earliest doctrine that emphasizes material authenticity is the Society for the Protection of Ancient Buildings (SPAB) Manifesto of 1877, penned by William Morris, who is well known as the leader of the Arts and Crafts movement. Written to carefully emphasize the need to retain as much historical fabric from a building as possible, the SPAB Manifesto equates restoration (i.e., scraping away historical building fabric) with destroying the "true" state in which a historical building should exist; Morris (1878, p. 7) would later clarify that the intent of the Manifesto was to require buildings to be "preserved in a genuine condition." In the immediate decades after the creation of the Manifesto, SPAB published a number of works to clarify the philosophical position of the Manifesto (e.g., SPAB, 1879, 1903; Peers, 1917; Powys, 1929), which established the primacy of retaining the purity of fabric and equating this behavior with moral and ethical correctness. This directive survives today in the verbiage that many preservation advocacy NGOs use that refer to a "preservation ethic" grounded in protecting historical fabric from adulteration. It is critical to understand how the SPAB Manifesto, which is still active and guiding contemporary doctrine and policy, normalized Western built heritage conservation precepts, culminating in the Venice Charter of 1964; the US Secretary of the Interior's Standards, written in 1977, is based on the Venice Charter, and, in essence, has operationalized the Manifesto into US contemporary preservation regulations for more than a half century (Hudgins, 2012). Other countries have similar regulations based on the Venice Charter as well (Jokilehto, 1999).

By the middle of the twentieth century, orthodox ideas about historical authenticity (i.e., historical integrity) were well established and centered on avoiding making buildings "lie," in part by safeguarding the purity of genuine building fabric and thereby avoiding a "false sense of history" (Grabar 1945, p. 182). Borrowing from Didron, the eighteenth-century French archaeologist, the National Park Service's (NPS's) public advocacy materials emphasized that "it is better to preserve than repair, better to repair than restore, and better to restore than to reconstruct" (Drury 1950, p. 30), thereby creating an ethically desired hierarchy of minimal (most desirable) to maximal (least desirable) interventions framed on most to least pure in character (Piper 1947, p. 88). Where interventions were unavoidable, the preferred solution to avoid a "false sense of history" was to emphasize the difference between old and new building fabric, which helped to highlight which fabric was pure and which was impure. This idea, originally proposed by the Italian architect Camillo Boito (1884) and later reified by art conservators, such as Max Friedländer (1942) and Paul Philippot (1976), became item nine in both the 1964 Venice Charter and the NPS's Secretary of the Interior's Standards for Rehabilitation.

The important takeaway about the relationship between historical integrity/material authenticity and purity is the way in which integrity is assessed. Historical buildings and places either have or do not have historical integrity (NPS, 1997a), and as such, retain their unadulterated material authenticity or lose it; there is no middle ground and no place for more nuanced arguments. Moreover, if this presence of historical fabric—ensuring that the historical object is genuine, and therefore authentic—is insufficient, then, also, in binary fashion, the building, place, and landscape is not of interest or value to the people who engage in historic preservation/built heritage conservation practice or to the doctrine and policy that guide their work. The historical object, in this latter case, has therefore lost its purity and is outside the scope of the discipline's interest.

ONTOLOGICAL PURITY

Orthodox historic preservation doctrine, in its grounding insistence of the purity of historical fabric, sidelined emotional ways of conveying authenticity by the 1930s. But, up until this point, the conflation of emotion and historic places by highly educated individuals, such as architectural critics and archaeologists, was still normalized discourse. For instance, Wendell

Phillips, a historic preservationist, abolitionist, and attorney, in his 1877 speech on preserving the Old North Church in Boston, spoke about how simply being in the presence of the bricks and mortar from which the church was constructed could instill a proper moral foundation in an individual; Phillips spoke as if the building's fabric had the ability to, through some kind of unseen, osmotic process, "educate" people (Phillips, 1878). Phillips's rhetoric, along with that of many other contemporary authors and orators, expressed emotional and religious values and meanings related to built heritage that were not very different from the public's (cf. Cram, 1917).

By the turn of the twentieth century, however, the language of preservation/conservation professionals began to change in response to the rise of the modern era and its emphasis on scientific rigor. Phillips's emotional appeals were increasingly replaced by calls for scientism and objectivity in built heritage conservation and an emphasis on the visual sense over other ways of understanding reality—i.e., only if material culture can be seen, can it then be documented and measured; if it cannot be seen or measured, it does not exist. In the United States and England, new words arose in building conservation literature, describing the objective and scientific goals of preservation/conservation, such as "accuracy" and "precision," while religiously affiliated words such as "revere," "sacred," and "profane" declined precipitously. Preservation/conservation work was increasingly legitimized based on principles of science, objectivity, and a search for a positivistic, visually empirical truth while pejoratively dismissing the subjective, emotional meanings of the public as "sentiment and tradition" (Lockwood, 1937, p. 49). In England, the SPAB began its practice of publishing books that focus on the appropriate scientific treatment of building fabric (e.g., Peers, 1917; Powys, 1929; SPAB, 1903); importantly, these books were imported and extensively read by preservation architects in the United States and influenced the development of preservation philosophy and, later, federal historic preservation policy.

Professionals who specialized in the older built environment, such as historians, architects, and archaeologists, responded to the calls of Modernism with a dramatic ontological shift in how proper preservation/conservation ought to be performed. In an attempt to make the burgeoning disciplines of built heritage conservation and archaeology more "scientific" (Carhart, 1895, p. 394; Connor, 2005, p. 450), these professionals made concerted efforts to identify and then eviscerate subjectivity in their work and, in its place, impose an empiricist-positivist ontological paradigm on the preservation/conservation discipline (Tainter & Lucas, 1983). This change in perspective helped to characterize the work of the built heritage conservator as "scientific" and "objective" and therefore difficult for the public to challenge (King, 2009; Muñoz Viñas, 2005; Smith, 2006); some authors go as far as to claim that some heritage professionals "misrepresent" themselves as scientists in order to gain authority in the eyes of the public (e.g., Hutchings & La Salle, 2015). As the twentieth century progressed, historians, architects, and archaeologists increasingly claimed built heritage conservation as their own, developing a unique professional discourse in which "the proper care of heritage, and its associated values, lies with the experts, as it is only they who have the abilities, knowledge and understanding to identify the innate value and knowledge contained at and within historically important sites and places" (Smith, 2006, pp. 29-30).

This rise of the scientific theory of conservation and the concomitant need for expert specialization drove a wedge between how the preservation/conservation professional and the public perceived and sustained the authenticity of historic places (Kunz, 1912; Muñoz Viñas, 2005, pp. 86-87). From the professional's perspective, maintaining material authenticity is a "truth enforcement operation" that seeks to retain the objective purity of the historical object (Muñoz Viñas, 2005, p. 91). Because of this emphasis on singular truths, professional discourse therefore developed into binary positions on the objective/subjective, true/false, and do/don't dichotomies in which the built heritage conservation professional is an objective scientist in opposition to the public's sentimental, emotionally-laden relationship with heritage (Kimball, 1935; Perry, 1935). These binary perspectives still survive in US local, state, and federal historic preservation policy, which is built on doctrine that embraces the modern era (e.g., Venice Charter) and rejects more recent, constructivist ideas on authenticity (e.g., the Nara Document).

Perhaps one of the best known orthodox preservation dichotomies, described in the previous section on fabric purity, is the need to differentiate "new" building fabric from "old" in order to make sure that the building cannot prevaricate about itself or convey a "false sense of history." Building on the ideas of its originator, Camillo Boito (1884), European art conservators—especially Cesare Brandi (1977), Philippot and Philippot (1959), and Friedländer (1942)—further developed this need to differentiate into a series of discrete techniques, guided by gestalt psychology, based on related dichotomies, such as "figure" and "ground." In building conservation, Modernist architects readily assimilated this objective through the moral imperative of "building in the spirit of our time" as Donald Insall (1958, p. 34) advocated and as SPAB had been advocating for most of the twentieth century. Insall even went as far as suggesting that a date be inscribed on all replacement fabric so as to not only differentiate old from new, but also to clearly indicate when the intervention took place. Today, this objective lives on in item nine in the Venice Charter of 1964, an international conservation doctrine, the US NPS's "Secretary of the Interior's Standards for Rehabilitation" (created in 1977), British Standard 7913 (created in 1998), and Standards and Guidelines for the Conservation of Historic Places in Canada (created in 2003), among many other international examples.

Dichotomies, like the need to differentiate fabric, provide evidence that orthodox built heritage conservation is based on an empiricist-positivist paradigm (Tainter & Lucas, 1983). This paradigm was first evident in the 1877 SPAB Manifesto, which introduced the idea that a historic building should exist in an objectively "true" (or pure) state. The Manifesto calls into operation a logical, objective binary between a desired state of preservation—retention of as much building fabric as possible—and an undesirable state—restoration—or the removal or scraping back of building fabric to earlier periods. In doing so, the SPAB Manifesto equated restoration with destroying the truthful existence of a building and, instead, causing it to exist in an adulterated state of falseness (Morris, 1878, p. 7). At the turn of the twentieth century, SPAB (1903, p. 10) reified this true/false dichotomy by characterizing restored buildings as "mere modern copies" or false versions of the original. Preservation, as the preferred treatment, was the only way to ensure the building's *"true* expression" of its authenticity (author's emphasis); restoration created a "forgery" and a "*falsified* historical record" (author's emphasis; SPAB, 1903, pp. 11, 13). William Lethaby (1898, pp. 18, 20), a prominent English preservation architect at the turn of the twentieth century, echoes SPAB's language in his message that "tampering" with a building (i.e., making any changes) destroys its truth: "It is the same everywhere; this tampering with old buildings is a disease of the age, which apparently will only die of want of material to be infected when all have been *falsified*. . . . An edifice is a document the most significant and authentic of all; to restore is to *falsify* testimony" (author's emphasis).

In order to avoid this "tampering" with buildings and maintain their truth, orthodox preservation/conservation doctrine developed the directive to accurately record buildings (e.g., photographs, measurements, drawings, materials analysis) in order to provide an objective, empirical basis for treatments that will, ideally, reveal this true way a building should be expressed and which maximize its historical authenticity and thus avoid making a building "lie" about itself. Scientific methods to record buildings, which are fundamentally based on an empiricist-positivist ontological paradigm, as well, mirrored the rise of scientism in the first half of the twentieth century. Literature from this era repeatedly justifies recording methods based on their ability to establish "historical accuracy" and "scientific accuracy." The search for scientific methods to record buildings is one reason why the built heritage conservation field readily adopted techniques first developed in archaeology. These new methods of recording, such as photography, ushered in a "revolution... in regard to scientific observation and treatment" according to a contemporary early twentieth-century account by A. Michaelis (1908, pp. 281, 303, 304), a professor at the University of Strasbourg. An early example of this transition to scientific recording processes was Joseph Chandler's 1907–08 restoration of Paul Revere's house in Boston. Unlike earlier, "sentimental" restoration work in the United States, such as the restoration of the White House in Washington, DC, a decade prior ("Restoration of White House," 1903), this project was a scientific enterprise that focused on an archaeological reading of the building's fabric, which was revolutionary at the time. An article from *The Architectural Record* ("Restoration of Paul Revere House," 1914) uplifts Chandler's work as an exceptional example of the use of scientific inference to restore a historic building. Chandler's (1944) own account of the restoration reinforces the way in which he treated the building as a storehouse of data that needed to be objectively read to understand its evolution. Similarly, the restoration of Congress Hall in Philadelphia placed important emphasis on the need for research and recording in order to ensure "historical accuracy" ("Congress Hall Restored," 1914). In other words, the objective reality of Congress Hall was to be found not only in paper documents, but in the historical fabric of the building itself, which could be scientifically read, just like a book, as C. R. Peers (1917, p. 65) elaborates: "To those who can read it, an old building offers a more intimate and authentic record of its makers than almost any other relic of past times." The preservation of buildings in New England in the teens was also driven by this emphasis on the building as document and on the ability of archaeology to reveal objective, scientific facts to guide restorations (Appleton, 1919). Thus, the building's fabric could potentially present more scientifically accurate evidence than could the written document.

The restoration, preservation, and reconstruction of Colonial Williamsburg in the 1930s greatly helped to normalize the scientific recording of buildings. The architects and archaeologists leading this work warned that any hint of "imagination" or "theatrical" methods adulterated the objectivity of decision-making processes. Only a "scientifically" pure approach that relied upon "substantial accuracy and perfection" could bring back the "original reality" of a historic building (Kimball, 1935, p. 359). To its inventors, Colonial Williamsburg was the "historic truth" based in "scientific fact" (Perry, 1935, pp. 370, 377). In creating Colonial Williamsburg, architects used what they described as scientific, archaeological methods to read original building fabric, which then guided their interventions. Where such evidence was not extant, facts found in written documents and old photographs substituted. There was a clear hierarchy of truth and accuracy established by using this method: the building's fabric told the purest and most objective form of factual information to the preservation architect; other information was more impure and not as trustworthy. Of all methods available to the preservation architect, oral history was the least trustworthy and most impure way to understand the past. This hierarchy remains true today in preservation/conservation scholarship, education, and practice.

By the middle of the twentieth century, preservation architects regularly wrote about how collected data from an older building should "tell" them how to preserve the "true nature" of the building. For instance, the English architect C. R. Peers (1931, p. 312) advocated that when deciding an intervention, "the treatment must suggest itself" based on the scientific analysis of the building fabric. If the data are reliable and accurate, as Colonial Williamsburg architect, William Graves Perry (1935, p. 363) directs, then the building can "speak to us plainly," a view reinforced by Harry Stuart Goodhart-Rendel (1944, p. 42), an English preservation architect. This perspective was still present in the late 1980s, when Nicholas Pappas (1985, p. 44), a retired American preservation architect, described how a building will tell us how it wants to exist: "If the building and its history are examined carefully . . . it might soon reveal what *it* wants to be." Orthodox preservation doctrine still maintains this idea that the building can and should tell a truth about how it needs to properly and accurately exist, while denying the possibility of more nuanced, pluralistic interpretations based on the public's perceptions.

The professional's craft in relating historical significance, as with material authenticity and recording methods, developed in similar ways that seek to create a more pure, objective historical account of the past. In orthodox historic preservation doctrine and policy, historical research, again, through this lens of positivism, treats historical narratives as the collection of enumerated facts that can then speak for themselves (NPS, 1997a). As applied to the work of the historian, historical positivism posits the existence of objective facts independent of interpretation; the more of such "facts" that one can gather, the stronger and more "accurate" the arguments and conclusions of a historian can be (cf. Dunning, 1914; Green, 1998). Historical positivism, because of its emphasis on scientism, attempts to link "facts" to historical causation and correlation; the historian then presents the past in teleological fashion, where a sequence of events can be assembled in neat fashion through time, culminating in some expected great event, series of related events, and/or people that, in turn, serve a grand, and expected, purpose in society (Wells, 2007). It is important to note that, in the 1970s, during the post-modern turn, academic historians largely abandoned positivism for an ontology that opened the possibilities for pluralistic and contradictory "facts" whose supposed objectivity relies on an interpretive frame, and more importantly, on who is doing the interpretation (Breisach, 2003). This more constructivist paradigm has yet to be incorporated into orthodox historic preservation work, which, instead, continues to uphold historical positivism as normalized practice.

The development of historical research methods in preservation/conservation doctrine and policy and ways to write significance statements mirror the rise of acceptable research methodologies and methods espoused by historians in the twentieth century, prior to 1960. In the 1930s, when the NPS developed its methods to record the histories of buildings for the Historic American Building Survey, which were later adopted into the criteria used in the National Register of Historic Places, it embraced historical positivism, which was the prevalent and widely accepted way in which the historian worked at the time (cf., Dunning, 1914). Henry Smith Williams (1904, p. 4), a well-known academic historian, explains how the prerogative of the historian is similar to the scientist: "The essential thing is that the modern historical investigator is fully actuated by the spirit of scientific accuracy and impartiality." The modern historian, as Floyd Matson (1957, p. 273) clarifies, is on a fact-seeking mission in which "the method of science ... fastens upon the fact."

Because the techniques and, especially, government policies to establish historical significance in historic preservation were already well established by the 1950s (Mackintosh, 1986; Sprinkle, 2014) and have not changed significantly in the twenty-first century, a postmodern perspective on history has not been able to significantly influence the majority of contemporary historic preservation doctrine and policy. Today, the orthodox method to establish the historical significance of a building is, by design, incapable of telling a full and inclusive story and continues to rely on significance arguments primarily to establish whether something is, or is not, officially historic, with nothing in between these extremes. As Caroline Cheong (2020, pp. 203–204) relates, in the third decade of the twenty-first century, "the historic register system at all levels functions in a binary: historic or not" and perpetuates the perception that the field "prioritizes elitist history—that is, the stories of white, wealthy, and usually male leaders—over all else." In simple terms, historical positivism, because of its elevation of the wealthy, White, male perspective and use of reductive, grand historical themes, sustains racial and ethnic bias in historical registers, such as the National Register of Historic Places. This situation is a major reason why the majority of National Register nominations created in the past half century tell a story from the perspective of the dominant socioeconomic and racial group in the United States while ignoring the experiences of people with minoritized identities (e.g., Kaufman, 2009; Loop, 2021; Magalong, 2017; McGhee, 2016). The bias in the National Register is also sustained by dated guidelines, such as National Register Bulletins, published by the NPS (NPS, 2017a, 2017b). These guidelines, first drafted in the early 1980s as federal government policy and widely replicated at state and local levels, direct researchers in dated, prejudicial techniques that unintentionally help to ensure the final nomination adheres to the core precepts of historical positivism. Specific directions include an emphasis on gathering as many objective "facts" as possible—without defining or explaining the culturally relative nature of facts or even what a properly "objective fact" is; the need to create a powerful, singular argument for significance that, in turn, ignores more nuanced and pluralistic historical narratives; and then relating this argument to a narrow range of predefined historical themes or "contexts," especially when such contexts are "associated with historic themes or trends that have been widely recognized and fully studied" (NPS, 1997b, p. 5). These guidelines ensure that the everyday, lived experiences of people who lack objective "facts" about their lives and whose experiences do not relate to widely known and studied historical themes/contexts will have difficulty rising to the standard set by the NPS to establish the historical significance of a place.

In sum, in the twentieth century, through a focus on scientism and objectivity, orthodox preservation/conservation doctrine introduced and then elevated three concepts to achieve an ontological purity in historical building conservation: 1) interventions in historical buildings should seek to avoid making such buildings "lie" (i.e., tell a "false sense of history"); 2) methods to record historic buildings must be scientifically substantiated; and 3) establishing why a building is historically important, or "significant," and thus, worthy of such treatment, is a truth-finding operation based on historical positivism. These concepts became the foundation of preservation/conservation theory in the 1950s and 60s and were institutionalized, through governmental preservation/conservation policy, in the 1960s and 70s and have not significantly changed to this day, especially in the United States (Avrami, Leo, & Sanchez, 2018; Bronin & Irwin, 2023; cf. Piper, 1947; Wells & Stiefel, 2019). To be sure, in the present, orthodox conservation doctrine is still fundamentally based on the kinds of true/false dichotomies presented here. Buildings either have, or they do not have, historical integrity (or material purity). They either have, or do not have, historical significance (factual purity). There is nothing in between these states, no gray area, and no place for more nuanced discussions on the essential concepts of authenticity and historical significance. This is the epitome of the positivism that upholds the ontological purity of orthodox preservation/conservation doctrine and, by extension, public policy.

EPISTEMOLOGICAL PURITY

Historic preservation, through the lens of epistemological purity, is a story about disciplines that were excluded from developing its doctrines, standards, and policies, but it is also a story of certain epistemological territorialization, based on specific disciplines developing a rhetoric around who owns, and does not own, specific knowledge.

The analysis and identification of the individuals who created preservation doctrines and policies, described in this chapter (see also appendix A), reveal these territories. Historians developed a rhetoric of "significance" based on historical positivism; architects developed a rhetoric of "integrity" (or "authenticity") based on an empiricist-positivist paradigm in which only things directly observable by the senses exist; art conservators developed a method for retaining the material authenticity of historic buildings and places based on gestalt psychology and the natural sciences; and processual archaeologists, who were rather late to the field, emphasized the scientific, informational value that could be contained in resources that were buried or otherwise hidden. In looking through these disciplines that are represented, however, it becomes obvious that many other disciplines are not represented, but certainly could have been. Anthropology, which has the potential to reveal much about cultural significance, including how groups of people, today, have a relationship with their built heritage, is not represented.[2] Sociology, which could help explain the relationship between social stratification/social power and the significance of the built environment (especially in relation to racial, ethnic, religious, or other marginalized groups) is not represented. Environmental psychology, which could greatly inform how individuals perceive and are emotionally affected by the age of places, could directly inform the treatment of the historic environment, but is not represented. The absence of this last discipline is especially puzzling given the interest that art conservators had in gestalt psychology, which is a precursor to contemporary environmental psychology—it would seem natural that this thread could have continued to the present, informed by better methods and theoretical understandings.

Humanistic geography had a brief cross-pollination with built heritage, especially through the writings of David Lowenthal (1985, 1998), Yi-Fu Tuan (1974, 1977), and Rowntree (1981), but this disciplinary perspective,

---

2. In the American higher education system, it is curious that archaeology is usually considered to be a subdiscipline of anthropology, yet archaeology students rarely have the opportunity, much less are required, to understand cultural heritage and the relationship of intangible heritage to people's interactions with the built environment.

and the associated area of environment and behavior research, never gained traction in either historic preservation or built heritage conservation. For instance, several decades ago, Philip Hubbard (1993, p. 369) argued that the use of historical facts, alone, to establish the significance (or value) of older buildings and places is misguided because "historicity in itself cannot act as an adequate basis for [heritage] conservation policy. Rather, it is apparent that the value of the familiar is not merely that people are used to it, but in the meanings that become associated with it over time." This perspective is especially important in light of the emotional attachments and identity, referred to by Hubbard as "the familiar," that many nondominant groups obtain from their older built environment; these places are more likely to have insufficient written records to establish their factual histories and lack high-style aesthetic values that often drive orthodox value assessments.

Other disciplines that were absent from the development of historic preservation doctrine and policy include environmental conservation and public policy, which are two areas that fundamentally intertwine with federal historic preservation policy, today. To be sure, environmental conservation and historic preservation policy are treated as overlapping by federal agencies during mandated environmental review processes, and many cultural resource management employers want employees to be as versed in the National Historic Preservation Act as they are in the Endangered Species Act (Wells, 2018). Seventy percent of historic preservation practice in the United States is driven by laws and regulations at the federal, state, and local levels (Wells, 2018), yet there is not a single public policy education program, center for preservation policy analysis, or tradition of scholarship that combines these two areas.[3] Lastly, with few exceptions (e.g., McLean, 2020; Milholland, 2010; Roberts, 2019; Rotenstein, 2019), research on historic preservation doctrine and public policy—i.e., beyond representation in policy-driven work and into investigating the structural elements of preservation policy—is largely absent from racial or ethnic study literature or programs but is sorely needed because the historic preservation discipline

---

3. An important reason why there has never been a center for the analysis of public preservation policy is that no funders in the United States have shown an interest in this topic.

is defined, in large part, by its traditional emphasis on White supremacy, which is sustained by such policy (Wells, 2021).

The key takeaway from this discussion, therefore, is that the disciplines of architecture, history, art conservation, and archaeology have owned the epistemological space of historic preservation for more than a half century, which manifests in the field's doctrinal norms and public policies; the fundamental involvement of these disciplines has also helped ensure that the epistemological purity of built heritage conservation is maintained by focusing only on these disciplinary perspectives. And, there appears to be little interest from these gatekeepers in allowing extradisciplinary perspectives from the social sciences, geography, public policy, environmental conservation, and ethnic/racial studies to gain a foothold.

SOCIAL PURITY

The history of the professionalism of historic preservation practice and the creation of federal historic preservation policy is, in part, a story of racial, ethnic, class, and gender bias. The traditionally accepted narrative of the history of the historic preservation movement in the United States is that it was founded on American patriotism (Hosmer, 1965; Murtagh, 1997; Tyler, Tyler, & Ligibel, 2018), which is not inaccurate, but it is a surface read of the stories that contribute to this movement. I will, instead, present a deeper, and more nuanced investigation of this history, which exposes the core impulse of this patriotism as a form of White supremacy. I begin this story with an overview of the sociocultural context in which the field of preservation was professionalized and then interpret the demographics of the people who made significant contributions to the development of historic preservation policy. Thus, "purity" in this context relates not only to bias, but also to the characteristics of the individuals who formed preservation policy.

In the early twentieth century, the professionalization of the historic preservation and environmental conservation movements paralleled the rise of eugenics. All three social movements focused on different permutations of "purity," with their main difference being their objects of attention: buildings, nature, or people, respectively. Historic preservation was founded on the need to preserve the "authentic" purity of building fabric; wilderness preservation was based on the exigency of needing to preserve "pristine" wilderness (Callicott, 1998); and eugenics was founded on the premise that the eminence of the White race was imperiled by other "impure" races, and thus the White race itself needed to be preserved (Basford & Levine, 2010).

As Garland Allen (2013) reveals, not only is the language used between these movements similar, but people overlapped in more than one of these "preservation" areas. For instance, many early environmental conservationists espoused the supposed logical necessity of the need to preserve the purity of a pristine wilderness as a prerequisite for preserving the "purity" of the mythological "Nordic" race; this assumption was based on the theory that the superior Nordic races were ennobled and purified through their ancient, spiritual relationship with pristine wilderness (Allen, 2013, p. 65; Spiro, 2009). Thus, for many early wilderness preservation proponents, there was a direct relationship between "preserving" the White race and preserving wilderness (Sommer, 2016; Spiro, 2009).

This racial supremacy context can readily be found in the origins of the European historic preservation movement, which sprang from a great reverence for Gothic architecture: of all the stylistic architectural forms, this style is uniquely associated with Nordic racial supremacy. Significant numbers of architects and preservationists alike at the turn of the twentieth century believed that that "the tradition of Gothic architecture is inherent in the Anglo-Saxon race and is a natural form of expression of the British Empire and its provinces," as *Architectural Review* ("Gothic design," 1908) observed. Certainly, John Ruskin (1849), well known for his singular emphasis on preserving Gothic cathedrals, would agree. Ruskin had documented racial biases, which included public support of the enslavement of African peoples and blatant anti-Indian discrimination (Arthur, 2001; Brantlinger, 1996), so even though his writings do not explicitly call out Gothic architecture for its expression of racial supremacy, there is, minimally, a strong implication of this association. Ruskin's compatriot Eugène Emmanuel Viollet-le-Duc was rather more direct in associating Gothic architecture with White supremacy when he wrote, "The human races are not equal and, to speak only of the two extremes, it is obvious that the white races that have covered Europe for three thousand years are infinitely superior to the Negro races that have lived since time immemorial in a large part of Africa" (Ramey, 2014, p. 23). The association of Gothic architecture with White supremacy, during this time, is also evident in other European countries, such as Germany. Alfred

Rosenberg (1893-1946), one of the most well-known Nazi intellectuals, frequently singled out Gothic architecture as a prominent example of the Nordic race's superiority over other "inferior" races (Rosenberg, 1939).

In sum, it is difficult to disentangle the nineteenth and early twentieth centuries' reverence for Gothic architecture (and the associated Arts and Crafts movement), from which historic preservation sprang, from White supremacy, as Nora Hanagan (2019, p. 498) explains:

> Especially troubling is the extent to which the Arts and Crafts movement reflected the patriarchal and racist sentiments of upper-class citizens. . . . While participants admired Asian designs, the movement was also pervaded by a sense of Anglo-American and European superiority. [William] Morris observed that the "Chinaman" is "a deft maker of pretty toys" whose techniques are not suited to the more imaginative "good workmen of our race." It is hardly surprising that a movement composed primarily of white middle- and upper-class Victorians would reflect prejudices that were common among Victorian elites. The extent to which the Arts and Crafts movement promoted race and gender stereotypes nevertheless undermines its claim to offer a universal vision of good design and also highlights why movements to promote democratic pleasure should not be elite driven.

To be sure, the early historic preservation movement was, as Hanagan intones, created by elites (e.g., Ruskin, Morris) to promote the admiration and preservation of old buildings by a much broader socioeconomic class, but the precepts and aesthetic values of this movement also embodied the racism that was endemic in the upper classes. And, a key aesthetic value collectively held by these elites was the inherent inferiority of vernacular, non-Western architecture, from Africa, India, and China, in particular, compared to northern European architecture (Coetzer, 2021).

Certainly, as Rosenberg's example shows, White supremacy and early preservation had more overt political contexts. European fascists capitalized on historic preservation as a political tool to promote White supremacy, and many intellectual leaders in the early preservation movement are associated with this party. Some prominent scholars who developed the Italian school of scientific/critical restoration, which is embodied in the international Venice Charter (ICOMOS, 1964) and the US NPS's Secretary of the Interior's Standards, such as Giulio Carlo Argan (1909-1994) and Gustavo Giovannoni (1873-1947), were members of the Italian fascist party (Aramini, 2020; Argan, 1931). A few authors of the international Athens Charter (Congress in Athens, 1931) and Venice Charter, such as Alois Kieslinger (1900-1975) and Gertrud Tripp (1914-2006), helped the Nazi regime's forced labor efforts in concentration camps and to steal art from Jewish people (Löscher, 2019; Mertz, 2020). According to Lucas Lixinski (2019, p. 114), during the 1930s and 40s, Nazi Germany sought to uphold historical monuments that the state uniquely believed to be associated with the aesthetic qualities of Nordic history; historic preservation therefore became a tool to enforce "a moral and racial purity of the national community [and to] produce and maintain Nazi ideology." Similarly, Benito Mussolini used historic preservation to "prove" the superiority of Roman precedents in Italian architectural design (Painter, 2007). The use of racial and cultural supremacy in promoting historic preservation was not limited to Europe, however; many early twentieth-century examples exist in the United States as well.

Charles Hosmer, the noted historic preservation movement historian, elevates the founder of the Society for the Preservation of New England Antiquities, William Sumner Appleton (1874-1947), as the first historic preservation "professional." According to Hosmer (1965), Appleton was one of the first individuals in the country to approach the preservation of buildings in a scientific, objective way that emphasized objectivity and careful documentation. Hosmer, however, did not detail one important aspect of Appleton's motivation: as a known eugenicist, Hosmer believed in preserving the colonial historic resources of New England as a way of promoting the racial superiority of the northern Europeans who built these structures (Lindgren, 1996).

There are many other examples in which White supremacy is the focus of an early preservation organization in the United States, such as the Association for the Preservation of Virginia Antiquities' founding on the premise of using historical monuments to advance the "lost cause" narrative of the American South (Meringolo, 2012). The Daughters of the American Revolution had a fundamental goal of "the conservation of the supremacy of the Anglo-Saxon race on this continent," according to Julia Green Scott (1839-1923), President General of the organization (Conservation Congress, 1911, p. 271). Another example is how the American Scenic and Historic Preservation society correlated historical significance with the degree to which a monument could demonstrate the superiority of "Anglo-Saxon civilization" in North America; a prominent example is Jamestown, which the Society promoted as "the garden of our people's [i.e., white people's] infancy in the

Western Hemisphere" (Hall, 1902, p. 105). These were "sacred memorials" that were "consecrated by the sacrifices and sufferings of a generation of [Anglo-Saxon] heroes" (Hall, 1902, p. 124). But, perhaps there is no better example than Colonial Williamsburg in Virginia.

Carefully crafted by architects and archaeologists in the 1930s, Colonial Williamsburg was reconstructed, restored, and preserved to capture the supremacy of northern European culture as it was translated into a North American context. By uplifting a purely "Anglo-Saxon" narrative of American's colonial past, the creation of Colonial Williamsburg erased the contributions of countless people of African origin and ignored the Indigenous peoples that were already present long before Europeans arrived. Some of these erasures were quite literal as the architects of the re-envisioned town saw the shacks in which enslaved people lived as "ugly" and aesthetically undesirable and proceeded to remove them, while preserving the much more aesthetically pleasing and "symmetrical" buildings constructed by White people, even if they were "modest" (Anders, 2009; Perry, 1935). For the first several decades after its creation, there was next to no mention of the institution of slavery, enslaved peoples, or Indigenous peoples in the interpretation of Colonial Williamsburg (Anders, 2009; cf. Kocher & Dearstyne, 1949).

These examples highlight the semiotic qualities of built heritage, but there is another story as well, which relates to the normalization of local history research, through the 1970s, as an endeavor that elevates the voices of White men while deprecating or ignoring the voices, and experiences, of people with other identities (Soleim, 2021). This development of public history through the early to mid-twentieth century is essential to understand the perspectives of the professional historians who created federal preservation policy, especially as embodied in National Register of Historic Places criteria. A place to start this understanding is by exploring the university education and training these individuals received. Most of the historians who helped developed the National Register criteria received their university degrees in history between about 1920 and 1955 (refer to appendix A). During their education, their professors, from whom these historians would have learned, would have likely elevated the work of a number of prominent historians with documented racial and ethnic biases:

- Frederick Jackson Turner (1861–1932), known for his "frontier thesis," which posited that because the white settlers of North America were "exceptional," the colonization of the frontier, and the dispossession of Indigenous lands, were justified. By the 1930s, about 60% of the top university history programs in the United States were teaching Turner's methods and thesis (Bogue, 1994). Biographers of Turner have noted the many racial and ethnic biases that were evident in his work (e.g., Washington, 1993).

- Samuel Eliot Morison (1887-1976), the noted author of *The Growth of the American Republic* (1930), which was one of the most influential books on American history through the mid-century and would have likely been a core textbook for courses on American history, expressed consistent racial bias toward people of African descent, especially in relation to their enslavement. Morison's work is considered to be part of the "Phillips school" of slavery historiography, which was named after Ulrich Bonnell Phillips (1877-1934) and noted for its benign or positive portrayal of slavery in American history (Gilmore, 1978). The NAACP publicly called out Morison's bias in his textbook in 1944 (Jumonville, 1999, p. 147).
- Madison Grant (1865-1937), noted eugenicist and conservationist, in his work *The Passing of the Great Race; or The Racial Basis of European History* (1916), emboldened other historians, of his era, to emphasize the supposed innate superiority of the White race in their work (Allen, 2013).
- William Archibald Dunning (1857-1922), a contemporary of Grant and the founder of the "Dunning school" of historiography, normalized the use of racial bias in historical interpretation, which was subsequently adopted into the early field of public history (Smith & Lowery, 2013; Soleim, 2021).

Most other historians in the early Modern era, however, rather than promoting White supremacy, simply omitted any histories in which White men were not involved. The work of their peers, some of whom are listed above, helped legitimize that the only valid history was one related to broad narrative themes in which important White men were involved.

With this sociocultural context in place, I will now explore the demographic characteristics of the individuals who created preservation policy. This exploration will answer basic questions about the race, gender, and education status of these professionals and provide needed empirical evidence for the claims that the people who developed historic preservation policy were largely White, male, and elite. In other words, this is a story of how a rather narrow demographic slice of the European and American populations was granted the power to decide about historical significance and authenticity for everyone else. These data will therefore help provide an answer to what kinds of social, cultural, and power norms these policymakers brought to the table when creating their various theories, doctrines, and finally, policies based on earlier theories and doctrines.

Just like people today, the individuals who were responsible for helping craft federal historic preservation policy, from about 1930 to 1970, would have had some degree of inherent racial or gender biases in their discussions and writings; based on sociocultural norms of the period in which they worked, such biases would have been more normalized than today, however. In other words, to expect that federal historic preservation policy, as written by these professionals, is entirely neutral and without bias is an unreasonable assumption. Thus, the question becomes to what *degree* might bias be present, and to induce this interpretation through an examination of the demographic characteristics of these individuals. In other words, there is a reasonable expectation that a White male working in 1960 would have been less likely to hold egalitarian principles for people with minoritized identities; and, conversely, someone with a specific minoritized identity—say, African American—would be less likely to hold a bias against those within their own group identity. I do not, however, make any assumptions that these individuals had an agenda to implement bias in their work; rather, I make the assumption that, as products of the society in which they were raised and educated, they will be likely to express the sociocultural norms of their day, in their work.

I also want to make clear that the point in this exploration is not to focus on specific individuals, but their characteristics in aggregate and how this speaks to the larger preservation enterprise. To be sure, while there are a few individuals who have documented racial and ethnic biases, most appear to not be in this category, based on the data I have found.

The method that I used in gathering these demographic data was to only collect information from individuals with the following characteristics:

- They had the power and, relative to the era in which they lived, socially recognized expertise to make theory, doctrinal, and policy recommendations and/or the implementation of these policies that were directly relevant to historic preservation/built heritage conservation;
- The influence and action of these individuals are well documented by other researchers and cited frequently in the literature;

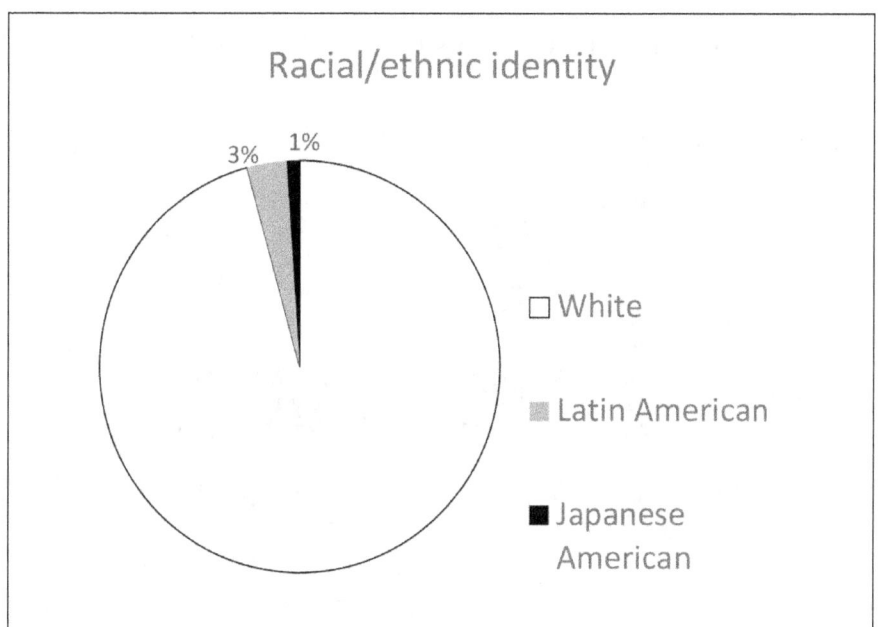

FIGURE 3.1. Racial or ethnic identity of professionals who helped create federal preservation policy

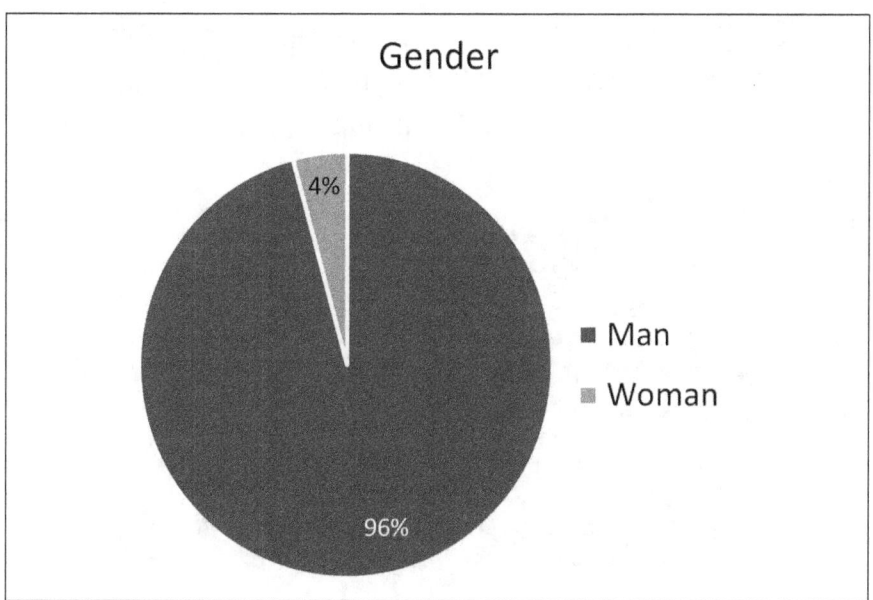

FIGURE 3.2. Gender identity of professionals who helped create federal preservation policy

- These individuals are recognized authors or coauthors of the recommendations and/or policies they have made that contributed to historic preservation/built heritage conservation.

Thus, using this methodology, while Lady Bird Johnson played a pivotal role in helping to pass the National Historic Preservation Act of 1966, no

FIGURE 3.3. Educational attainment of professionals who helped create federal preservation policy

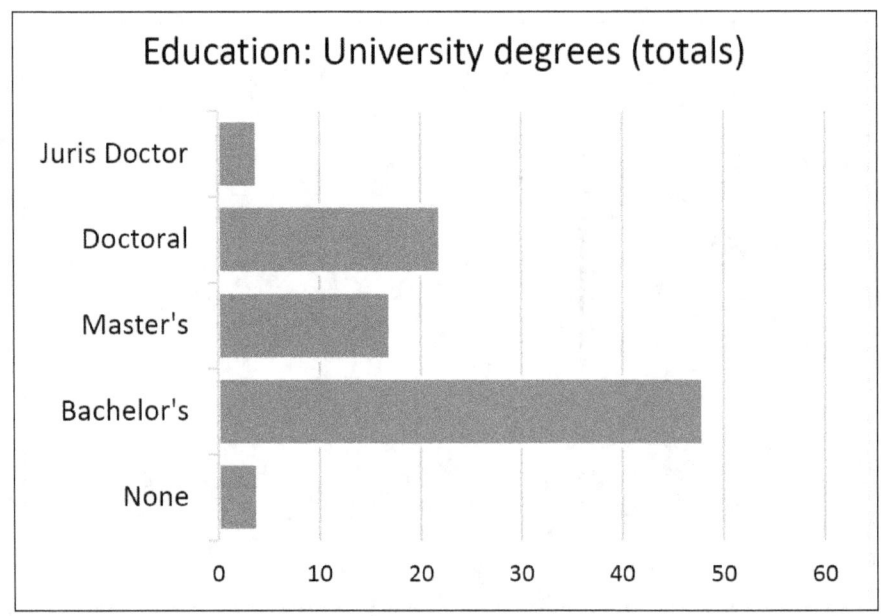

FIGURE 3.4. Professionals with a degree from an elite university who helped create federal preservation policy

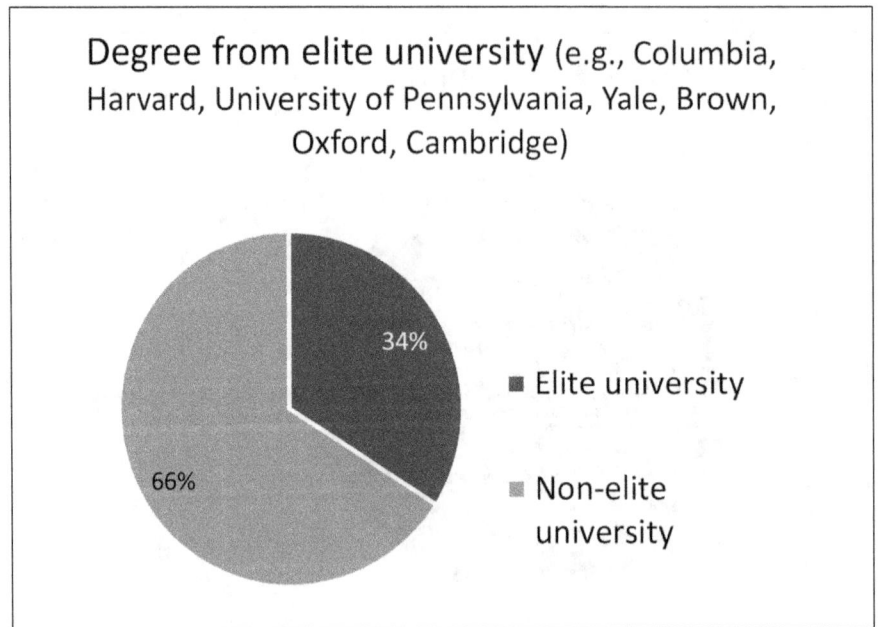

scholars have indicated that she contributed to the theoretical, doctrinal, or specific policy debates in historic preservation and she has no publications, with her name as an author, that documents such contributions. Similarly, while Jane Jacobs has had a significant influence on urban planning and preservation practice, during the 1960s, when much of the finalization of

National Register policy was being made, her contributions to the planning field were not yet widely recognized; it was only later that her importance was realized, as it should have been, originally. Unfortunately, no scholar has recognized Jacob's work in connection with the development of federal historic preservation policy.

I also make the concession that it is possible that other people, who did not publish their contributions to preservation theory, doctrine, or policy, possibly participated in these areas, but their contributions were not recorded by others; and it would therefore not be possible for me to include them in the data. On the other hand, from the mid-nineteenth century to the early 1970s, the likelihood that women and people with minoritized racial and ethnic identities would have been welcomed in these discussions seems somewhat improbable, unfortunately. Perhaps the best example of this is that in the seven-member team that the NPS assigned to create the significance and integrity criteria for the National Register, the only woman, of the seven, served as the "secretary" (Kathryn [Kay] Thomas; Mackintosh, 1986); I include her in these data as it seems likely that in her role in recording information, she undoubtedly was able to make significant contributions.

Using this methodology, I identified 95 people who contributed to the development of the policy that led to the creation of the US National Register of Historic Places criteria and the US Secretary of the Interior's Standards. They are listed in appendix A. These data empirically show that the people responsible for developing today's National Register criteria and the Standards:

- Were nearly all white men (Figures 3.1, 3.2);
- Were highly educated with an unusually large number (especially for the time) of people with doctoral degrees and who taught in universities (Figures 3.3, 3.4);
- Often held degrees from elite universities;
- Have some documented racial and ethnic bias.

What is the takeaway, therefore, from this analysis of the demographics of the professionals who helped craft federal historic preservation policy? There are now data to substantiate the claim that very few—that is 95—White men, who were highly educated and from elite schools, helped to create federal historic preservation policy. In other words, you could put all these individuals into a single, medium-sized room, and their collective, homogenous identity would be incapable of representing the broader diversity of Americans, much less humanity.

NAKED HERITAGE: A RETURN TO THE EMBODIED EXPERIENCE OF THE BUILT ENVIRONMENT

If one strips away the defining characteristics that purified orthodox historic preservation doctrine and policy—fabric purity, ontological purity, epistemological purity, and social purity—what is left is an "impure" concept of heritage, or the meanings and values that the creators of this discipline discarded. But, this process of baring the cryptic meanings and values of heritage also leaves them naked and exposed because their defenders are largely absent. I choose the word "naked" for another reason as well, and that is to convey an embodied aspect of heritage meanings that has long been ignored, not only by historic preservation proper, but by many allied fields, including heritage studies and environmental design (i.e., environment and behavior research). One cannot understand what it is to be naked without realizing your body is an interface to the environment; and it is this person–place relationship that characterizes naked heritage.

For scholars familiar with the history of historic preservation doctrine, this embodied experience and its relationship with meaning in the older built environment should be familiar, as it is the perspective that Ruskin (1849) took in writing his chapter on the "Lamp of Memory" in his book *The Seven Lamps of Architecture*. The concepts he explored, including the "golden stain of time" in reference to patina, and how the centuries of human feet and hands that touched building fabric left an intangible imprint in these materials are grounded in a deep and profound, emotional experience of being embedded in certain historic environments. The Italian art conservators of the early twentieth century who created the theories around how historic fabric should be treated to retain its authenticity were deeply influenced by gestalt psychology. Brandi (Matero, 2007), for instance, developed his conservation theories using his body as an instrument to record how the experience of completeness and authenticity in art could be altered by changing the kinds of treatment used for these historic objects. The method Brandi used is called a first-person phenomenological reduction and is still used as a research method in environmental psychology (Moustakas, 1994; van

Manen, 1990). Phenomenological reductions are particularly useful in understanding the person–place interaction and how the environment (natural and cultural) impacts human behavior. Today, however, it is more likely for a psychologist to use a *third-person* phenomenological reduction in order to access and understand the prereflective, embodied experiences of others (e.g., Wells & Baldwin, 2012).

And, this perspective, outside of one's own body, is precisely what orthodox historic preservation doctrine is missing: all these theories were developed using a first-person, rationalistic perspective, in which empirical evidence from other people's experiences were either not considered, or rejected (Wells & Stiefel, 2019). From Ruskin, to Morris, Boito, and Brandi, orthodox preservation/conservation theory has been addressed exclusively from this rationalistic, first-person perspective, which could only be reflective of these individuals' homogenous social, racial, and gender identities. Thus, orthodox preservation/conservation theory, which has been embedded in US historic preservation policy, and built heritage conservation policy internationally, is defined, in part, by excluding available, empirical evidence about other people's lived experiences—especially the experiences of people whose racial and ethnic identities are dramatically different from the elite, highly educated, White men who created these doctrines.

And these everyday lived experiences that characterize naked heritage are often about the "charm" and "magic" of older places. To be sure, they can go as far as literally expressing a belief that there are spirits embedded in place—witness the growth in "dark" tourism, for instance, in which ghost stories play a fundamental role in the interpretation of "historic" places. It is simply not possible in orthodox heritage conservation practice, while adhering to accepted doctrine and policy, to discuss and give full consideration of this kind of magical lived experience, including spontaneous fantasies, and be taken seriously (again, the concept of heritage is not sufficiently pure—based in the physical reality of fabric, objective, and supportive of the epistemology and reality of conventional experts). Simply put, there is no place in which the everyday lived experiences of heritage can be legitimately considered within accepted preservation/conservation doctrine and public policy that drives most of the field's practice.

Thus, naked heritage is about a return to understanding the embodied, lived experience of being in the historic environment, but unlike what happened a century ago, we can look at this experience through the individual eyes, ears, and voices of other people, and especially people whose participation in historic preservation has traditionally been marginalized because of their racial and ethnic identities. The next chapter will explore the qualities of naked heritage and environmental heritage.

CONCLUSION

This chapter examined the historic preservation/built heritage conservation discipline through four fundamental characteristics: fabric purity, ontological purity, epistemological purity, and social purity. What was outside of this discourse became "impure" heritage, tainted by subjectivity, emotion, and popular sentiment. Stripping away this professionally imposed veneer of purity found in the discipline's doctrine and policies lays bare many of the important, fundamental reasons people value and give meaning to built heritage through their lived, emotional experiences. Rather than looking at impure heritage in a critical, negative light, how do these values and meanings, held by the public, appear when exposed and naked in all their vulnerability? The next chapter will answer this question in the context of changing preservation doctrine and policy that embraces and capitalizes on the magic of old places.

Works Cited

Allen, G. (2013). "Culling the herd": Eugenics and the conservation movement in the United States, 1900-1940. *Journal of the History of Biology*, 46(1), 31-72.

Anders, G. (2009). *Creating Colonial Williamsburg: The restoration of Virginia's eighteenth-century capital*. University of North Carolina Press.

Appleton, W. S. (1919). Destruction and preservation of old buildings in New England. *Art and Archaeology*, 8(3), 131-183.

Aramini, D. (2020). A racist and anti-Semitic Romanità: The Racial Laws of 1938 and the Institute of Roman Studies. *Trauma and Memory*, 8(2), 161-196.

Argan, G. C. (1931). La teoria di architettura di Sebastiano Serlio. Tesi datt. Torino: Regia Università, Facoltà di Lettere e Filosofia.

Arthur, T. (2001). Economics, slavery and Victorian reformers. *Economic Affairs*, 21(2), 49-52.

Avrami, E., Leo, C.-N., & Sanchez, A. S. (2018). Confronting exclusion: Redefining the intended outcomes of historic preservation. *Change Over Time: International Journal of Conservation and the Built Environment*, 8(1), 102-120.

Basford, A., & Levine, P. (Eds.). (2010). The Oxford handbook of the history of eugenics. Oxford University Press.

Becher, T. (1981). Towards a definition of disciplinary cultures. *Studies in Higher Education*, 6(2), 109-122.

Bogue, A. G. (1994). Frederick Jackson Turner reconsidered. *The History Teacher*, 27(2), 195-221.

Boito, C. (1884). *I restauratori, conferenza tenuta all'esposizione di torino, il 7 giugno 1884*. Florence.

Brandi, C. (1977). *Teoria del restauro*. Einaudi.

Brantlinger, P. (1996). A postindustrial prelude to postcolonialism: John Ruskin, William Morris, and Gandhism. *Critical Inquiry*, 22(3), 466-485.

Breisach, E. (2003). *On the future of history: The postmodernist challenge and its aftermath*. University of Chicago Press.

Bronin, S. C., & Irwin, L. R. (2023). Regulating history. *Minnesota Law Review*, 108(1), 241-331.

Callicott, J. B. (1998). The wilderness idea revisited. In J. B. Callicott & M. P. Nelson (Eds.), *The great new wilderness debate* (pp. 337-366). University of Georgia Press.

Carhart, H. S. (1895). The educational and industrial value of science. *Science*, 1(15), 393-402.

Chandler, J. E. (1944). Notes on the Paul Revere house. *The Walpole Society Note Book*, 15-20.

Cheong, C. S. (2020). Connecting historic preservation and affordable housing. In E. Avrami (Ed.), *Preservation and social inclusion* (pp. 201-212). Columbia University Press.

Coetzer, N. R. (2021). Earthly beings and the Arts and Crafts discourse in the Cape: Conflicted and contradictory (non)appropriations of vernacular traditions. In J. Mascarenhas-Mateus & A. P. Pires (Eds)., *History of construction cultures* (vol. 1, pp. 262-267). Taylor and Francis, CRC Press.

Congress Hall Restored. (1914, January). *The Architectural Record*, 35, 97-100.

Congress in Athens. (1931). *The Athens Charter*. First International Congress of Architects and Technicians of Historic Monuments.

Connor, C. D. (2005). *A people's history of science*. Nation Books.

Conservation Congress. (1911). *Proceedings of the second national conservation congress at Saint Paul, September 5-8, 1910*. National Conservation Congress.

Cram, M. (1917). *Old seaport towns of the South*. Dodd, Mead & Company.

Drury, N. B. (1950). A symposium on principles of historic restoration: The National Park Service. *Antiques*, (July), 29-49.

Dunning, W. A. (1914). Truth in history. *American Historical Review*, 19(2), 216-230.

Foucault, M. (1991). *Discipline and punish: The birth of the prison*. Penguin.

Friedländer, M. J. (1942). On restorations. In *On art and connoisseurship* (pp. 267-272). B. Cassirer.

Gilmore, A. T. (Ed.). (1978). *Revisiting Blassingame's The slave community: The scholars respond*. Greenwood Press.

Goodhart-Rendel, H. S. (1944). Preservation. *The Architect and Building News*, 179(July 21), 41-44.

Gothic design in Regina competition. (1908, March). The *Architectural Review*, 39-43, 47.

Grabar, I. (1945). The restoration of Russian architectural monuments. *American Slavic and East European Review*, 4(1/2), 182-184.

Grant, M. (1916). *The passing of the great race, or the racial basis of European history.* Charles Scribner's Sons.

Green, H. L. (1998). The social construction of historical significance. In M. A. Tomlan (Ed.), *Preservation of what, for whom? A critical look at historical significance* (pp. 85-94). National Council for Preservation Education.

Hall, E. H. (1902). Jamestown: The first permanent English settlement in America. In *The eleventh annual report of the American Scenic and Historic Preservation Society* (pp. 105-124). J. B. Lyon Company.

Hanagan, N. (2019). The citizen, the baker, and the candlestick maker: What Democrats can learn from the Arts and Crafts and Slow Food movements. *American Political Thought: A Journal of Ideas, Institutions, and Culture,* 8(4), 479-503.

Hosmer, C. B. (1965). *Presence of the past: A history of the preservation movement in the United States before Williamsburg.* Putnam.

Hubbard, P. (1993). The value of conservation: A critical review of behavioural research. *Town Planning Review,* 64(4), 359-373.

Hudgins, C. (2012). *Transcription of W. Brown Morton III, Hon. AIA, interview.* Clemson/College of Charleston Historic Preservation Graduate Program.

Hugo, V. (1888). *The hunchback of Notre-Dame.* Little, Brown, and Co. (Original work published 1831)

Hutchings, R., La Salle, M. (2015). Why archaeologists misrepresent their practice—a North American perspective. Journal of Contemporary Archaeology, 2(2), S11-S17.

Insall, D. W. (1958). *The care of old buildings: A practical guide for architects and owners.* SPAB.

International Council on Monuments and Sites (ICOMOS). (1964). *The Venice Charter.* https://www.icomos.org/en/participer/179-articles-en-francais/ressources/charters-and-standards/157-thevenice-charter

Jokilehto, J. (1999). *A history of architectural conservation.* Butterworth Heinemann.

Jumonville, N. (1999). *Henry Steele Commager: Midcentury liberalism and the history of the present.* University of North Carolina Press.

Kaufman, N. (2009). *Place, race, and story: Essays on the past and future of historic preservation.* Routledge.

Kimball, F. (1935, December). The restoration of Colonial Williamsburg in Virginia. *The Architectural Record,* 78(6), 359.

King, T. F. (2009). *Our unprotected heritage: Whitewashing the destruction of our cultural and natural resources.* Left Coast Press.

Kocher, A. L., & Dearstyne, H. (1949). *Colonial Williamsburg, its buildings and gardens: A study of Virginia's restored capital.* Colonial Williamsburg.

Kunz, G. F. (1912). *The imperishable records of the ancients: Compared with methods in use up to the present time.* American Scenic and Historic Preservation Society.

Lethaby, W. R. (1898, December). How they restore. *The Architectural Review,* 5, 14-20.

Lindgren, J. M. (1996). *Preserving historic New England: Preservation, progressivism, and the remaking of memory.* Oxford University Press.

Lixinski, L. (2019). *International heritage law for communities: Exclusion and re-imagination.* Oxford University Press.

Lockwood, A. G. (1937). Problems and responsibilities of restoration. *Old Time New England,* 28(October), 49-59.

Loop, J. (2021). The 1992 uprising: Historic preservation and the durability of Whiteness. *Carolina Planning Journal*, 46, 50-57.

Löscher, N. (2019). Gertrude Tripp: 30 May 1914 - 17 April 2006. Lexikon der österreichischen Provenienzforschung. https://www.lexikon-provenienzforschung.org/en/tripp-gertrude.

Lowenthal, D. (1985). *The past is a foreign country*. Cambridge University Press.

———. (1998). *The heritage crusade and the spoils of history*. Cambridge University Press.

Mackintosh, B. (1986). *The National Historic Preservation Act and the National Park Service: A history*. US Department of the Interior, National Park Service.

Magalong, M. (2017). Politics of representation and participation in federal historic preservation programs [Doctoral dissertation, University of California, Los Angeles].

Matero, F. G. (2007). Loss, compensation, and authenticity: The contribution of Cesare Brandi to architectural conservation in America. *Future Anterior*, 4(1), 45-58.

Matson, F. W. (1957). History as art: The psychological-romantic view. *Journal of the History of Ideas*, 18(2), 270-279.

McGhee, F. L. (2016). Heritage dispatches from the American approaches of hell: Public housing, historic preservation, and environmental impact analysis. *Environmental Practice*, 18(3), 192-204.

McLean, K. (2020). Reclaiming time and space: Bringing historical preservation into the future [Master's thesis, Massachusetts Institute of Technology]. https://hdl.handle.net/1721.1/127624

Meringolo, D. D. (2012). *Museums, monuments, and national parks: Toward a new genealogy of public history*. University of Massachusetts Press.

Mertz, G. (2020). "Das braun der erde." Die träger der Haidinger-Medaille der Geologischen Bundesanstalt und der Nationalsozialismus. *Jahrbuch der Geologischen Bundesanstalt*, 160(1-4), 359-408.

Michaelis, A. (1908). *A century of archaeological discoveries*. John Murray.

Milholland, S. (2010). In the eyes of the beholder: Understanding and resolving incompatible ideologies and languages in US environmental and cultural laws in relationship to Navajo sacred lands. *American Indian Culture and Research Journal*, 34(2), 103-124.

Morison, S. E. (1930). The growth of the American republic (2 vols.). Oxford University Press.

Morris, W. (1878). Annual report of the SPAB - I. *The Architect*, (6 July), 7-8.

Moustakas, C. E. (1994). *Phenomenological research methods*. Sage Publications.

Muñoz Viñas, S. (2005). *Contemporary theory of conservation*. Elsevier.

Murtagh, W. J. (1997). *Keeping time: The history and theory of preservation in America*. John Wiley & Sons.

O'Donnell, E. (1998). *National Register bulletin 39: Researching a historic property*. US Department of the Interior, National Park Service.

Painter, B. W. (2007). *Mussolini's Rome: Rebuilding the eternal city*. Palgrave Macmillan.

Pappas, N. (1985). Scape and anti-scrape: Wherein we explore the treacherous jungle between these two extremes; discover the perils hidden therein; and seek the path to Eldorado. *APT Bulletin*, 17(3/4), 43-50.

Peers, C. R. (1917, March). The care of ancient monuments. *The Architectural Review*, 41, 65-66.

———. (1931). The treatment of old buildings. *RIBA Journal*, 38(10), 311-320.

Perry, W. G. (1935, December). Notes on the architecture [of Colonial Williamsburg]. *The Architectural Record*, 78(6), 363-382.

Philippot, A., & Philippot, P. (1959). Le problème de l'intégration des lacunes dans la restauration des peintures. *Bulletin De L'Institut Royal Du Patrimoine Artistique*, 2.

Philippot, P. (1976). Historic preservation: Philosophy, criteria, guidelines. In S. Timmons (Ed.), *Preservation and conservation principles and practices*. Preservation Press.

Phillips, W. (1878). *Speech of Hon. Wendell Phillips for aid in the preservation of the Old South Meeting-House [Speech to Massachusetts Legislature, Committee on Federal Relations]*. Alfred Mudge and Son.

Piper, J. (1947, September). Pleasing decay. *The Architectural Review*, 102, 85-94.

Powys, A. R. (1929). *Repair of ancient buildings*. J. M. Dent & Sons.

Ramey, L. T. (2014). *Black legacies: Race and the European Middle Ages*. University Press of Florida.

Restoration of the Paul Revere House, Boston. (1914, July). *The Architectural Record*, 36, 80.

The Restoration of the White House. (1903, February 29). The American Architect and Building News, 79, 67.

Roberts, A. R. (2019). "Until the Lord come get me, burn it down, or the next storm blow it away": The aesthetics of freedom in African American vernacular homestead preservation. *Buildings & Landscapes: Journal of the Vernacular Architecture Forum*, 26(2), 73-97.

Rosenberg, A. (1939). *Der mythus des zwanzigsten jahrhunderts*. Hoheneichen-Verl.

Rotenstein, D. S. (2019). The Decatur Plan: Folklore, historic preservation, and the Black experience in gentrifying spaces. Journal of American Folklore, 132(526), 431-451.

Rowntree, L. B. (1981). Creating a sense of place: The evolution of historic preservation of Salzburg, Austria. *Journal of Urban History*, 8(1), 61-76.

Ruskin, J. (1849). *The seven lamps of architecture*. Smith, Elder, and Co.

Scott, J. C. (1998). *Seeing like a state: How certain schemes to improve the human condition have failed*. Yale University Press.

Smith, J. D., & Lowery, J. V. (Eds.). (2013). *The Dunning school: Historians, race, and the meaning of reconstruction*. University Press of Kentucky.

Smith, L. (2006). *Uses of heritage*. Routledge.

Society for the Protection of Ancient Buildings (SPAB). (1879). *"Restoration" in East Anglia. No.1, A report to the Society for the Protection of Ancient Buildings upon the condition and prospects of the cathedrals of Ely and Norwich, and certain other churches and buildings of East Anglia*.

Society for the Protection of Ancient Buildings (SPAB). (1903). *Notes on the repair of ancient buildings*.

Soleim, S. A. M. (2021). "To make history the living force": The professionalization of public history—1880-2000 [Doctoral dissertation, North Carolina State University].

Sommer, M. (2016). *History within: The science, culture, and politics of bones, organisms, and molecules*. University of Chicago Press.

Spiro, J. P. (2009). *Defending the master race: Conservation, eugenics, and the legacy of Madison Grant*. University of Vermont Press.

Sprinkle, J. H. (2014). *Crafting preservation criteria: The National Register of Historic Places and American historic preservation*. Routledge.

Tainter, J. A., & Lucas, G. J. (1983). Epistemology of the significance concept. *American Antiquity*, 48(4), 707–719.

Tuan, Y.-F. (1974). *Topophilia: A study of environmental perception, attitudes, and values.* Prentice-Hall.

Tuan, Y.-F. (1977). *Space and place: The perspectives of experience.* University of Minnesota Press.

Tyler, N., Tyler, I. R., & Ligibel, T. (2018). *Historic preservation: An introduction to its history, principles, and practice.* W. W. Norton & Company.

US National Park Service (NPS). (1997a). *National Register Bulletin: How to apply the National Register criteria for evaluation.*

US National Park Service (NPS). (1997b). *National Register Bulletin: How to complete the National Register registration form.*

van Manen, M. (1990). *Researching the lived experience.* University of Western Ontario.

Washington, M. (1993). African American history and the frontier thesis. *Journal of the Early Republic*, 13(2), 230–241.

Wells, J. C. (2007). The plurality of truth in culture, context, and heritage: A (mostly) post-structuralist analysis of urban conservation charters. *City and Time*, 3(2:1), 1–13.

———. (2017). Are we "ensnared in the system of heritage" because we do not want to escape? *Archaeologies: Journal of the World Archaeological Congress*, 13(1), 26–47.

———. (2018). Challenging the assumption about a direct relationship between historic preservation and architecture in the United States. *Frontiers of Architectural Research*, 7(4), 455–464.

———. (2021). 10 ways historic preservation policy supports White supremacy and 10 ideas to end it. University of Maryland, College Park faculty papers. https://doi.org/10.13016/hyol-8vgp

Wells, J. C., & Baldwin, E. D. (2012). Historic preservation, significance, and age value: A comparative phenomenology of historic Charleston and the nearby new-urbanist community of I'On. *Journal of Environmental Psychology*, 32(4), 384–400.

Wells, J. C., & Stiefel, B. L. (2019). Introduction: Moving past conflicts to foster an evidence-based, human-centric built heritage conservation practice. In J. C. Wells & B. L. Stiefel (Eds.), *Human-centered built environment heritage preservation: Theory and evidence-based practice* (pp. 1–30). Routledge.

Williams, H. S. (1904). *The historians' history of the world.* The Outlook Company.

Younès, C. (2006). Doctorates caught between disciplines and projects. *The Journal of Architecture*, 11(3), 315–321.

CHAPTER 4

Transforming Historic Preservation Policy to Manage Charm

INTRODUCTION

Now that the previous chapters have established the nature of the person-patina relationship and a theory of practice based on it, this chapter delves into pragmatic ways to actualize this theory. The next logical step would be to begin to manage, through new and reformed public policy, the character, degree, and type of charm—more specifically, emotional affect—ascribed by people to certain heritage places. The goal would then be to manage the overall affective character of a place in a way that maximizes people's emotional attachment to it. Or, in another sense, this chapter focuses on how to implement the management of "charm" through public policy, which was discussed in the introduction.

 This chapter is guided by the assumption that built heritage conservation must, first and foremost, benefit people. To be sure, orthodox preservation/conservation doctrine and policy primarily focus on immovable and inanimate objects, while failing to consider and articulate how preservation/conservation work directly affects people, for good or bad—especially people outside of the dominant racial, ethnic, and socioeconomic groups (see chapters 1 and 3). After all, without people, why bother to engage in preservation/conservation at all (Wells, 2020)? Thus, this chapter is guided by Kyle Ezell's (2022) recommendation that planning for the public should always foreground three "essential questions" to remind us to ask who our work impacts and how this impact manifests: "Who is helped? Who is harmed? Who is missing?" To this list, I would also add the question "Who am I?" Asking this latter question is characteristic of a reflexive practitioner. Preservation/conservation policy should therefore be transformed from an assumption that *people must help older places* to challenging policy to show *how preservation/conservation benefits, or potentially harms, people*. By using empirical evidence related to "Being Affected by Old Places" (BAOP), the reasons to engage in built heritage conservation can be greatly expanded, especially through how the person–patina relationship facilitates the magic of old places (see chapter 2).

I will begin by introducing the importance of conventional experts adopting the role of facilitator, instead of enforcer/reeducator, through grassroots, community-based participatory research. Since meetings form one of the most common ways that this work occurs—i.e., community workshops—this chapter will describe effective ways to organize and facilitate these meetings. Data from environmental psychology—which undergirds an understanding of BAOP—can also help to inform policy, and some suggested areas of focus will be recommended. Lastly, this chapter will provide important considerations for how to convert outcomes from community-based participatory research and environmental psychology research into policy directives.

THE IMPORTANCE OF HERITAGE FACILITATORS AND CIVIL EXPERTS IN CHANGING POLICY

Charm management first requires considering how power manifests and is expressed through orthodox historic preservation policy. There has been much literature written on this topic (see chapter 1), but the basic premise is that orthodox preservation/conservation policy is a top-down process, controlled by conventional experts in which the public's values and meanings (largely the meanings of civil experts) are sidelined through laws, regulations, and/or guidelines to ensure efficiency, reproducibility, and predictability. Thus, within orthodox policy, conventional experts are expected to educate the public on orthodoxy and enforce it within their everyday work—in a more pejorative sense, used by some authors (e.g., Emerick, 2014; Hall, 2016; Kisić, 2022), these experts are heritage policy "police." The opposite of this perspective is a process that is grassroots, or bottom-up, wherein everyday people (i.e., civil experts) work hand-in-hand with conventional experts to identify, address, and solve a problem or achieve an objective (e.g., Garcia, 2018; Roberts, 2018; Silverman et al., 2019). The result can be messy, contradictory, and time intensive, but that is the fundamental nature of grassroots, public engagement and cannot be avoided; the assumption, however, is that the outcome is more likely to represent the needs, values/perceptions, and ideas of specific constituents who engage in this process.

Facilitators guide a process but step back and let others make decisions, develop and direct the identification of problems, propose methods to address them, and choose and test solutions. Wickens and Gupta (2022, pp. 323–324) describe how this "stepping back" should look within the context of heritage conservation and how to let others in the process "lead":

> Not only do we need the excluded to tell us how to include them, those of us in leadership roles have to make way for them. We have to stop setting the agenda, teaching people to do things our way, and welcome people into our world. We need to let go of power. There are many others who can and should lead. We must let others take the good work we have done and shape it into something we never thought possible, and maybe never even imagined.

The key description here, that fits within the frame of "heritage police," is the directive to "let go of power." Facilitated community workshops are fundamentally about moving power from conventional experts to civil experts. Conventional experts remain part of the process and provide information, guidance, and, where appropriate, suggestions, but do not attempt to control, direct, or enforce doctrine or policy within these deliberative contexts.

Within the fields of public health, community-based archaeology, and environmental conservation, there is a precedent to achieve these goals to equalize power between civil and conventional experts: action research and, especially, community-based participatory research, which is a form of action research. In this chapter, I will often use the phrase "participatory research" to encompass both traditions, which are closely related (Castellanet & Jordan, 2004; Fals-Borda, 1987; Freire, 1970; Kemmis & McTaggart, 2005). It is important, however, to not be biased by the word "research," as these techniques are quite clearly focused on real-world problems, pragmatic methods, and community-led change. They are, by design, not academic, erudite, or abstruse; rather, they have been designed for easy accessibility, applicability, and functionality.

In participatory research, everyone involved in the project becomes a coresearcher, which purposely blurs the lines between who is the "researcher" and the "subject." Participatory research is emancipatory because of this goal to equalize power (Kemmis & McTaggart, 2005). In particular, the participants are always fully aware of their choices and can therefore choose not to engage in certain activities, as they wish; conversely, participants are also aware that they have the power to suggest and lead processes, as the group feels is appropriate. Participatory research can thus be defined as a community that researches itself in a process facilitated by a conventional expert (or "researcher" in orthodox parlance). In traditional social science methodologies, the researcher and the subject are clearly and permanently delineated, even in those methodologies (such as ethnographies) that seek an emic or insider's perspective. In participatory research, it is not possible to make this distinction because of the fluidity of the roles that community members play in the process. Louise Fortman (2008, p. 2) refers to participatory research as "interdependent science" because some "questions are best answered in collaboration."

Interdependent science is defined by "local knowledge" or "situated knowledge" by "civil" experts as opposed to "conventional" experts who are defined, in part, by their use of scientific knowledge (Fortman, 2008, pp. 2-4, 8). Participatory research therefore embodies a kind of epistemological agnosticism, readily accepting any form of knowledge as long as it is defined and accepted by community participants. Bendremer and Thomas (2008, p. 65) emphasize respect for this epistemological flexibility, directing conventional experts to "stop privileging academic inquiry and assign equal standing to Indigenous belief systems, decision-making bodies, and sensibilities." Fortman (2008, p. 6) refers to the academy's preference for conventional experts' scientific knowledge as an "epistemic injustice" because all people have the potential to be "credible knowers" regardless of their education or social status.

Conventional experts, however, can be full participants in participatory research, performing as equals with their community members. The conventional expert, however, does not control the process and seeks to equalize power structures. In this frame, the expert serves as a facilitator of the overall process, providing input and suggestions, when appropriate, but deferring to the community members in terms of decision-making endeavors. In addition, sometimes experts train community members how to perform certain research methodologies. Bergelin et al. (2008, pp. 146–161) offer the advice that conventional experts should listen carefully and not be "controlling" and strive to be "open and humble, persistent and strong." This hands-off approach, as Arora-Jonsson et al. (2008, p. 246) emphasize, manifests as "local people [being] treated, not as data sources, but as colleagues in producing new knowledge."

While there are a number of different flavors of participatory research, they all focus on issues of social justice and social action. The premise is that through coresearch, communities are empowered to identify problems and create and implement possible solutions. In this sense, participatory research has much in common with participatory democracy by maximizing the opportunity for a community to make its own decisions. This process, as Timothy Pyrch (2012, p. xiv) advocates, "opens up the world of knowledge-making to people long silenced by forces intent on controlling knowledge for the educated elite." This characteristic is one reason why participatory researchers typically work with disempowered communities in developing countries, but it can and has been applied to a wide variety of cultures in Western as well as non-Western contexts.

Kemmis and McTaggart (2005), who are often cited in participatory research literature, define a model for participatory research that employs an overall cycle of planning for change, acting on the change, and reflecting on the action, which then repeats:

- Planning a change;
- Acting and observing the process and consequences of the change;
- Reflecting on these processes and consequences;
- Replanning;
- Acting and observing again;
- Reflecting again, and [repeating the process].

Thus, participatory research is inherently an iterative process that continues until the participants decide they are done—e.g., the problem has been addressed.

Per the theoretical assumptions of participatory research, the coresearchers (i.e., the participants) in a study are free to define the methods that they will use to collect and analyze data. These possible methods might include interviews, journaling, participant and nonparticipant observation, photo elicitation, and even artistic expression (e.g., dance, painting/drawing, music). In my work in community-based participatory research, I found that the iterative framework of "participatory evaluation in community initiatives" presented by Fawcett et al. (2003) to be particularly useful. It consists of the following steps that are repeated until the participants achieve satisfaction:

- Naming and framing the problem/goal;
- Developing a logic model for achieving success;
- Identifying research questions and methods;
- Documenting the intervention and its effects;
- Making sense of the data;
- Using information to celebrate and make adjustments.

The use of this framework assumes that knowledge is coproduced by all participants (including conventional experts) in the process.

The recommendations in this chapter are therefore guided by the overarching goal of coproducing policy, which assumes that the public benefits achieved through public policy are better maximized by conventional experts working, in tandem, with civil experts (e.g., residents, stakeholders) through a process that equalizes the distribution of power (Stoudt et al., 2016). While there are many contexts in which participatory research can occur, the community workshop—where a group of participants convene to work collaboratively—is one of the most common. These facilitated meetings are therefore fundamental to participatory research.

CHANGING POLICY THROUGH PARTICIPATORY RESEARCH AND COMMUNITY WORKSHOPS

What does a facilitated community workshop look like? While these meetings, on the surface, look like many of the so-called "public" meetings convened by governmental entities, or their contractors, there are some key differences in how this kind of meeting is organized and run. The core difference is that community workshops are focused on equalizing power, and therefore, increasing participation. To ensure this balance, however, requires expert facilitation, which is dependent on clearly defined roles and meeting objectives, participant engagement, preparation, and facilitation techniques. In addition, these gatherings are more than just a "meeting;" they are a place where all the participants are expected to *work*—hence, the phrase community *workshop*. The recommendations below are from my extensive experience in helping to train facilitators for community workshops, as well as performing this role, myself, to address heritage issues.

Not everyone will be comfortable serving as a community workshop meeting facilitator, but for those who enjoy working with people, it can be a highly rewarding experience. In the realm of built heritage conservation, these kinds of community workshops have been used by urban planners to inform comprehensive and small area plans and to help make decisions about what is important about heritage (e.g., Bashforth et al., 2015). What makes the community workshop meeting different in the context of participatory research is that there is a further emphasis on community empowerment. Unlike community workshops held by urban planners, there is an expectation with community-based participatory research that the participants will actually engage in some of the action items that have been identified. While there is no promise that community-based participatory research will always work in all situations, where a community is actively engaged in a problem, this methodology can be particularly useful.

What Is the Difference Between a Facilitated and a Nonfacilitated Meeting?
In a public meeting, power and information flow primarily in one direction. Many disciplines—especially planning—use community workshops as a way

FIGURE 4.1. Typical layout for a public meeting which visually emphasizes that power emanates from the front of the room (photo by author)

FIGURE 4.2. By placing smaller tables, that are ideally round, in a room with chairs around each table, power differentials are visually equalized (photo by author)

to engage defined groups in an open atmosphere that encourages sharing and participatory democracy. In the United States, it has long been fashionable to call these community workshop meetings "charrettes" (sometimes spelled "charette"), but functionally, they are essentially the same. These workshops need to be facilitated, but what exactly does "facilitation" mean in this context? The answer relates to how power is distributed among the individuals involved in the meeting.

For an example, we can analyze the room where a typical "public meeting" takes place; public meetings are a very common communication tool that governments around the world use, especially at the local level. The chairs in these meetings are arranged much like a church, with many rows of chairs facing the front of the room (Figure 4.1). Elected officials and staff sit at the front of the room, often on a dais (raised platform). The physical arrangement of the room is designed to convey not only the directional flow of information—front to back—but also differentials in power. What this tells us is that the people at the front of the room have more power than those in the audience and that the expected information flow is from those in power to those with less power. And, in practice, this is usually what happens. While audience members can participate, minimally, the time and topic in which they can speak is very limited. Moreover, elected officials and government staff are not necessarily obligated to act on or even pay attention to the meanings the audience is conveying. (An important note is that elected officials ought to care about their constituency, but in practice this may vary considerably across different countries, regions, and cultures.) Clearly, a public meeting is not an example of a facilitated meeting.

In a facilitated meeting, the chairs in the room are arranged in circles where people face each other (Figure 4.2). Sometimes the chairs are arranged around circular tables, which is ideal. Most people, therefore, are not facing the front of the room, and as such, this part of the room does not play an important role in how the meeting is conducted. In other words, no one sits at the front of the room, facing the people sitting in circles, and no one is on a raised platform.

The difference between a facilitated meeting and one that is not facilitated is therefore defined by the expression of power differentials between people: in a facilitated meeting, all participants (ideally) are equal in terms of their capability of contributing to the process, and as such, a facilitated meeting is innately democratic. Conversely, in nonfacilitated meetings, a few people ultimately have the ability to control how others can express meanings and which ones receive attention.

The Role of a Facilitator
The facilitator is the person who helps organize, structure, and guide a meeting in a way that empowers the participants to identify and act on issues. The facilitator of a meeting cares about the process, but (ideally) has no vested interest in the outcome. The facilitator therefore strives to be neutral party to the process, does not take sides, and is there to make sure that as many people contribute as possible in an open environment. Some meetings have one facilitator while others can have multiple people performing this role, depending on the workload required.

To understand this role better, we return to the idea of power differentials in a room. If a facilitator directly contributed to the content of a meeting and controlled the decisions being made-in other words, assuming a partial position-then the power flow in the room is adversely affected. The "facilitator" then becomes the person in the room with the most power. In this example, the role of facilitator is replaced by the new role of a chairperson, manager, or in simple terms, the person who "runs the meeting." Most business meetings are conducted in this manner, where one person controls the power flow and makes the final decision. Typically, this person is a manager, or a person who already is assumed to have more power than the rest of the people in the meeting. For this reason, it is important to be aware of how a community will perceive a person's power and authority before considering using this individual as a meeting facilitator, because even if this person strives to equalize power, it is not possible to erase people's preconceptions.

What kind of person makes a good facilitator? Even though a facilitator focuses on process and not content, it can be very helpful if the facilitator understands the subject under discussion. There are organizations and individuals who can be hired to perform this role, but because heritage conservation is still perceived as a niche discipline, finding a professional facilitator who knows heritage conservation can be rather difficult. Urban and regional planning experts often do have good facilitation skills along with knowledge of heritage conservation, but it is important to keep in mind the ramifications of using a planning official from a government agency as a facilitator with a community over which this individual has decision-making power. University students, with sufficient training and appropriate background, can make excellent facilitators precisely because they are nonthreatening to participants.

The Facilitator's Specific Objectives During the Meeting

There are some specific objectives that a facilitator uses to achieve the overall goal of helping organize, structure, and guide the process of a meeting without controlling its content:

- Recognizing who is affected and how: Be aware of how actions being discussed may help some people, harm others, and ask who may be missing and should be included in the discussion.
- Following an agenda: There should be a clear purpose for the meeting and a series of tasks that need to be accomplished. The participants should be free to change this agenda if there is a consensus.
- Active listening: A facilitator should be a good listener and provide regular feedback to participants to make sure that he or she is (or they are) understanding what is being discussed.

- Getting people to participate: A community workshop is not useful if people choose not to participate in the discussions and activities that are planned. Some people will innately want to participate while others will be much less motivated. A good facilitator will identify these less participative individuals and constructively encourage them to participate; many group activities can be planned in a way that encourages participants to engage people who are passive.
- Making sure that no one dominates: In almost every meeting, there will be one or more individuals who tend to monopolize the conversation, are overly dominant, and suppress the participation of others. This is perhaps one of the most difficult problems a facilitator will encounter; some suggestions for addressing this issue are below.
- Summarizing information: When working with groups of people, discussions can become blurred and the focus of topics disjointed. A facilitator will see when this problem is happening and offer to summarize and center the conservation.
- Consensus building: A consensus is the general agreement of all participants on a certain topic or subject. It is not, as is sometimes misunderstood, 100% agreement of all participants. Consensus is the democratic principles of a community workshop in operation: the facilitator tries to see where consensus is being reached and helps clarify it for the participants, recognizing that some people will not always be in agreement.
- Achieving meeting outcomes: At the end of the workshop meeting, the facilitator helps in creating work plans or a series of action steps that the participants have agreed to perform. The facilitator does not dictate what should happen, but rather should be acutely aware of what the participants wish to do and then help them achieve it.

Techniques for Engaging Participants

How does a facilitator actually engage the participants in a community workshop? While there are many techniques available, there are a few that are commonly used because of their simplicity and effectiveness:

- Brainstorming: This is a process where the facilitator asks the participants to list ideas on a certain topic. The facilitator then writes these ideas down, typically on a flip chart or whiteboard, and attempts to organize them into common categories based on input from the participants. Other variations include having participants write their ideas on sticky notes and then bring them to the facilitator who organizes them under categories.

- Small group discussion: The reason why many community workshops are based on small groups sitting in a circle is to help facilitate small group discussions. Upon consensus from the participants, discussions can be broken down into these small groups. Typically, one person in each group is a recorder, responsible for writing down information that the group expresses. The recorder then summarizes what was discussed and reports back to the larger group.
- Role playing: Role playing can be particularly effective if participants are polarized on a subject. It is a way of helping participants understand others' perspectives. Role playing can take many forms, such as a skit or play or asking the participants to pretend to be someone else and respond to questions and ideas as if they were this other person.
- Journaling/diary: The facilitator asks participants to write down ideas/concepts/meanings as they occur. This can be in the context of a meeting or can even take place outside of the meeting. Where multiple meetings occur, the participants are asked to come back and discuss what they recorded.
- Round robin discussion: Round robin discussions are great ways to get everyone to participate. The facilitator asks each person to respond to a particular question, one at a time.

There are also more unusual participatory techniques that are more common to participatory research strategies where creative works embody problems, questions, meanings, and concepts, such as:

- Art, such as drawing and painting;
- Music;
- Plays in which a problem and its potential resolution are conveyed by actors in a performance;
- Poetry;
- Story telling/folklore.

Participants can create these items in the workshop or create them outside of the workshop meeting and then discuss them at a later meeting. Sometimes these creative works are shared with the community at large in public performances. In addition to these possible techniques, participants are free to define any other methods in which they can share meanings and ideas. Many of these additional techniques will be highly specific to certain cultures. The important thing to remember is that the participants must be allowed to define and engage in methods in which meanings are shared that are normal for their particular culture. Be careful about imposing your norms about the legitimate ways knowledge must be known and presented; openness in this respect is very important.

Preparing for the Community Workshop

LOCATION AND TIME

One of the most important items to consider for the meeting is its location. All locations—buildings and outdoor meeting places—have specific meanings associated with them that need to be considered from the perspective of the participants. For instance, if the topic of the community meeting is to address a perceived failing on the part of a municipality, it would not make sense to hold the meeting at the municipality's city hall. Because the city hall symbolically represents the city, participants would be less likely to attend and will be more guarded in sharing their concerns. For this reason, the most neutral location possible is desirable.

Other factors for the meeting location include its size—how many people can the location hold—and comfort factors. Will it be too cold or hot? If it is outside, what happens if it rains? Is it quiet and without disruptions? Can people easily get to the location? Is there a need for disability access? Cost factors should be considered as well.

The choice of meeting days and times is also critical because these need to be chosen from the perspective of the potential participants. For this reason, evening or weekend meetings may work better than meetings in the middle of the workweek, depending on job schedules. In some communities, people may have very little free time because of the need to work multiple jobs. Be understanding and compassionate about people's time.

It is important to have food and beverages at the meeting because it helps to make people comfortable. This need not be complicated or expensive but is always desirable. Consider food and drink that is familiar to your invited participants. Alcohol, even if it is permitted in your meeting location, can be more trouble than it is worth because, while it may relax people and increase participation, the resulting lack of social inhibition can result in behavior problems with participants that are best avoided.

Lastly, check to make sure your meeting location can accommodate chairs arranged in small circles of no more than about 10-12 people.

MEETING RULES

Prepare a list of rules ahead of time for acceptable behavior in the meeting. All individuals should agree to these rules prior to being allowed to participate in the meeting. These rules should be flexible and can be changed upon consensus from the participants. The purpose of these rules is to encourage the kind of respectful discussion that is necessary for a community workshop to function well.

Some basic rules might include asking participants to agree to:

- Respect the instructions given by the workshop facilitators;
- Be on time for the community workshop meetings;
- Have an open mind for new ideas and concepts;
- Ask questions;
- Not interrupt people when they are speaking;
- Help make sure that there is only one conversation happening at the same time;
- Treat people with respect; it is OK to judge and critique ideas, but not people. No personal attacks are allowed;
- Keep professional jargon to a minimum and use simple language;
- Encourage people who are quiet to speak;
- Encourage people who talk too much to let others speak;
- Help keep the conversation focused on relevant topics;
- Not use your cell phone during the meetings, unless it is an emergency;
- Avoid arguments that rely on authority for their validity;
- Not reveal to others outside of the community workshop meetings who is participating or what specific individuals have said or written;
- Try to have fun and enjoy the process.

Be prepared to remind people about these rules during the meeting if they are not followed, especially if they interfere with the conduct of the meeting.

Facilitating the Community Workshop Meeting
While the facilitator should pay close attention to the agenda of the meeting to help keep topics on track, there are a series of recommended steps that should be in all these kinds of meetings.

STARTING THE MEETING—MAKING PEOPLE FEEL COMFORTABLE
AND AT EASE WITH "ICEBREAKERS"

In community workshops, always assume that some people will not know each other. It is therefore important to help make everyone as comfortable as possible through a process of introductions and warm-up exercises, also known as "icebreakers." The intent of these techniques is to encourage cooperation and openness. If people are uncomfortable, they will contribute less and the meanings they share will be thinner and less useful. It is important not to underestimate the importance of the warm-up in ensuring a successful meeting.

There are many ways that you can help warm up your participants. The first technique would be to simply have people introduce themselves and explain what they would like to get out of the workshop. This can be done in round-robin fashion. Typically, other people will respond with questions and interest. The other kind of technique is to have the participants engage in a collaborative activity that has no direct connection with any of the topics in the meeting—in other words, a nonthreatening topic.

For example, the technique of "rain making" can be an easy and effective way to warm up participants and make them feel comfortable. In the technique, all the participants are asked, in sequence, to start making the sound of rain falling by rubbing their hands together, then progressing to rubbing harder to increase the sound, then moving to clapping hands, and then finishing with people clapping against their thighs. Then, the facilitator instructs the participants to reverse the process. So, in effect, the participants have created an artificial rainstorm.

You might also consider having people organize into pairs and then share personal experiences with each other in a structured way. Participants then report back to the group what the other persons told them. There are also culturally-specific exercises that may work particularly well for helping people warm up; consult with community leaders for their advice.

Facilitating the Main Part of the Meeting

Again, the facilitator should make sure that the meeting keeps on track, based on the agenda. The facilitator should be open to, and at times, encourage changes in the agenda based on a consensus of the participants. Often, meanings will be shared that necessitate a change in focus or direction;

rigidly sticking to the agenda can be as unhelpful as not using an agenda at all. Remember that the beneficiaries of the meeting are the participants, so the meeting's structure needs to always accommodate their needs.

End of Meeting Summaries and Next Steps

Sometimes, there is only one community workshop meeting, which at the end, only requires that the facilitator attain a consensus from the participants on a summary of what was shared. Oftentimes, however, there will be multiple meetings, especially when the participants wish to identify a problem and create potential solutions as is found in participatory research methodologies. In this latter case, the facilitator needs to work with the participants to summarize what the next steps are that should be taken, including helping the participants create a work plan and task assignments which are expected to be completed by the time of the next meeting.

Addressing Problems in Facilitating Community Workshops

Sometimes things will not go so well in a meeting, so a good facilitator should be prepared to deal with some common problems, which include:

- Dominators: These are people who will not let other people talk, they talk over other people, and generally monopolize conversations.
- People who are quiet: Some people find it difficult to talk in large groups; the facilitator should help in making sure that the meeting environment is safe and comfortable, which will help to encourage participation. There are also some useful participatory techniques (see below) that can be helpful.
- Disinterested people: Sometimes individuals in the workshop may not be particularly interested in a topic and will not contribute to the discussion.
- Goofing off and not being serious: While the goal of the workshop should be to have fun, some people fail to take enough of the workshop seriously so that the topics and discussion are constantly off track. Keep in mind that there are some cultural differences in terms of what is and is not acceptable, so be careful of imposing your cultural expectations on others. The key indicator whether there is a problem is if the participants are clearly annoyed by the behavior of a specific individual.
- People who obsess: Similar to a dominator, some people will not let a topic drop and continually bring up the same thing over and over again.

As with people who goof off, pay attention to the other participants. If
they are clearly annoyed, the facilitator should help address the situation.

This list is not meant to be all-inclusive, but represents most of the common issues that a facilitator will likely encounter in community workshops. While there is no perfect, one-size-fits-all tool to address some of these problems, I have learned that there are some techniques that a facilitator can use that are often effective.

THIRD PARTY MEDIATOR TO SUMMARIZE

When there are two people who disagree strongly with each other, it may be useful to have another participant function as a kind of mediator to help with clarity in communication. This technique works best in groups as singling out two individuals from all participants can be embarrassing and threatening to these individuals. The way this works is as follows:

- Find a participant who is willing to serve as a mediator;
- Have the mediator listen to the first person and repeat, word for word, exactly what this person said. During this process, the person whose words are being repeated cannot speak until the process is done;
- The mediator then summarizes what the first person said, confirming that the important meanings were all conveyed and were accurate and correct;
- The mediator then listens to the second person and repeats, word for word, exactly what this person said using the same process;
- The mediator then summarizes what the second person said, again confirming that the important meanings were all conveyed and were accurate and correct.

SHARING FEELINGS AND CONCERNS OPENLY

The facilitator arranges people in small groups and asks that they share things that are really bothering them about the meeting itself or the way that people are behaving. In these small groups, each person, in round-robin fashion, starts with the statement, "One thing that really bothers me about this meeting is . . . ," and then completes the sentence with the one thing that is really bothering them. When this person is speaking, no one else can speak. After the person is done speaking, then others can respond. When the process is done with all the groups, the facilitator should help clarify if there are specific, common problems that have emerged and ask the participants how they would like to address them.

REVERSE ROLE PLAYING

Similar to the role playing technique described earlier, this is a specific application meant to address a particular problem in the meeting. To use this technique, the facilitator helps to define two sides to an issue or problem. Half of the participants assume the perspective of one side of the issue, and the other participants assume the perspective of the other side. The participants are then arranged in pairs of opposing sides. At certain points in the role playing process, the facilitator asks people to freeze and then immediately take the opposite side. This process can be particularly useful in helping people understand perspectives contrary to their own.

LEARNING HOW TO BE A REFLEXIVE FACILITATOR— ASK "WHO AM I?"

A reflexive practitioner continually seeks to understand their relationship with others by being aware of power differentials, being a good listener, working against internal biases, and empathizing with others. In essence, this kind of individual is able to express a genuine interest in listening to and understanding people who may have very different life experiences from their own. These skills are essential to be an effective facilitator as well as a more effective historic preservation practitioner. For example, Stephanie Ryberg-Webster (2017, p. 20) recommends that preservation professionals need to "constantly be reflexive practitioners" to avoid assuming that marginalized communities will always benefit from preservation activities; what she means is that a reflexive stance instead assumes "first understanding (ideally from the community's perspective) what benefits are needed and then determining if and how preservation can contribute." A failure to take this critical approach increases the likelihood that these communities will view facilitators and preservation practitioners as agents of social injustice rather than partners for positive change.

INCREASING PARTICIPATION FROM GROUPS THAT GOVERNMENT HAS TRADITIONALLY IGNORED

It is well known, by planners who work in local government, that people who are White, wealthier, older, and have higher levels of education will

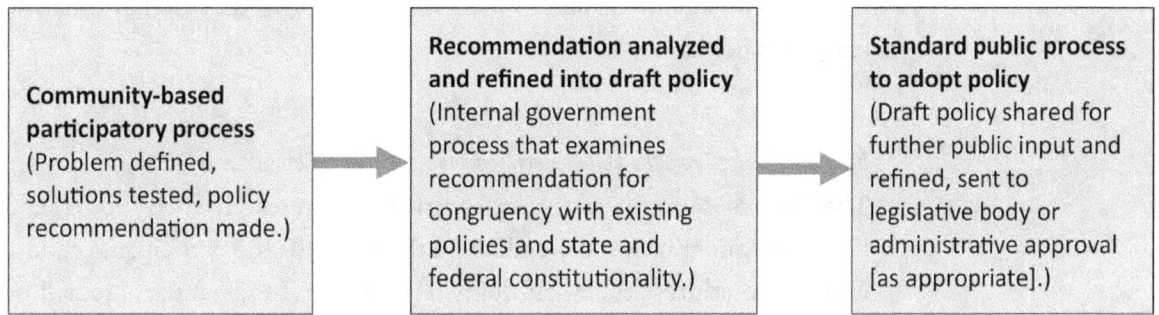

FIGURE 4.3. The three-step process to convert community-driven recommendations into new or reformed public policy

disproportionately participate in publicly-engaged processes (Silverman et al., 2019). Conversely, people with marginalized racial, ethnic, and ability identities, who are on the lower end of the economic spectrum, and are younger, are very unlikely to participate. Some of the reasons for this situation, in addition to a history of systemic racism, in which government has engaged, is that many people, without substantial economic means, work multiple jobs and have jobs that are much less flexible than higher-paid individuals. In addition, there are substantial numbers of people who are not US citizens, but who could add valuable input in these processes, but fear government-sanctioned actions that might lead to deportation—even for people who are legally in the county (e.g., permanent residents). Awareness of these issues is critical in planning for community participation in order to provide potential solutions.

Wherever possible, consider paying people to participate in community-based participatory projects. This could be in the form of hourly pay, stipends, or the reimbursement of expenses, such as childcare and transportation. Consider working with major employers to help them encourage their employees to participate in these processes and perhaps even pay for such participation. Be aware of accessibility issues in choosing the venue for participation, including easy access to public transportation. Encourage youth and young adult participation by working with schools and teachers. And, lastly, if the community in which you are working has many non-English speakers, make sure that materials are presented in other languages and that interpreters are available and present.

Identify and work with community leaders, who can be found in local churches, nonprofit groups, informal community advocacy groups, and schools to gain their trust and then ask that they help recruit participants. People are much more likely to participate if the "ask" comes from someone that they consider to be part of their social network—they already trust and know this person.

Informing Policy From the Data Generated From the Participatory Research Process
The kinds of data created through participatory research will be both qualitative and quantitative, depending on the methods the participants choose in order to address their self-defined problems. In general, there will be a three-step process to convert the recommendations developed through the community-based participatory process into reformed or new policy (Figure 4.3). This process is largely identical to existing policy-making but positions the community participation as the first step that then is used by conventional experts, in a governmental entity, to develop a draft policy. It is critical, however, that participants be encouraged to try to independently create policy ideas, including recommended administrative processes. As many participants may not be familiar with public policy and the legislative and administrative roles of government, this potential knowledge gap means that facilitators may need to provide some basic education to participants as to what "policy" is. This process ensures that community-led ideas will surface while being vetted by conventional experts to make sure that they do not violate existing, related policies and are congruent with state and federal constitutions. In my experience, categories that participants address are broad and varied, but in a well-facilitated workshop, in which the participants stay on track to address heritage problems and solutions, these categories often consist of:

- Storytelling in which participants describe their shared and individual values, perceptions, experiences, and meanings that relate to their built and natural environments; participants will usually agree on which places are the most important and specific reasons why.
- Identification of threats to heritage places, the reasons why these places are threatened (i.e., the "problems"), and stories that relate to people's personal experiences where they learned of these threats.
- Potential solutions to identified problems, including community-led workplans in which specific governmental and nongovernmental actors are identified.
- Ways to test solutions and refine them to improve their efficacy.

As long as the participants represent the broad diversity of a community, with a preponderance of civil experts, these data almost always relate to naked heritage meanings (see chapter 3). Expect to hear stories that center feelings and unseen phenomena, such as "ghosts"; facilitators should let these stories play out and foster participants' respect for meanings that diverge from orthodoxy—this is especially important for any conventional experts who are present and have been trained to "educate" people on the "correct" way the public should value older places (see the sections on "purity" in chapter 4).

If too many conventional experts are in these workshops, I have found that the civil experts will nearly always defer to the former group's values and recommendations. If you see this kind of differential in power surfacing between conventional and civil experts in a community workshop, either the facilitation process needs to change, or potentially, different participants need to be involved that better represent civil experts. In addition to limiting the membership of conventional experts in community workshops, consider a two-step process in which civil experts meet first and are then empowered to invite conventional experts, at a later stage, to the community workshop meetings. Conventional experts are, however, especially useful in later phases where potential solutions are being explored and tested because of their knowledge and experience working within orthodox policy.

Data from community workshops can, potentially, be used to inform the entirety of historic preservation policy at the local, state, and federal levels but is perhaps best utilized at the local level where there is a close association between the environmental experiences of the participants and their geography. Common regulatory processes, such as listing buildings and districts and the protection of the material authenticity of these places could change to accommodate the recommendations from these community workshops, which will fundamentally relate to BAOP (see chapter 2) and will therefore challenge the purity of orthodox preservation policy (see chapter 3). In addition, there is a potential for historic preservation policy (e.g., laws, regulations, guidelines, and/or official government action) to begin to embrace intangible heritage—which it does not do today, for the most part. In my experience, participants in heritage-based community workshops will identify what conventional experts would categorize as intangible heritage, how it is threatened, and ways to sustain it. Government leaders should therefore be open to considering these recommendations, as they arise, and whether they are best implemented by changing laws, regulations, guidelines, or other official governmental actions.

CHANGING POLICY BY BRINGING PHENOMENOLOGY TO THE PEOPLE (WITHOUT CALLING IT THAT)

A well-established and reliable methodology to access the precognitive, emotional meanings associated with being in certain places is the phenomenology (see chapter 1); this technique also has close associations with gestalt psychology upon which the Italian school of architectural conservators based their theories, which then informed the Athens and Venice charters and the Secretary of the Interior's Standards (see chapter 2). As Jack Elliott, Jr. (2002, p. 54), a retired historical archaeologist for the Mississippi Department of Archives and History (the state historic preservation office), describes, phenomenology is uniquely suited to informing historic preservation policy:

> The phenomenological approach is of particular relevance when dealing with the questions of significance for preservation.... If a historical place is such a phenomenon, then the term "significant" should be used in preservation to describe places whose physical character and matrices of historical, mythical, and social associations can and do evoke experiences of awe, wonder, beauty, and identity, among others.

Elliott is clearly relating the importance of the emotional experience of being in certain older places. I would ask the reader to remember a particularly emotional encounter with an old building or place. Maybe you even had a physical sensation, like your spine tingling, because you saw something out of the corner of your eye. Or perhaps you simply felt physically and emotionally connected with some past event. In my research, I have found nearly everyone seems to have these experiences with old places, which is why a tool to access, relate, and understand these experiences, in order to inform policy, is essential.

The emotional connection with place is a very different way of looking at historical significance than the methods required by orthodox preservation/conservation policy. It does not rely on facts about the past, architectural history, or objective measures of authenticity and integrity. Instead, the value of a historic place is predicated on people's emotional attachment to a place. On the face of it, this seems like a terribly obvious way to value things; after all, the people in our lives we value the most are the ones we love the most. Why should place be treated any differently? The answer is that it is very difficult to translate an emotion, such as love, into something that has enough objectivity so that it can be used to define policy. But, does this mean policy should simply ignore a fundamental reason why people value historic places? I believe the answer is no; we need better answers as well as better tools to understand this emotional connection to historical places. Once we understand this phenomenon better, then we might be able to adapt heritage management practices to accommodate it.

A phenomenology is one of the most effective tools for understanding emotion. The nursing discipline has long used this methodology to understand how patients experience pain, through a specific technique known as an existential phenomenology (Nay & Fetherstonhaugh, 2012). Other fields, such as architecture (e.g., Christian Norberg-Schulz, 1980) have used a different technique, known as a hermeneutical phenomenology, to understand "genius loci" or "sense of place." In the built environment, the largest users of existential phenomenology are humanistic geographers who desire to understand people's emotional experience of being in certain places. Yi-Fu Tuan (1977, pp. 194, 198) briefly explored some aspects related to built heritage conservation policy, arguing that orthodox policy has nothing to do with how people are affected by place or attached to place. With few exceptions, however, phenomenology has not been used to research the historic environment in any depth. The only two examples that I know of are my own work (e.g., Wells & Baldwin, 2012) and that of Ingrid Leman Stefanovic (1998).

What Is Phenomenology? The Technical Explanation
Phenomenology, as a general concept, is first credited to Kant (1934/1787) when he separated objects into "phenomena" and "noumena." Phenomena alone are generated from perception and experience; noumena can exist purely as an intellectual concept without a concrete presence. Hegel (1937/1807) later refined these ideas into a study of consciousness and the phenomenon of the mind. The modern concept of phenomenology was developed by Husserl in the early part of the twentieth century and focused on "being of the world" and transcendence, or the process of "conferring

meaning by the knowing ego [and] reflecting on itself" (Ray, 1994, p. 119). The goal is to "attain the genuine and true form of the things themselves" (Ray, 1994, p. 119). This emphasis on the true and genuine quality of things has led to the label of "pure" phenomenology for Husserl's methods.

As opposed to Husserl, Heidegger (Husserl's student) focuses on "being in the world"; for Heidegger "being, as such, already is present in the world. . . . Presuppositions are not to be eliminated or suspended, but are what constitute the possibility or intelligibility of meaning" (Ray, 1994, p. 120). Most phenomenological researchers use Husserl and Heidegger as a division between the two major strands of phenomenology. While Husserl represents a pure or transcendental phenomenology, Heidegger stands for an interpretive or hermeneutical perspective. Husserl's methodology insists that "phenomenological research is pure description and that interpretation (hermeneutics) falls outside the bounds of phenomenological research" (van Manen, 1990, pp. 25–26).

Phenomenology is the study of the essences of human perception; the goal is to find definitions for these essences based on perception and consciousness (Merleau-Ponty, 1962, p. vii). It is the "explication of phenomena as they present themselves to consciousness" (van Manen, 1990, p. 9). Phenomenology seeks to describe and understand the preontological ramifications of "being in the world" (Heidegger, 2005/1924) and "experiential meanings as we live them" (van Manen, 1990, p. 11). Seamon (1982, p. 119) describes phenomenology as a "science of beginnings" that dispenses with "assumed notions and perspectives [in order to] return to the foundations of meanings, things, and experiences." According to van Manen (1990, p. 9), phenomenology "differs from almost every other science in that it attempts to gain insightful descriptions of the way we experience the world prereflectively, without taxonomizing, classifying, or abstracting it."

Phenomenological research focuses on the experience. What is it like to be in a certain environment? What senses are called into action? What kind of feelings are engaged? For instance, Merleau-Ponty (1962, p. 4) spends many pages describing the experience of the color red: "This red patch which I see on the carpet is red only in virtue of a shadow which lies across it, its quality is apparent only in relation to the play of light upon it, and hence as an element in a spatial configuration." Phenomenological research requires the researcher to become in part a philosopher, reflecting on the experience of the self and of others.

TABLE 4.1. Orientations in phenomenological research, themes, and origins

Orientation	Basic themes	Origins
Transcendental	intentionality, eidetic (mental images) reduction, and constitution of meaning	Husserl, Stein, and Fink
Existential	lived experience, modes of being, ontology, and lifeworld	Heidegger and Merleau-Ponty
Hermeneutical	interpretation, textual meaning, dialogue, preunderstanding, and tradition	Heidegger, Gadamer, and Ricoeur
Linguistical	textual autonomy, signification, intertextuality, deconstruction, discourse, and space of the text	Foucault and Derrida based on earlier ideas of Heidegger, Merleau-Ponty, and Gadamer
Ethical	otherness, responsibility, I-Thou, the vocative, and (non)relationality	Levinas and Scheler based on ideas of Husserl, Heidegger, and Sartre
Experiential (application of phenomenology to social science)	Applied research originating in the human sciences such as education, clinical psychology, nursing, medicine, and specializations such as psychiatry or midwifery, but based on philosophical approaches	Binswanger (field of psychiatry in the 1940s)

TYPES OF PHENOMENOLOGY

Max van Manen (1990) divides phenomenology into transcendental, existential, hermeneutical, linguistical, ethical, and experiential "orientations" (Table 4.1). A phenomenological researcher may draw on all the phenomenological orientations described by van Manen. While the hermeneutical approach appears to dominate most research because of its interpretive basis, existential phenomenology is most useful in understanding BAOP because of its emphasis on the emotional experience of being in the world.

Existential phenomenologies can be divided into two major types: first person and third person. In a first-person phenomenology, the researcher experiences the phenomena directly and reflects on this experience; in a third-person phenomenology, the researcher collects data, usually by interviews, from people who explain their experience.

A PHENOMENOLOGICAL METHOD

There is a lack of a general consensus in the field of phenomenology as to how one should conduct a phenomenological inquiry. Some researchers believe that by rigidly defining a series of steps, unwanted postcognitive meanings compromise the collection of data. Probably the most detailed method I have found is from Patricia Munhall (2007) from the field of nursing. Max van Manen's (1990) guide to conducting a phenomenology is the most widely used reference, but it is not prescriptive and only provides general principles and guidelines, which are as follows:

- Empty your mind of any preconceived notions about the phenomenon you are trying to understand; try to experience the phenomenon on its own terms as if you have never encountered it before. (I like to think that the researcher assumes the perspective of a toddler, who is experiencing nearly everything in the world for the first time—a kind of childlike wonder about the world.)
- Focus as much as possible on precognitive emotions and states. For example, suppose you are trying to understand the experience of a breeze on your face. You would describe how it feels (e.g., cool, tickles, smells), the feelings it elicits (calmness), and any memories that are catalyzed without your conscious effort (the smell of the ocean makes you think of spending time at the beach with your mother).
- Avoid any higher-order information or meaning processing, which could take the form of comparing how cool the breeze is today with the breeze yesterday or whether the ocean really smells like seaweed.

As David Seamon (1982) writes, this process is "radically empirical" where you want to focus on the essence of experience in all its richness. This should result in lots of descriptive terms of experience.

There are lots of variations to this process, but it is important to remember that you want to focus on elements of experience just as they enter your consciousness but before you have started analyzing their meaning.

These instructions assume a first-person phenomenology, but they also apply to a researcher trying to understand others' experience of the world as well.

After collecting data, a common technique is to look for patterns and themes in the data that were collected and use these patterns to answer a particular research question. (This step has much in common with many qualitative research methodologies, such as ethnographies.)

The Nontechnical Explanation of Existential Phenomenology
Most of the materials on phenomenology are rather difficult for most people to understand because they are written for academic researchers. I will attempt to describe, in as simple language as possible, the characteristics of an existential phenomenology and how someone can use it in understanding emotional responses to the environment.

It is not possible to experience the world without your body. All experience is therefore mediated through your body. Phenomenology seeks to understand this experience of "being in the world." Another way of looking at this condition is that there is no way to understand the world without your body. Therefore the assumption is that experience and your body are inseparable; the factual nature of the experience is not what is important. Understanding your body's reaction to this experience is fundamental. Focus on describing the way your body experiences the world in as much rich detail as possible, focusing on emotional states and feelings and raw description.

An existential phenomenology is an appropriate technique to use when there is a desire to learn as much as possible about how you or other people experience, on the most fundamental, emotional level, different environments. There are much better methodologies to use if you want to understand cultural values, beliefs, or other meanings that require higher-order cognitive processing. A phenomenology needs to focus on the most "naked" elements of environmental experience. In other words, what is the most basic, fundamental way you can describe a particular experience in the most detail possible? This is how one conducts a phenomenology.

Can Lay People Be Taught to Conduct an Existential Phenomenology?
In the context of community-based participatory research, it is possible to train participants (assuming that they are interested and curious) to use a first-person phenomenology in order to understand the experience of being in certain environments. Rather than this process being one-ended—data going to the researcher—the goal is for the participants in the community workshop to share their experiences with each other, and through this process, come up with their own patterns and themes to answer questions that they think are important. Refer to appendix B for a guide to how this could be implemented in a community workshop.

Workshop facilitators who are considering the use of an existential first-person phenomenology in a community workshop should keep the following items in mind:

- Never use the word "phenomenology" with participants. No one will know what it means and its multisyllabic and erudite qualities will probably not work very well in terms of warming up a group of community workshop participants. Instead, tell participants that they will be learning how to connect with and express the emotions they experience by being in old places. You might refer to this as "old place meditation" or "learning how to meditate on old places," for instance.
- Provide instructions to participants in a very simple way (similar to what is described in the section above), focusing on personal feelings and emotions.
- Suggest to participants that they write down words that describe emotions and feelings in a journal during a particular experience so that it is fresh and vivid.
- Consider suggesting that participants take photos of places that are particularly meaningful to them and then discuss the photographs in the community workshop meeting, focusing on the emotional experience of being in that particular environment.

Undoubtedly, you will encounter other areas of ambiguity in exploring BAOP with participants, but it is important to realize that there is no one way to implement a phenomenological approach and that, through exploring different ways of helping people understand BAOP, there is always value in discovery and understanding, even if the frame is not "perfect." Using a phenomenological approach in community-based participatory research is novel, but the instructions here show how it can be implemented in a practical way for lay people.

CHANGING POLICY TO LEGITIMIZE BAOP

Chapter 2 describes two concepts that are critical in managing the charm of old places: BAOP and the related person–patina relationship. While this chapter summarizes the work of many environmental psychology researchers, how might these data be used to influence historic preservation policy with the goal of managing the affective character of heritage places to maximize place attachment? Before answering this question, it is important to discuss how this growing body of knowledge can be accessed by practitioners, who have largely been excluded from these conversations. To reiterate, this book, while targeted, in part, to academics, is also meant to be used by built heritage practitioners—especially people who work in areas that are directly influenced by policy. It is therefore important for the reader to know that the ability to use data and recommendations from this body of knowledge *does not* require one to be an environmental psychologist, an academic, or a social scientist.

Because BAOP rests upon a technical base of environmental psychology, it would be natural to conclude that only environmental psychologists would be able to translate phenomena into potential policy ideas. This assumption, however, is not often the case, as understanding BAOP only requires an interest and a willingness to look at academic literature, read abstracts, and, on occasion, read relevant papers. As I have told my students, the introduction, discussion, and especially conclusions in these papers will present information in a way that is accessible; policymakers do not need to know how research methodologies work or how they are implemented to understand what a researcher's conclusions are.

For those readers who are not academics and do not have access to academic library database subscriptions, there are still ways to get access to new BAOP research. Google Scholar (scholar.google.com) has, in the past decade, become one of the primary tools to find all published research on a topic; this database includes most peer-reviewed journals and books published by university presses, along with gray literature. The caution, here, is that sometimes resources will be available through Google Scholar that may have lower levels of reputability and reliability, but generally speaking, this literature is, by far, minimal in most results.

Another tool from Google, which is indispensable, is Google Books (books.google.com). It is now commonplace for academic presses to provide the full text of their books to Google prior to releasing them to the public. Google then adds these books to their database. The issue, however, is that most book publishers want some (or in rarer cases, all) of the text redacted to encourage people to buy the book. But, you can still perform full text searches in all the books that are in Google Books' corpus; while you may not see the exact results in context with a page—sometimes you just get a snippet or just an indication that your search terms are somewhere in the book—you will always know if the book contains material germane to your search. Lastly, an increasing number of academic journal publishers are making their published articles freely available (no charge) via their websites, and authors are now regularly posting their book and paper preprints to the Research Gate (researchgate.net) and Academia.edu sites. What all of this means is that, even for people who do not have the resources of an academic at their fingertips, it is still possible to at least access most of the same materials.

If a municipality, or state or federal government office, wants to inform their historic preservation policy through BAOP research, the other option, of course, is to hire an expert to prepare a white paper, study, or literature review that would be able to inform policy changes. Such an expert would need a deep understanding of orthodox historic preservation policy, environmental psychology, and environment-behavior research germane to the older built environment. While these experts can be difficult to find, there are organizations, such as the Environmental Design Research Association (EDRA) in the United States and the International Association of People-Environment Studies (IAPS) in Europe that can help locate such expertise. These experts can also be found through their publications—in particular, Environment & Behavior and the Journal of Environmental Psychology represent the work of many experts, although not all would be familiar with research that addresses the older built environment.

In the hopefully not too distant future, existing historic preservation advocacy organizations, such as the National Trust for Historic Preservation, the National Alliance of Preservation Commissions (NAPC), the Historic Preservation Education Foundation, the International Council on Monuments and Sites (ICOMOS; and the US chapter), and the International Centre for the Study of the Preservation and Restoration of Cultural Property (ICCROM) (among other possibilities) would offer educational materials, training, and policy analysis tools that address ways in which BAOP research could and should influence historic preservation policy changes. Certainly, there is a place for the National Park Service (NPS) and the Advisory Council on Historic Preservation (ACHP) to play a role, as well, because of their long-esteemed leadership in historic preservation policy at all levels of government. Lastly, educational leaders in historic preservation degree programs could expand their curricula to focus on BAOP, especially because this area of research, and the evidence it presents, is almost entirely absent from these programs (Wells, 2021b); by doing so, future historic preservation practitioners would be more familiar with BAOP research and ways to apply it in practice, especially within a policy frame.

Informing Policy from BAOP Data

As opposed to data from community-based participatory research, BAOP data, collected from conventional academic research, will likely be narrowly focused on specific contexts and, as such, harder to apply in a general way that is useful for developing or changing policy. This characteristic, however, does not make such data irrelevant, but rather, caution is warranted before overgeneralizing from research results.

For reference, specific themes in BAOP research are summarized in chapter 2. Some key takeaways from this literature, relevant to policy, are as follows:

- From the public's perspective, the main value of retaining old building fabric is in its ability to convey age through its patina, which then engenders emotional attachments to place through spontaneous fantasies; in this respect, there is a great deal of compatibility between orthodox and BAOP approaches to preservation policy in that they both greatly respect older building fabric.
- Changes to buildings, places, and landscapes should preserve environmental patina (i.e., evidence of age) to sustain and grow people's emotional attachments to places.
- The natural elements (e.g., trees, plants) of landscapes are as important as older buildings in defining the age of places and increasing people's emotional attachment to these places.
- For some people with minoritized racial or ethnic identities, the style of buildings can be traumatic, by reminding them of their ancestors' struggles.
- People have the innate, psychological ability to differentiate between new and old building fabric, which diminishes orthodox policy's insistence to purposefully exaggerate this difference through materials and design.
- People who self-select to work in the field of historic preservation are more likely to find surface decay/patina of old building fabric to be more pleasing and to believe this fabric is newer, compared to the public.

The future promises to bring new research, based on neuroscience, to our understanding of BAOP, but, to date, little work has happened in this area (Wells, 2021a). There is a great need for more interest in researching the BAOP from environmental psychologists, which would likely increase if policymakers were to also show an interest.

EXAMPLES OF COMMUNITY-BASED PARTICIPATORY AND BAOP RESEARCH INFLUENCING PUBLIC POLICY

While examples of community-based participatory research, and action research, more generally, can be readily found in community-based archaeology, environmental conservation, and, especially, public health, only the latter field has a number of successful examples of using this research methodology to directly influence public (i.e., government) policy. To date, with the exception of the action research project, sponsored by the Organization of American States (OAS) and led by Coherit Associates LLC, to help create a policy for Caribbean nations to list historic places (OAS, 2017), there are very few such examples where this participatory methodology has directly influenced built heritage conservation policy. To give a sense, however, of how community participation can lead to public policy change, a few examples from public health are warranted. These public health examples apply to addressing environmental toxins, reducing addictive substances, and controlling infectious disease. Residents had, for many years, been dealing with these situations and local and state governments were not responding, much less offering assistance. Through partnership with leaders from local nonprofits and universities, who facilitated the process, and residents who participated as coresearchers, each of these cases resulted in policy changes, including direct government action to address the respective issues.

In the United States, it has long been common for companies to dump toxic waste near low-income communities, often because residents lack political power to object to this practice. But, a growing amount of evidence is showing that these toxins negatively affect the health of residents—especially children. In Buffalo, NY, Williams et al. (2016) describe how a community, tired of government inaction, started an investigation of a possible correlation between exposure to toxic waste and the incidence of autoimmune diseases. Community members, facilitated by experts from nonprofit organizations, coresearched the issue, which led to the city securing the site and a resolution to clean up the site; legislators were also compelled to secure funding. In the first decade of this century, in Baltimore, MD, small cigar sales to teenagers were rising, causing concern among residents and community health advocates. In a study by Milam et al. (2012), African American youth, facilitated by academics, helped lead the collection of data on small cigar usage in inner communities in the city. The data and information that were collected allowed the participants to help create bills for city and state legislators. Lastly, many cities have long battled the spread of HIV in their communities but have struggled with effective prevention policies. In Philadelphia, PA, using participatory research, a team of African American community leaders developed an HIV prevention policy memo for the City of Philadelphia City Council, which successfully resulted in changes to the city's policies around HIV prevention (Nunn et al., 2015).

Similarly, while there are no specific examples where environmental psychology or environment-behavior research has directly influenced heritage policy, there are examples in planning literature. In their work for Ohnan Town in Shimane Prefecture, Japan, to create a vision, Shirotsuki, Otsuki, and Sonoda (2017) implemented a methodology to help local residents use their sense of place in the visioning process. It is noteworthy that external reviewers, who did not participate in the visioning process, ranked the vision in which sense of place was centered as better than a traditional vision. This has direct applications in how historic preservation is often a featured component of comprehensive plans in the United States. While "sense of place" may be mentioned in these documents, there is usually not an attempt to articulate what this means for residents and then translate these meanings into public policy, as was done in Ohnan Town.

Urban design, and especially design guidelines, have benefited from environmental psychology research, which informs public policy. An example of this approach is when Szczepańska and Skorupka (2010) looked at central Warsaw, Poland, and used methods from environmental psychology to inform the development of the city's public plan for the area. The researchers interviewed residents, as they were walking through the area, to understand their psychological experiences along with observational studies and surveys. The results were recommendations, made to city planners, to address transportation connectivity and to ensure design changes promoted a "relaxing atmosphere" and addressed areas considered to be "unsafe," "unattractive," and "empty." In the United States, this focus—design and, especially, design guidelines—is a fundamental part of local historic preservation policy, in which historic preservation commissions use design guidelines in their assessment of property owners' applications to change their historic buildings in some way that is under control of a municipality's ordinance. These guidelines, which are almost always based on or derivative of the Secretary of the Interior's Standards (see chapters 1 and 3), are not empirically based and could benefit greatly from being informed through environmental psychology.

CHALLENGES

Public historic preservation policy in the United States has become as defined by its ossification as it is by its directives (see chapters 1 and 3). While disarming the regimes that uphold public policy is required to leave heritage naked, vulnerable, and exposed (see chapter 3), this is an unclear and difficult task. There have been many others in this space before that have failed to influence orthodox historic preservation policy at the local, state, or federal levels—Thomas King (2009), Randall Mason (2002, 2006), Ned Kaufman (2009), Laurajane Smith (2006), David Lowenthal (1985), and Richard Longstreth (2008), among others. Fundamental changes to local, state, and federal historic preservation policy in the United States that would enable facilitation and balance power more equally between civil and conventional experts are required. To make this transition requires policy leaders (e.g., elected officials, political appointees, and supervisors) to first recognize that the enforcement of orthodox preservation policy is a form of cultural hegemony. It is a hegemonic process because, as Višnja Kisić (2022, p. 89) explains, it simultaneously sidelines public values and sentiment while presenting these actions as "natural and commonsensical [and] apolitical and neutral." But, as Kisić and many others observe (see chapter 1), orthodox historic preservation policy is inherently biased, unnatural (from the perspective of the public), and, to be sure, lacks common sense.

More specifically, there is also a related challenge in helping elected leaders, political appointees, and supervisors in local, state, and federal government to consider the inevitability of recognizing and codifying emotional meanings related to heritage places and then developing a management plan to support these subjective meanings that correlate with overall well-being. But, this pill is easier to swallow when one realizes that public policy need not necessarily be exclusively regulatory. The City of San Francisco, for instance, has been using cultural heritage districts to recognize these kinds of meanings, which then influence the overall, official activities in which the city engages, including comprehensive and small area plans (Buckley & Graves, 2016).

Case Study: The Protection of Intangible Heritage as Nonregulatory Local Governmental Policy

The concept of governmental policy is broad and cryptic, but in the public eye, it tends to be exclusively synonymous with laws and regulations. This perspective is overly narrow and misleading, however. Governmental policy (or, more accurately, public policy) consists of all decisions and actions that a governmental entity officially undertakes from spending on arts programs to ensuring that zoning updates are congruent with a comprehensive plan, even if these activities are not narrowly required by a specific statute or ordinance (Cairney, 2020). Historic preservation within local governments is a case in which this public perception, however, is largely accurate. In this latter context, nearly all activities undertaken by a public entity, in the name of historic preservation, derive from quite specific, legally required rules in a "preservation" ordinance. In my (unpublished) work analyzing the official, published job duties of city preservation staff across the country, on average, about 95% of staff duties are to narrowly implement only and exactly the rules stated in these ordinances. (This is a characteristic shared with city building code inspector duties, which I further detail, below.) In addition to my research, I have also worked in preservation programs within city government, including leading the Landmark Preservation Program for the city of Denver, Colorado (USA) and have directly observed the phenomena I describe.

Within the United States, the City of San Francisco is unique in that it created an ordinance to protect heritage that does not depend on city staff narrowly following rules for its implementation. In this respect, this unique ordinance is fundamentally different than the traditional historic preservation ordinance because it advocates for broad, voluntary action to protect intangible heritage rather than legally demanding it through narrowly prescribed rules. This ordinance, which establishes "cultural heritage districts," is also unique because of its focus on intangible, as opposed to tangible, heritage.

For the past several decades, the ethnic, racial, and social diversity of San Francisco's central neighborhoods has been declining, and with this change, the heritage places and businesses associated with these groups have also been declining (Buckley & Graves, 2016). While regulations, through historic preservation commissions, have long been used by local municipalities to identify and protect tangible historic places (e.g., buildings, structures, districts), community and city leaders wanted to expand this tool beyond regulations and into nonregulatory planning policy.

FIGURE 4.4. Peace Pagoda located in San Francisco's Japantown, one of its cultural heritage districts (sketch by author)

Most municipalities in the United States have not been able to undertake historic preservation planning (as opposed to regulating) on par with the way in which cities have undertaken urban planning, for a number of reasons, chiefly related to a lack of resources. In fact, most municipalities do not have any form of historic preservation plan (Mason, 2009). In comparison, while urban planning does incorporate regulations—chiefly land use regulations, such as zoning—much of the work of planning professionals involves gathering and analyzing data and then making recommendations on the future policy directions of a municipality. A prime example is the comprehensive plan, which a group of city planners craft, in close partnership with local residents and business owners, to guide (i.e., not control, through rules and regulations) the way in which land is used, buildings and places are designed, and infrastructure is created while also focusing on incentives for private developers and the development partnerships to facilitate these changes. A comprehensive plan does not, on its own, establish regulations, but elected officials often use such plans as a framework to guide the creation of new city regulations with the aim of helping to implement the vision established by a comprehensive plan (Rouse & Piro, 2022).

Even though, in city government, the work of historic preservation is typically undertaken by professionals with the title of "historic preservation planner," the work of these professionals is more closely allied with building code inspectors than it is with urban and regional planning (cf. Voss, 2024). In the case of building inspectors, their charge is to enforce specific building code regulations. Similarly, the main job of historic preservation planners, in local government, is to enforce historic preservation regulations, either directly or through their work as staff to a historic preservation commission. In close parallel to the work of a building inspector, some preservation planners are charged, by their municipality, with directly enforcing stop work orders on properties that did not receive a proper "certificate of appropriateness" from the historic preservation commission; in other cases, preservation planners closely work with their city's building code enforcement staff to issue such orders. On any given day, historic preservation planners are more likely to work with building inspectors than they are with urban and regional planners. The point, in this explanation, is to clearly circumscribe the work of traditional historic preservation "planning" in local municipal government and to show how these professionals' nomenclature is misleading; nearly universally, across the United States, the work of these professionals fails to entertain the kind of long-term planning that could guide the creation or changes in the regulatory environment that could specifically impact older buildings and places.

This situation is why San Francisco has been rather remarkable in the creation of its cultural heritage districts because it is a clear departure from tradition. This city is one of the first, in the country, to attempt to take the work of local historic preservation, in a city government, outside of a largely regulatory scope and into the traditional purview of urban and regional planning practice. It is, in short, a unique perspective on historic preservation policy, within local government, that is nonregulatory and driven by intangible, rather than tangible, heritage priorities.

Officially, a cultural heritage district is "a geographic area of location within the City and County of San Francisco that embodies a unique cultural heritage because it contains a concentration of cultural and historic assets and culturally significant enterprise, arts, services, or businesses and because a significant portion of its residents or people who spend time in the area or location are members of a specific cultural, community, or ethnic group that historically has been discriminated against, displaced, and oppressed" (SF municipal code, sec. 107.1). As opposed to the normative process of creating a traditional local historic district, wherein the Landmarks Board recommends the creation of a district to the Board of Supervisors (an elected legislative body), "any supervisor," the mayor, or a city department can request the creation of a cultural heritage district by the Board of Supervisors (SF municipal code, 107.4a). This latter process more closely mirrors how, for instance, a planning department recommends that its elected leaders (e.g., a city council) adopt a comprehensive or small area plan.

The fundamental purpose of a traditional local historic preservation district is to preserve the material authenticity of buildings and places; changes to listed buildings and places must go through a regulatory process for approval using criteria derived from the Venice Charter, such as the US Secretary of the Interior's Standards or a local derivation thereof (Bronin & Irwin, 2023). The purpose of a cultural heritage district, however, is not a focus on material authenticity but rather to sustain the cultural continuity of unique places threatened by displacement that have suffered a historical pattern of oppression (SF municipal code, 107.2b); in other words, a cultural heritage district is intended to protect the intangible heritage associated with these places. Cultural heritage districts therefore serve as planning documents that encourage useful partnerships between the city and local communities in protecting and sustaining culturally significant places. These characteristics are fundamentally different than the work traditionally undertaken in a local municipality's historic preservation program.

San Francisco's cultural heritage districts effectively sustain intangible cultural heritage by encouraging voluntary design guidelines and economic incentives. As part of the environmental review process used by the city, threats to cultural heritage districts are officially recognized and recommendations to mitigate negative changes are made. While none of these recommendations are legally mandated, the voluntary process has resulted in the protection of the cultural characteristics identified in these districts, although there have been some issues around implementing economic incentives that would benefit specific businesses (Buckley & Graves, 2016).

Reconceptualizing public historic preservation policy's potential to influence governmental decisions, as San Francisco has, needs to be a key part of policy reform. The answer for this reform, as this chapter has shown, is not to create a new set of rigid guidelines that attempt to narrowly codify a process, as has been done for Section 106, but rather, through action research, it is important to allow members of the public to define—at least in part—what this process should be on a dynamic, case-by-case basis. Thus, the decision-making process becomes much more collaborative than is currently practiced. Conventional heritage and policy experts have a clear role to play, not in enforcing a rigid process and making all the decisions, but by helping members of the public to think holistically and consider potential issues that may not have been discussed. And, through this more democratic process, decisions about built heritage and places with heritage meanings can start to become more inclusive and participatory. The challenge, in this transformation, will be for conventional heritage experts to think of their role as facilitators rather than decision-makers or rule enforcers.

Lastly, there are some legal issues if a local municipality were to base its design review process around community-based participatory research rather than codify specific design criteria, as is currently the case (Wells & Lixinski, 2017). In other words, giving residents the power and authority to make design review decisions, on the fly, without preadopted criteria, may not be possible without changes to the way in which administrative law works. Administrative law, which, in the United States, gives governmental entities the ability to translate legislative will into administrative action, through implementing regulations, has a required concept known as "finality." Finality assumes that public input happens during the process of creating a regulation and thus also assumes that public input that would then redefine how the regulation is implemented cannot occur. In other words, administrative law cannot, currently, be used for dynamic processes. (For reference, this is also a fundamental issue for proposed regulatory management processes in environmental conservation [Craig & Ruhl, 2014].)

CONCLUSION

To be sure, the idea of managing the charm of older places through historic preservation policy reform is novel. With the exception of Russell Staiff (2017), there do not seem to be previous, published attempts to use this normal human experience in the management of heritage. While Staiff only addresses interpretation, this chapter has focused on changes to orthodox public policy, which would require a much more grassroots, participatory process in defining how places are significant and how they ought to be treated in order to maximize people's emotional attachment. It would also require that preservation policy, for the first time, be informed by environment-behavior and environmental psychology research.

Functionally, these changes can be achieved if there is an interest and a will in policymakers to be open to, and ideally, embrace the idea that one of the fundamental ways that older places become unique to the public is through their emotional experiences. Within these broad goals are many possibilities for how policy reform can happen, be it through laws, regulations, guidelines, or other official governmental actions. Because of the unique constitutional framing of states' and local governments' rights it is here, at the local level, where the most promise exists for a people- and human-centered historic preservation policy to bear fruit.

Works Cited

Aurora-Jonsson, S. (2008). "Research sounds so big . . .": Collaborative inquiry with women in Drevdagen, Sweden. In L. Fortmann (ed.), Participatory research in conservation and rural livelihoods: Doing science together (pp. 130-145). Wiley-Blackwell.

Bashforth, M., Benson, M., Boon, T., Brigham, L., Brigham, R., Brookfield, K., Brown, P., Callaghan, D., Calvin, J.-P., Courtney, R., Cremin, K., Furness, P., Graham, H., Hale, A., Hodgkiss, P., Lawson, J., Madgin, R., Manners, P., Robinson, D., . . . Turner, R. (2015). How Should Heritage Decisions be Made? Increasing Participation From Where You Are. Project Report. Connected Communities: Arts & Humanities Research Council.

Bendremer, J. C., Thomas, E. L. (2008). The tribe and the trowel: An Indigenous archaeology and the Mohegan archaeological field school. In S. Silliman (ed.), Collaborating at the trowel's edge: Teaching and learning in Indigenous archaeology (pp. 50-66). University of Arizona Press.

Bergelin, A., et al. (2008). Where peace comes dropping slow: The forests and nature for us. In L. Fortmann (ed.), Participatory research in conservation and rural livelihoods: Doing science together (pp, 146-161). Wiley-Blackwell.

Bronin, S. C., & Irwin, L. R. (2023). Regulating history. *Minnesota Law Review*, 108(1), 241-331.

Buckley, J. M., & Graves, D. (2016). Tangible benefits from intangible resources: Using social and cultural history to plan neighborhood futures. *Journal of the American Planning Association*, 82(2), 152-166.

Cairney, P. (2020). *Understanding public policy: Theories and issues*. Red Globe Press.

Castellanet, C., & Jordan, C. F. (2004). *Participatory action research in natural resource management*. Taylor and Francis.

Craig, R. K. & Ruhl, J. B. (2014). Designing administrative law for adaptive management. *Vanderbilt Law Review,* 67(1), 1-87.

Elliott, J. D. (2002). Radical preservation: Toward a new and more ancient paradigm. *Forum Journal*, 16(3), 50-56.

Emerick, K. (2014). *Conserving and managing ancient monuments: Heritage, democracy, and inclusion*. Boydell & Brewer.

Ezell, K. (2022). *Three essential questions for better planning; PAS Memo 110*. American Planning Association.

Fals-Borda, O. (1987). The application of participatory action-research in Latin America. *International Sociology*, 2(4), 329-347.

Fawcett, S. B., Boothroyd, R., Schultz, J. A., Francisco, V. T., Carson, Bremby, R. (2003). Building capacity for participatory evaluation within community initiatives. Journal of Prevention & Intervention in the Community, 26(2), 21-36.

Fortman, L. (2008). Doing science together. In L. Fortmann (ed.), Participatory research in conservation and rural livelihoods: Doing science together (pp. 1-17). Wiley-Blackwell.

Freire, P. (1970). *Pedagogy of the oppressed*. Continuum.

Garcia, I. (2018). Community participation as a tool for conservation planning and historic preservation: The case of "Community As A Campus" (CAAC). *Journal of Housing and the Built Environment, 33*(3), 519–537.

Hall, E. (2016). From regulation to community action: The expanding role of preservation commissions. *Forum Journal, 30*(2), 64–69.

Hegel, G. W. F. (1937). *The phenomenology of mind* (J. B. Baillie, Trans.). Harper Torchbooks. (Original work published 1807).

Heidegger, M. (2005). *Introduction to phenomenological research* (D. O. Dahlstrom, Trans.). Indiana University Press. (Source material derived from lectures in 1923 and 1924)

Kant, I. (1934). *Critique of pure reason* (J. D. D. Meiklejohn, Trans.). Everyman. (Original work published 1787).

Kaufman, N. (2009). *Place, race, and story: Essays on the past and future of historic preservation.* Routledge.

Kemmis, S., & McTaggart, R. (2005). Participatory action research: Communicative action and the public sphere. In N. K. Denison & Y. S. Lincoln (Eds.), The Sage handbook of qualitative research (pp. 559–604). Sage.

King, T. F. (2009). *Our unprotected heritage: Whitewashing the destruction of our cultural and natural resources.* Left Coast Press.

Kisić, K. (2022). Beyond the good, the neutral and the consensual: Heritage between the police and the political. In F. Hammami, D. Jewesbury, & C. Valli (Eds.), *Heritage, gentrification and resistance in the neoliberal city (pp. 83–103).* Berghahn Books.

Longstreth, R. W. (Ed.). (2008). *Cultural landscapes: Balancing nature and heritage in preservation practice.* University of Minnesota Press.

Lowenthal, D. (1985). *The past is a foreign country.* Cambridge University Press.

Mason, R. (2002). Assessing values in conservation planning: Methodological issues and choices. In M. Torre (Ed.), *Assessing the values of cultural heritage* (pp. 5–30). The J. Paul Getty Trust.

———. (2006). Theoretical and practical arguments for values-centered preservation. *CRM: The Journal of Heritage Stewardship, 3*(2), 21–48.

Mason, R. F. (2009). Preservation planning in American cities. *Forum Journal, 23*(2), 38–44.

Merleau-Ponty, M. (1962). *Phenomenology of perception: An introduction* (C. Smith, Trans.). Routledge.

Milam, A. J., Bone, L., Furr-Holden, D., Coylewright, M., Dachille, K., Owings, K., Clay, E., Holmes, W., Lambropoulos, S., & Stillman, F. (2012). Mobilizing for policy: Using community-based participatory research to impose minimum packaging requirements on small cigars. *Progress in Community Health Partnerships, 6*(2), 205–212.

Munhall, P. (2007). A phenomenological method. In P. Munhall (Ed.), *Nursing research: A qualitative perspective* (pp. 145–210). Jones and Bartlet.

Nay, R., & Fetherstonhaugh, D. (2012). What is pain? A phenomenological approach to understanding. *International Journal of Older People Nursing, 7*(3), 233–239.

Norberg-Schulz, C. (1980). *Genius loci: Towards a phenomenology of architecture.* Rizzoli.

Nunn, A., Sanders, J., Lee, C., Thomas, G., Cornwall, A., Towey, C., Lee, H., Tasco, M., Shabazz-El, W., Yolken, A., Smith, T., Bell, G., Feller, S., Smith, E., James, G., Dunston, B. S., & Green, D. (2015). African American community leaders' policy recommendations for reducing racial disparities in HIV infection, treatment, and care: Results from a community-based participatory research project in Philadelphia, Pennsylvania. *Health Promotion Practice,* 16(1), 91-100.

Organization of American States (OAS). (2017). *A model for inventories and national registers of heritage places: Expanding the socio-economic potential of cultural heritage in the Caribbean.*

Pyrch T. (2012). Breaking free: A facilitator's guide to participatory action research practice. Lulu.

Ray, M. A. (1994). The richness of phenomenology: Philosophic, theoretic, and methodologic concerns. In J. M. Morse (Ed.), Critical issues in qualitative research methods (pp. 117-133). Sage.

Roberts, A. (2018). Performance as place preservation: The role of storytelling in the formation of Shankleville community's Black counterpublics. *Journal of Community Archaeology & Heritage,* 5(3), 146-165.

Rouse, D. C., & Piro, R. (2022). *The comprehensive plan: Sustainable, resilient, and equitable communities for the 21st century.* Routledge.

Ryberg-Webster, S. (2017). Beyond rust and Rockefeller: Preserving Cleveland's African American heritage. *Preservation Education & Research,* 9, 7-23.

San Francisco municipal code. Chapter 107: Cultural Districts. https://codelibrary.amlegal.com/codes/san_francisco/latest/sf_admin/0-0-0-59520

Seamon, D. (1982). The phenomenological contribution to environmental psychology. *Journal of Environmental Psychology*, 2(2), 119-140.

Shirotsuki, M., Otsuki, S., & Sonoda, M. (2017). Bridging the gap between planning and environmental psychology: An application of sense of place for visioning of public policy. *Asian Journal of Environment-Behaviour Studies*, 2(2), 11-22.

Silverman, R. M., Taylor, H. L., Yin, L., Miller, C., & Boggs, P. (2019). Are we still going through the empty ritual of participation? Inner-city residents' and other grassroots stakeholders' perceptions of public input and neighborhood revitalization. *Critical Sociology,* 46(3), 413-428.

Smith, L. (2006). *Uses of heritage.* Routledge.

Staiff, R. (2017). *Re-imagining heritage interpretation: Enchanting the past-future.* Routledge.

Stefanovic, I. L. (1998). Phenomenological encounters with place: Cavtat to Square One. *Journal of Environmental Psychology,* 18(1), 31-44.

Stoudt, B. G., Torre, M. E., Bartley, P., Bracy, F., Caldwell, H., Downs, A., Greene, C., Haldipur, J., Hassan, P., Manoff, E., Sheppard, N., & Yates, J. (2016). Participatory action research and policy change. In C. Durose & L. Richardson (Eds.), *Designing public policy for co-production: Theory, practice and change* (pp. 125-138). Policy Press.

Szczepańska, J., & Skorupka, A. (2010). Evidence based planning in the city of Warsaw: Environmental psychology methods employed in research projects informing urban planning processes. In M. Aboutorabi & A. Wesener (Eds.), *Urban design research: Method and application proceedings of the international conference held at Birmingham City University, 3-4 December 2009* (pp. 215-225). Birmingham City University.

Tuan, Y.-F. (1977). *Space and place: The perspectives of experience.* University of Minnesota Press.

van Manen, M. (1990). *Researching the lived experience.* University of Western Ontario.

Voss, E. H. (2024). *Become a construction and building inspector.* BrightPoint Press.

Wells, J. C. (2020). Is there such a thing as tangible heritage? *Forum Journal,* 32(4), 15-24.

———. (2021a). Attachment to older or historic places: Relating what we know from the perspective of phenomenology and neuroscience. In R. Madgin & J. Lesh (Eds.), *People-centred methodologies for heritage conservation* (pp. 16-38). Routledge.

———. (2021b). Does intra-disciplinary historic preservation scholarship address the exigent issues of practice? Exploring the character and impact of preservation knowledge production in relation to critical heritage studies, equity, and social justice. *International Journal of Heritage Studies*, 27(5), 449-469. https://doi.org/10.1080/13527258.2020.1799059.

Wells, J. C., & Baldwin, E. D. (2012). Historic preservation, significance, and age value: A comparative phenomenology of historic Charleston and the nearby new-urbanist community of I'On. *Journal of Environmental Psychology*, 32(4), 384-400.

Wells, J. C., & Lixinski, L. (2017). Heritage values and legal rules: Identification and treatment of the historic environment via an adaptive regulatory framework (part 2). *Journal of Cultural Heritage Management and Sustainable Development*, 7(3), 345-363.

Wickens, J. D. J., & Gupta, A. (2022). Leadership: The act of making way for others. *Studies in Conservation*, 67(sup. 1), 319-325.

Williams, E. M., Terrell, J., Anderson, J., & Tumiel-Berhalter, L. (2016). A case study of community involvement influence on policy decisions: Victories of a community-based participatory research partnership. *International Journal of Environmental Research and Public Health,* 13(515), 1-9.

CHAPTER 5

Overcoming Historic Preservation's "Resistance to Research"

Creating an Informed Policy

INTRODUCTION

When many people hear the word "research," they immediately jump to the lone academic and the ivory tower, in isolation from the real world and its pragmatic exigencies. For this reason, when I considered writing this chapter, I hesitated in using this word because of this association. While not entirely inaccurate, the kind of research which I discuss, in this chapter, is very much the opposite of this stereotype: It is pragmatic, applied, and deeply embedded in specific contexts. "Research," as I use this word, in this chapter, is about problem solving. And the big problem in the historic preservation field is how public preservation policy has long been ossified and highly resistant to change—especially change that considers the magic of old places and the importance of this phenomenon to the public.

To recap, from chapters 1 and 3, US historic preservation policy has been uniquely resistant to change, since its foundations began to be fixed in the late 1960s through the formalization of federal regulations and guidelines in the 1970s and early 1980s. When a preservation law, ordinance, or regulation has been adopted, its rules have tended to remain unchanged for many decades until the present; and if there are, on occasion, minor amendments, they are not substantial, meaningful, or significant because they seek to preserve the *status quo*. Unlike other areas of public policy, such as public health, the historic preservation field does not have a tradition of using research to collect data to provide evidence for the effectiveness of existing policies in order to catalyze needed policy changes. To be sure, the only place that this kind of evidence has been used by advocates is through economic analyses, primarily as a way to influence the US Congress to fully fund historic preservation activities as was originally promised in the National Historic Preservation Act of 1966.

Historic preservation education, and especially the scholars who teach in higher education within historic preservation degree programs, also appear to be unusually resistant to change. As my own work has shown, the exigent issues in the historic preservation field that have arisen in the past couple of decades, such as the need for better community engagement, climate change, and diversity, inclusion, equity, and social justice, have been significantly underrepresented in the research of these scholars (Wells, 2021b). To be sure, as I uncovered in my research, the general issue with historic preservation faculty is that they tend to do substantially less research—theoretical or applied—as compared to other disciplines. Moreover, when research is undertaken, it is largely done to uphold orthodox historic preservation practice, such as the preparation of National Register nominations and historic structure reports, rather than to challenge the *status quo*. Critically, there is next to no research that examines preservation practice or the effectiveness of public preservation policy on any level other than its influence on the economy. Thus, research, on the occasions it is conducted in the preservation discipline, is unlikely to significantly influence or change practice, much less public policy. There simply is no evidence being produced that would be necessary to drive change. The idiom of "out of sight, out of mind" is an apt characterization of the issue.

I have not been alone in observing this phenomenon, to which Ned Kaufman (2019) refers as "resistance to research." This situation appears to be driven by the field's pragmatic focus on just "getting the work done" and sidelining research that is not narrowly within the frame of satisfying a client's needs as King and Lyneis (1978, p. 889), Otero-Pailos (2007, p. viii), and Smith (2000, p. 314) observe. Other perspectives are more direct, in that the field expects historic preservation practitioners to be "indifferent to thinking" and desirous of advancing an anti-intellectual agenda (Elliott, 2019; Russell, 2014). Kaufman (2019, p. 309) provides further illumination on the overall lack of the historic preservation field's curiosity about its own activities:

> I should clarify what I mean by research. I do not mean investigations into architectural or landscape history, or into the chemistry of adhesives or

the statics of structures. These investigations concern the things on which preservation works, but they do not, except in matters of detail, determine what preservation seeks to do or how. They have little bearing on whether or not we should have a National Register of Historic Places, or tax credits, or programs to address climate change, or on whether local landmark regulations are on the whole too strict or not strict enough, or whether testimony from the public that "We have always lived in this place and like it as it is" should or should not be considered relevant. They tell us little if anything about how well existing policies accomplish their objectives, what unintended impacts they might have, or what options might be preferable. By research, I mean the kinds of investigations that do help answer these and similar questions: research that bears on the policies beneath the preservation enterprise, the assumptions that drive them, the forces that shape them, their impact on the world. Whenever I refer to Resistance To Research, I shall mean specifically this kind of research.

Although he does not mention it by name, Kaufman's focus is on public preservation policy and the field's insistence on uncritically preserving its own policies rather than questioning their effectiveness. Surely, historic preservation ought to be focused on preserving buildings and places, not on preserving its own policies, yet this is the situation in which the field and discipline finds themselves.

There are no easy solutions for magically injecting an attitude of curiosity, intellectual vigor, and critical thinking into historic preservation education, much less the field as a whole, but an area ripe for such change is an openness to research that intersects environmental psychology and the older built environment in order to inform public policy. Recognizing a need for the preservation field to adopt tools from the public policy and planning fields that would enable the analysis of public policy is a significant, and sorely needed, first step.

INFORMING ORTHODOX HISTORIC PRESERVATION POLICY THROUGH THE POLICY ANALYSIS

Most people who work in the historic preservation field have heard of "policy," but few can specifically identify what it means in the context of practice, often confusing "policy" as a synonym for "regulation," which is inaccurate. Fewer still will be able to accurately report the extent to which professional historic preservation practice is driven by public policy. None will likely have ever conducted a historic preservation policy analysis, much less read one. These are significant issues and contribute to why orthodox historic preservation policy in the United States has not changed in a half a century.

The first step, to address this myopia, is to teach students and help current practitioners understand that the majority of historic preservation practice in the United States—70%—is driven by policies at the local, state, and federal levels (Wells, 2018). Although Murphy, Leibowitz, and Hudson (2018, p. 423) note that the public knows that historic preservation, especially as it applies to private property rights at the level of local government, "comes with restrictions and more regulation than most people care to deal with," many professional and academic preservationists have long resisted this characterization. To be sure, there are many preservationists who bristle with defensiveness when faced with this actual character of the field and respond by denying or ignoring its policy-driven nature (e.g., Barrett, 2016; Cook, 2016; Hall, 2016; Michael, 2011; Rypkema, 1997). The way that the denial often comes across is through a kind of embarrassment, where the author is avoiding the admission that professional historic preservation work is mostly regulatory in nature, and inherently driven by public policy, and thus sidelines the entire discussion in hope of "moving beyond . . . regulatory duties" (e.g., Hall, 2016). The reality, supported by evidence (Wells, 2018), is quite clear: The majority of paid historic preservation practice centers around regulatory compliance, regardless of how hard these authors strive to deny the fact. But, additionally, historic preservation policy also consists of fundamentally important guidelines, such as how the National Park Service (NPS) expects National Register nominations to be prepared, and official government action (or inaction). These latter categories are not often called "policy" by historic preservationists, yet they most certainly are under this umbrella.

It almost seems as if, because of this embarrassment felt by academic and professional preservationists, the field has long been engaged in a mass denial of public policy as its central drive. If "preservation policy" is not central to historic preservation practice, then it conveniently disappears as an object of research. Other, more interesting and less embarrassing topics, like architectural history or architectural materials conservation, surface and dominate. The messiness of people and their values and meanings which intertwine with policy, regress into the background. And, indeed, this is the case in terms of the topics upon which most academic researchers in historic preservation focus: safe, objective, and inherently nonsociopolitical (Wells, 2021b). But, the net effect has been a decades-long neglect by academics and professionals in analyzing how the preservation policies, first established a half century ago, have performed. We know very little about this kind of performance because hardly anyone is asking about it—with some notable exceptions (e.g., Avrami, Leo, & Sanchez, 2018; Bronin & Irwin, 2023; Wells, 2021a). Instead of being a very minor player in historic preservation research, policy should be the most dominant topic, in reflection of its prominence in driving practice. To be sure, this situation is not unique to historic preservation. Critical heritage studies has also largely failed to focus on policy, even though, on an international level, heritage policy is equally as important in driving built heritage conservation practice as well as allied areas, such as tourism (Rodenberg & Wagenaar, 2023).

The reality is that, since the passage of the National Historic Preservation Act of 1966, there has never been a center or institute in the United States that has focused on public historic preservation policy, specifically. And, problematically, government entities and foundations typically only provide funding that upholds orthodox preservation policy, not that challenges or examines it. To date, no US funder has offered funding that specifically targets the effectiveness of federal, state, or local historic preservation policy in the United States. The situation is very different in Europe and Australia, however. In the United Kingdom, the Arts and Humanities Research Council (AHRC) regularly funds social science, participatory, and policy research that addresses the historic environment. Some successfully funded AHRC examples include:

- Siân Jones (University of Manchester): "Wrestling with the Social Value of Heritage: Problems, Dilemmas and Opportunities," funded for £29,598.[1]
- Alex Hale (Royal Commission on the Ancient and Historical Monuments of Scotland): "Linking Communities to Historic Environments," funded for £32,556. Hale's research identified ways that various communities can participate in activities related to the conservation of the historic environment.[2]

---

1. https://gtr.ukri.org/projects?ref=AH%2FL005654%2F1.
2. https://gtr.ukri.org/projects?ref=AH%2FJ501448%2F1.

- Susan Ashley (Northumbria University), "(Multi)Cultural Heritage: New Perspectives on Public Culture, Identity and Citizenship," funded for £138,838 to investigate how "(multi)cultural organisations, their stakeholders and audiences ... might participate more extensively in heritage and cultural policy-making."[3]

In addition, AHRC specifically provides research funding for heritage policy analyses, such as a £100,000–£135,000 fellowship to "inform policies for culture, heritage and the creative industries."[4]

In the European Union, some examples of research that the European Commission funded include:

- Università degli Studi Roma Tre: "Social Platform for Holistic Heritage Impact Assessment," funded for €1,511,070.[5]
- Université Libre de Bruxelles: "Intangible cultural heritage policies in Europe: what 'participation' of which 'communities'?" funded for €159,100.[6]
- Coventry University: "Re-designing access to cultural heritage for a wider participation in preservation, (re)use and management of European culture," funded for €1,499,981.[7]

In Australia, the Australian Research Council (ARC) provided AU$340,000 in funding for Tracy Ireland's (University of Canberra) proposal to address what "Everyday Heritage is about [and] the things and places that ordinary people value and how these can be better acknowledged." Ireland's research will also "focus on groups that haven't traditionally had a voice or a strong presence in the national story."[8]

In the United States, the likelihood that any of these projects, if applied to a US context, would be funded is infinitesimally small. This situation needs to change for the benefit of the public, but much more awareness of

---

3. https://gtr.ukri.org/projects?ref=AH%2FP008984%2F1.
4. https://www.ukri.org/opportunity/inform-policies-for-culture-heritage-and-the-creative-industries/.
5. https://cordis.europa.eu/project/id/870954.
6. https://cordis.europa.eu/project/id/252786.
7. https://cordis.europa.eu/project/id/769827.
8. https://www.canberra.edu.au/about-uc/media/newsroom/2021/august/everyday-heritage-wins-arc-linkage-grant.

this issue is needed by funders in the United States. If one accepts the premise for the social justice issues in historic preservation policy presented in chapters 1 and 3, then the onus is on preservation and social science funders to be more aware of what is happening in the cultural heritage sector in the United States; to continue to uphold and sustain orthodox historic preservation with their funds can potentially be creating social justice issues. Given the ossification of historic preservation policy in the United States, establishing funding priorities in this area is extremely important.

What Is a Policy Analysis in the Context of Historic Preservation?
What is a policy analysis, what does it aim to achieve, and how is it implemented? The answers to these questions should be well-known to all practitioners in the preservation field, especially the people who work in the 70% of the field in which policy is central to their work. This is even more critical in higher education, given that historic preservation degree programs do not educate their students in this technique (Wells et al., 2022).

In simple terms, a policy analysis is used to understand how public policies (i.e., laws, regulations, guidelines, and/or official government action) are made and to provide lawmakers, politically appointed leaders, and supervisors with information that can help them make better informed decisions about policies (Fischer, Miller, & Sidney, 2007). There are usually six general steps in conducting a policy analysis, based on the rational theory of policymaking, in which policy moves from idea to implementation (Spicker, 2006):

1. Assessment of the environment: Decisions have to be taken in the light of existing situations;
2. The identification of aims and objectives: Aims and values have to be identified and established as criteria by which decisions can subsequently be evaluated;
3. Consideration of the alternative methods which are available: Different ways of achieving the aims and objectives are identified. This is a question of what is possible;
4. Selection of methods: The possible consequences of all the possible methods are judged against the aims and objectives in order to decide their likely effectiveness. The selection of particular methods of working is then guided by consideration of efficiency and practical constraints;
5. Implementation: The policy is put into practice;

6. Evaluation: The consequences of policy are monitored and fed back into a reassessment of the environment, at which point the process begins again.

While there are other kinds of policy analysis methods, these steps are almost always present, in some fashion. Importantly, what drives the need for this analysis is a desire for government to continually improve public service, especially as sociocultural and economic conditions change. In some fields, such as public health, the policy analysis is central to the professional's identity and their desire to serve the public better. As Warren Walker (2000), Professor of Policy Analysis at Delft University of Technology, warns, "without [a policy] analysis, important policy choices are based on hunches and guesses—sometimes with regrettable results." And therein lies the most succinct definition of a policy analysis: ensuring that the actions of government are in the best interest of the public by basing policy on continually updated evidence in order to avoid "regrettable results."

While policy analyses have traditionally relied on quantitative research, in the past couple of decades, qualitative data and data generated from grassroots community research (e.g., action research) have been used for these analyses as well (Bartels & Wittmayer, 2018; Sadovnik, 2017; Smith & Ingram, 2002). Broadly speaking, there is no prescribed limitation on the kinds of data used, nor on how they may be collected, within the frame of a policy analysis. Nor is there necessarily a limitation on the kinds of public policy that can be examined or specific issues within a particular policy. For instance, the policy analysis has also been used to identify and address issues of systemic racism in public policy, such as in public education policy (Dowd & Liera, 2018), child welfare policy (Baron, Goldstein, & Ryan, 2023), and employment policy (Vohra-Gupta, Kim, & Cubbin, 2021), as well as federal historic preservation policy (Wells, 2021a).

NEED FOR MORE RESEARCH TO UNDERSTAND BEING AFFECTED BY OLDER PLACES (BAOP)

Chapter 2 established the reasons why an understanding of BAOP is important and the ready relationship that this phenomenon has to environmental psychology research. But, while there was a brief period of attention to the possibilities of using environmental psychology to influence built heritage conservation policy in the 1980s and early 1990s (Hubbard, 1993), the promise has yet to be fulfilled. In general, the field of environmental psychology has paid little attention to heritage environments, and few publications have resulted. The most prominent advocacy organizations for environment-behavior research and environmental psychology, as applied to the built environment, are the Environmental Design Research Association (EDRA), the International Association of People-Environment Studies (IAPS), and the Man-Environment Research Association (MERA). With the exception of EDRA, none focus on heritage environments, and EDRA only added a knowledge network area related to the historic environment in 2008, due to the author's efforts. In Australia and New Zealand, the People and Physical Environment Research Organization did have an extensive focus on the historic environment but folded at the turn of this century and is no longer active. Division 34, which is part of the American Psychological Association, and calls itself the "Society for Environmental, Population and Conservation Psychology," does focus on environmental psychology mostly as applied to the natural environment but not on heritage environments. The City University of New York has long had a graduate environmental psychology program, and some of its graduates have produced theses focused on heritage environments, but it is not a specific area of focus in the program. In the United States, faculty lines in environmental psychology have consistently been eliminated as faculty have retired. All these examples point to a general apathy toward the historic environment and environmental psychology, more generally.

Part of this issue is due to an apparent lack of interest in environmental psychology and especially as it is applied to any element of the built environment. In the late 1960s and into the 1970s and 80s, there was a great deal of excitement over the rise of environment-behavior research and environmental psychology as directed toward the built environment, but the growth in this area of research plateaued by the early 1990s and has not grown substantially since this time, instead becoming a marginal affair largely confined to postoccupancy studies (Galan-Diaz & Martens, 2015; Rapport 2008). Membership in EDRA, IAPS, and MERA has long stabilized and not grown. Many authors have advanced theories as to why this might be the case. Rapport (2008, p. 279), for instance, offers that environment-behavior research does not have "a philosophical base, clear definitions, agreement on terms and concepts, generalization, and [needs to develop a] conceptual frame."

But, this epistemological argument appears to be in the minority. There are other, more salient factors in play as well.

To be sure, the most consistent argument for the sustained lack of interest in environmental psychology research is simply that psychologists are not motivated to understand the "noise" of the physical world, preferring, instead, to remain fixated on inner worlds. As Gieseking (2014, p. 591), relates, "psychologists still assume the [physical] environment is background noise rather than a variable or component of study." Gary Moore (1991, p. 321) expands on this observation, noting that psychologists are too fixed on the internal world of the mind and are not nearly as interested in how the mind engages with the discrete elements of the physical world: "many [psychology] researchers continue to explore the categories of mind, without giving equal attention to the categories of environment—place types, the structure of the environment, and environmental cues." And, not surprisingly, in looking at much of the research in psychology, the physical world, indeed, does not seem to exist within the authors' research questions, research methodologies, or analyses and conclusions. Perhaps this condition is simply more of a reflection of the internal motivations of researchers than on other external factors, such as funding, epistemological limitations, or a discipline's structure. It is also likely a reflection on higher education's failure to bring together, in an interdisciplinary sense, psychology and built environment programs thereby sabotaging the potential for such collaborative research.

Outside of the specific discipline of environmental psychology—regardless of the authors' disciplines—scholarly articles, chapters, and books that address built heritage from a social science perspective rarely use methods from environmental and/or social psychology, which has not gone unnoticed by scholars. Fogarasi and Dúll (2021, p. 276) note that "very few studies deal with the psychological impact of built historic environments on individuals, communities and society, taking into account the . . . environmental psychological constructs of place attachment and place identity." To be sure, with few exceptions, research methods from psychology in the social science literature that addresses built heritage are absent. Some prominent examples of these exceptions are the work of Ahn (2013); Askari, Dola, and Soltani (2014); Herzog and Gale (1996); Herzog and Shier (2000); Levi (2005); Uzzell (2009); Wells and Baldwin (2012); Sektani et al. (2021), and Wells (2017). These outliers show the possibility of this ap-

TABLE 5.1. Built heritage publications in common social science disciplines

	Disciplinary affiliation of authors	No. of scholarly books	No. of journal articles and book chapters	Authors represented
	Anthropology	>100	>1000	>60
	Sociology	2	21	11
	Psychology	0	8	7

proach and help to validate the psychology of heritage places as an acceptable and needed area of research.

It is also helpful to position psychology against other social science disciplines, which are much more active in their investigations into built heritage topics. Overwhelmingly, anthropologists represent the vast majority of this literature, but sociology and especially psychology are seriously underrepresented. This conclusion is based on the number of scholarly publications on this topic in which anthropologists are substantially overrepresented (see Table 5.1). Part of this disparity could be that anthropology has always, to some extent, had a focus on the past and people's cultural relationship with it that sociology and psychology have not. But, even so, it is worth asking why anthropologists have come to own this space? And, should their perspective be exclusive to heritage? Is there value in disrupting this hegemony for a more pluralistic and nuanced understanding of heritage, especially intangible heritage? There are no clear answers, but this issue presents heritage meanings with a clear bias toward culture while largely ignoring social behavior and especially individual lived experience. There is value for these other social science perspectives to inform built heritage values, meanings, and perceptions.

Lastly, it is informative for me to relate my own experiences in relation to advocating for and encouraging an interest in the intersection of environmental psychology and built heritage. In the last institution in which I was employed as an associate professor, with an appointment to a historic preservation program, I made a concerted effort to find environmental psychologists with whom I could establish a potential research partnership. This was a flagship state university, with campuses distributed throughout the state; in total there are nearly 25,000 faculty employed at these campuses. In the entirety of the state, I was able to locate only one faculty member who was a psychologist trained in environmental psychology, and she was a postdoc (i.e., she did not have a tenure-track appointment). In addition, in the United States, no governmental or nonprofit organization funds environmental psychology work related to the older built environment. The *coup de grâce*, in my experience, was when, several years ago, I was a coeditor for a special issue in a well-respected, refereed psychology journal that focused on environmental psychology and built heritage. In total, I sent out several thousand solicitations for abstracts to psychologists, across the globe, many of whom identified themselves as "environmental psychologists" (most of this latter group lived in Europe). I personally contacted about forty people and engaged in a conversation to solicit interest in submitting a paper abstract. In the end, after an initial call and a repeat call, over a period of six months, my coeditors and I received a handful of submissions.

While the contexts that I relate are troubling, the fact that there still are a few researchers, including myself, who show an interest in this topic is encouraging. The National Trust for Historic Preservation (US) has an interest in this topic, which adds to this sense of encouragement (Mayes, 2017, 2018; Meeks, 2016). The U.K.-based National Trust has also shown a strong interest in environmental psychology and, especially, neuroscience (National Trust, 2017). And, Jorge Otero-Pailos, Director of Columbia University's Historic Preservation Program, notes that "preservation is so much about people's emotions and memories, and neuroscience is transforming the way we think of the relationship between landmarks and people" (Hudson, 2018). If we, like these organizations and this individual, assume that there is value in a psychological approach to built heritage, which could then inform public policy, how then do we encourage people to research environment-behavior interactions in this area and especially heritage environments? And, if we have more empirical evidence, how might environmental psychologists play a role in determining how historic environments are conserved? These are more open questions with few answers, but they ought to be asked more frequently, especially by leaders in historic preservation education and policy.

SOME FINAL THOUGHTS ON NORMALIZING RESEARCH IN HISTORIC PRESERVATION

As a student, first in an undergraduate and then in a graduate historic preservation program, I narrowly understood research in the field as something that either helped create an argument for historical significance or could be used to devise and test ways to conserve the fabric of old buildings. But, it was not until I entered a doctoral program that I genuinely learned what "research" actually was—a process in which a problem is defined, a question that relates to this problem is asked, a methodology and method is chosen to answer the question, data are gathered and analyzed, and, then, finally, there is an attempt to answer the question, using the analyzed data. While there are other research traditions that are not quite as linear as this definition, the basic elements are there: research is used to understand the nature of a problem. But, critically, research is not, and should not, be restricted to the proverbial ivory tower. In many fields, such as microelectronics, research is used in a highly applied way by industry, such as solving the ongoing problem of making computer chips smaller while also making them faster.

Why should historic preservation be any different? In the example of microelectronics and the allied field of computer science, applied research has totally redefined what these fields are since their origins more than half a century ago. A computer today is almost entirely different than in the 1970s—far smaller, with a graphical user interface, running a totally different operating system, and running programs coded in languages that were not even dreamed of fifty years ago. And, most importantly, computers are ubiquitous: they are in our phones, on our wrists, and in our refrigerators. Yet, in comparison, the majority of historic preservation practice—the 70% of the field driven by policy—looks much the same as it did in the 1970s. We use the same "code"—that is, the same doctrine—and the same "operating system"—that is, the same policies. Significance is still, like a command-line computer, reliant on a textual description using historical facts even though, in a multimedia world, there are many other ways to identify and relate what is "significant" from the perspective of the public. And, the areas in which one can find historic preservation policy—local design review, National Register nominations, Section 106—are largely identical to how they existed in the 1970s and early 1980s, which, again, is radically different from the way computers have become ubiquitous. Why has historic preservation not become ubiquitous as well? I would argue that one of the answers is its inherent resistance to research. Until we normalize the ability to query the relevancy, efficiency, and functionality of preservation policy, it cannot and will not expand. It will, instead, be preserved. But, is that what we really want of historic preservation policy—to preserve it?

To answer this question, the major preservation advocacy organizations in the United States, such as the National Trust for Historic Preservation, Preservation Action, National Conference of State Historic Preservation Officers, and many others, need to step up and start asking these questions and advancing the possibility of normalizing policy research in the field, informed by social science research—especially from environmental psychology. The NPS and the Advisory Council on Historic Preservation (ACHP), because of their centrality in establishing and promoting orthodox policy in the United States, should play a leading role in normalizing policy research and potentially even providing funding for it. And, historic preservation education could be teaching policy analysis in its degree programs. All these actions could radically reform the relevancy of the field to the public and make, for the first time, historic preservation/built heritage conservation a ubiquitous practice.

Works Cited

Ahn, Y.-K. (2013). Adaptive reuse and historic churches. *Preservation Education & Research*, 6, 25-40.

Askari, A. H., Dola, K. B., & Soltani, S. (2014). An evaluation of the elements and characteristics of historical building façades in the context of Malaysia. *Urban Design International*, 19(2), 113-124.

Avrami, E., Leo, C.-N., & Sanchez, A. S. (2018). Confronting exclusion: Redefining the intended outcomes of historic preservation. *Change Over Time: International Journal of Conservation and the Built Environment*, 8(1), 102-120.

Baron, E. J., Goldstein, E. G., & Ryan, J. (2023). The push for racial equity in child welfare: can blind removals reduce disproportionality? *Journal of Policy Analysis and Management*, 42(2), 456-487.

Barrett, J. (2016). Getting away from "no": Straight talk to local advocates. *Forum Journal*, 30(2), 46-49.

Bartels, K. P. R., & Wittmayer, J. M. (2018). *Action research in policy analysis and transition research*. Routledge.

Bronin, S. C., & Irwin, L. R. (2023). Regulating history. *Minnesota Law Review*, 108(1), 241-331.

Cook, W. J. (2016). How preservation law lays the groundwork for a "movement of yes." *Forum Journal*, 30(2), 4-18.

Dowd, A. C., & Liera, R. (2018). Sustaining change towards racial equity through cycles of inquiry. *Education Policy Analysis Archives*, 26, 65.

Elliott, J. D. (2019). The mystery of history and place: Radical preservation revisited. In J. Wells and B. Stiefel (Eds.), *Human-centered built environment heritage preservation: Theory and evidence-based practice* (pp. 89-100). Routledge.

Fischer, F., Miller, G. J., & Sidney, M. S. (2007). *Handbook of public policy analysis: Theory, politics, and methods*. CRC/Taylor & Francis.

Fogarasi, B., & Dúll, A. (2021). Inside the mind and heart of Homo aedificator: Towards revealing the psychological meaning of historic buildings and sites. *Építés – Építészettudomány*, 49(1-2), 267-287.

Galan-Diaz, C., & Martens, D. (2015, September 3). Architecture's brief love affair with psychology is overdue a revival. *The conversation*. https://theconversation.com/architectures-brief-love-affair-with-psychology-is-overdue-a-revival-45896.

Gieseking, J. (2014). Environmental psychology. In T. Teo, M. Barnes, Z. Gao, M. Kaiser, R. Sheivari, & B. Zabinski (Eds.), *International encyclopedia of critical psychology* (pp. 587-593). Springer.

Hall, E. (2016). From regulation to community action: The expanding role of preservation commissions. *Forum Journal*, 30(2), 64-69.

Herzog, T. R., & Gale, T. A. (1996). Preference for urban buildings as a function of age and nature context. *Environment and Behavior*, 28(1), 44-72.

Herzog, T. R., & Shier, R. L. (2000). Complexity, age, and building preference. *Environment and Behavior*, 32(4), 557-575.

Hubbard, P. (1993). The value of conservation: A critical review of behavioural research. *Town Planning Review*, 64(4), 359-373.

Hudson, E. (2018, February 26). Interview with Jorge Otero-Pailos. *Architectural Record*. https://www.architecturalrecord.com/articles/13257-interview-with-jorge-otero-pailos.

Kaufman, N. (2019). Resistance to research: Diagnosis and treatment of a disciplinary ailment. In J. C. Wells & B. L. Stiefel (Eds.), *Human-centered built environment heritage preservation: Theory and evidence-based practice* (pp. 309-316). Routledge.

King, T., & Lyneis, M. M. (1978). Preservation: A developing focus of American archaeology. *American Anthropologist*, 80(4), 873-893.

Levi, D. J. (2005). Does history matter? Perceptions and attitudes toward fake historic architecture and historic preservation. *Journal of Architectural and Planning Research*, 22(2), 149-159.

Mayes, T. (2017, July 21). *Show me the studies! Environmental design research and historic preservation*. National Trust Preservation Leadership Forum. https://forum.savingplaces.org/blogs/tom-mayes/2017/07/21/show-me-the-studies-environmental-design-research-and-historic-preservation.

———. (2018). *Why old places matter: How historic places affect our identity and well-being*. Rowman & Littlefield.

Meeks, S. (2016). *The past and future city: How historic preservation is reviving America's communities*. Island Press.

Michael, V. (2011, December 6). A new LEED for preservation? *Time Tells: Vince Michael on history, preservation, planning and more*. https://vincemichael.wordpress.com/tag/stephanie-meeks/.

Moore, G. T. (1991). Life-span developmental issues in environmental assessment, cognition, and action: Applications to environmental policy, planning, and design. In T. Gärling & G. W. Evans (Eds.)., *Environmental cognition and action: An integrated approach* (pp. 309-332). Oxford University Press.

Murphy, J., Leibowitz, J., & Hudson, A. (2018). Conservation for the long-haul: Protecting cultural and natural resources through financial, legal, and programmatic strategies. In C. A. Brebbia, E. Marco, J. Longhurst, & C. Booth (Eds.), *WIT transactions on ecology and the environment: Sustainable development and planning* (pp. 417-428). WIT Press.

National Trust (UK). (2017). *Places that make us: Research report*.

Otero-Pailos, J. (2007). Conservation cleaning/cleaning conservation. *Future Anterior, 4*(1), iii-viii.

Rapport, A. (2008). Environment-behavior studies: Past, present, and future. *Journal of Architectural and Planning Research, 25*(4), 276-281.

Rodenberg, J., & Wagenaar, P. (2023). Understanding the governance of heritage: A plea for using public administration theories in heritage studies. In J. Rosenberg, P. Wagenaar, & G. J. L. M. Burgers (Eds.), *Calling on the community: Understanding participation in the heritage sector, and interactive governance perspective* (pp. 7-27). Berghahn Books.

Russell, R. (2014). First Pete and then repeat? Fundamental differences in intention between undergraduate and graduate preservation programs in the United States. In B. L. Stiefel & J. C. Wells (Eds.), *Preservation education: Sharing best practices and finding common ground* (pp. 42-56). University Press of New England.

Rypkema, D. (1997). *Preservation and property values in Indiana*. Historic Landmarks Foundation of Indiana.

Sadovnik, A. R. (2017). Qualitative research and public policy. In F. Fischer, G. Miller, & M. S. Sidney (Eds.), *Handbook of public policy analysis* (pp. 443-454). Routledge.

Sektani, H. H. J., Khayat, M., Mohammadi, M., & Roders, A. P. (2021). Erbil City built heritage and wellbeing: An assessment of local perceptions using the semantic differential scale. *Sustainability, 13*(7), Article 3763.

Smith, L. (2000). "Doing Archaeology": Cultural heritage management and its role in identifying the link between archaeological practice and theory. *International Journal of Heritage Studies, 6*(4), 309-316.

Smith, S. R., & Ingram, H. (2002). Rethinking policy analysis: Citizens, community, and the restructuring of public services. *The Good Society, 11*(1), 55-60.

Spicker, P. (2006). *Policy analysis for practice: Applying social policy*. Policy Press.

Uzzell, D. (2009). Where is the discipline in heritage studies: A view from environmental psychology. In M. L. S. Sørensen & J. Carman (Eds.), *Heritage studies: Methods and approaches* (pp. 326-333). Routledge.

Vohra-Gupta, S., Kim, Y., & Cubbin, C. (2021). Systemic racism and the Family Medical Leave Act (FMIA): Using critical race theory to build equitable family leave policies. *Journal of Racial and Ethnic Health Disparities, 8*(4), 1482-1491.

Walker, W. E. (2000). Policy analysis: A systematic approach to supporting policymaking in the public sector. *Journal of Multi-Criteria Decision Analysis, 9*(13), 11-27.

Wells, J. C. (2017). How are old places different from new places? A psychological investigation of the correlation between patina, spontaneous fantasies, and place attachment. *International Journal of Heritage Studies, 23*(5), 445-469.

—— (2018). Challenging the assumption about a direct relationship between historic preservation and architecture in the United States. *Frontiers of Architectural Research*, 7(4), 455–464.

——. (2021a). *10 ways historic preservation policy supports White supremacy and 10 ideas to end It*. University of Maryland, College Park faculty papers. https://doi.org/10.13016/hyo1-8vgp.

——. (2021b). Does intra-disciplinary historic preservation scholarship address the exigent issues of practice? Exploring the character and impact of preservation knowledge production in relation to critical heritage studies, equity, and social justice. *International Journal of Heritage Studies*, 27(5), 449–469.

Wells, J. C., & Baldwin, E. D. (2012). Historic preservation, significance, and age value: A comparative phenomenology of historic Charleston and the nearby new-urbanist community of I'On. Journal of Environmental Psychology, 32(4), 384–400.

Wells, J. C., Chalana, M., Hoffman, S., & Stiefel, B. (2022, February). A summary of preservation education in relation to diversity, inclusion, equity, and social justice and some recommendations: A report by the Equity and Inclusion in Preservation Education Committee of the National Council for Preservation Education. Submitted for publication in *Preservation Education & Research*.

CHAPTER 6

Time for Change

It is a bright morning in August, 2073, and Jimena is in the process of readying herself to perform the role of facilitator as a place conservation manager for the city of Cantamen. As she thinks back over the past decade, and all the residents from her city that she's listened to, empathized with, and, at times, had congenial disagreements, her face glows with appreciation. She really likes what she does. On her way out the door, she looks at herself in the mirror and chuckles softly as she repeats, "I'm a charm manager."

Fifteen years ago, Jimena entered an undergraduate degree program in place-based preservation and conservation. Her coursework, while broadly inclusive of the humanities and the sciences, focused on history, the social sciences (anthropology, sociology, environmental psychology), community-based participatory methods in planning, critical heritage studies, environmental and climate change studies, and public administration. All her courses included readings and lectures by people with traditionally minoritized racial, ethnic, ability, gender, sexual, and religious identities, and she learned to approach her work by first understanding how her identity (Latina, African American) intersected with other people's identities and then identifying and working against her inherent biases. Jimena often thought how grateful she was for her course on intersectionality, which she referenced almost on a daily basis, and especially like today, when she would be coresearching with local residents.

On this day, Jimena was facilitating a community-led process to consider a property owner's application to add a new addition onto her house. While Jimena's municipality had the final say in the approval, this process relied on residents, from the neighborhood in which the property was located, to help research how this change might impact where they lived. All of the participants in this process received training in "learning how to meditate on old places" (otherwise known as a first-person existential phenomenology) to help them understand how they were affected by their neighborhood's environment and to consider how this would change with the proposed addition. Jimena also received this training, which helped complement the information on new "Being Affected by Old Places" (BAOP) research periodically distributed to her by a national advocacy organization. She loved reading about this new research, especially from neurobiology. Cantamen had, many years ago, revised its design guidelines to incorporate BAOP and general principles from environmental design and behavior research from environmental psychologists. Jimena's coresearchers also relied heavily on a community-led report, prepared a few years earlier, that explored and related the history and heritage meanings, perceptions, and values that most residents believed defined where they lived; much of the information in this report came from interviews, storytelling, and observations and was supplemented by archival, factual research.

Jimena remembered that she needed to stop by the childcare facility, provided by the city of Cantamen, on her way to work, to let them know that some of her coresearchers would be needing their help. She was so grateful that the city provided childcare in this way and also paid her coresearchers. Cantamen also set up agreements with some of the local employers to encourage their lower-paid employees to participate as her coresearchers. So many of these efforts made the difference in ensuring the participants represented economic diversity as well as other demographics that helped make the process more equitable. Equitable. Jimena tossed this word around her head and remembered her grandfather.

Back when she was a child, Jimena's grandfather used to tell her stories about how, when he was a historic preservationist (such a strange, archaic term!), working for the city of Cantamen, as staff to the local historic preservation commission, he used to prepare "staff reports," which basically told the volunteers on the commission how they should rule on an application to make changes to a historic property. How strange, she thought, that cities used to have these kinds of commissions to provide the appearance of political independence from the city, yet the city's efforts sure looked a lot like controlling the decisions of the commission members. And, how strange it felt when her grandfather said that all the commission members were White, with master's and doctoral degrees, and were rather well-to-do. How different things were today, in Cantamen.

Back in the 2050s, shortly after the city engaged in a community-based participatory process to explore and rewrite their heritage conservation ordinance, Jimena became one of the first volunteers in the same process that she is helping facilitate, today. It was through this experience that she first really became interested in heritage and, especially, how older places made her feel. She knew, even as a child, that there was something magical about downtown Cantamen and especially the old farms around the town that still had their ancient fields and barns. And, wow, she remembered that when she was eight years old, looking up at a great, old oak tree, how she felt so much in awe, she shuddered. She remembered trying, and failing, to encircle the trunk with her little arms. She remembered her reverence in believing the tree was like a long-lost great, great grandparent embracing her with its massive canopy. Old things were truly magical.

But, as much as Cantamen has magical places, it also has places with very dark histories, where terrible things had happened—like the former slave labor camps. No one calls or thinks of these places as "magical," but they still have power, and they still stoke the imagination. And one of Jimena's greatest memories, in working for Cantamen, was when she facilitated a project to consider what to do with some of these city-owned properties. Her coresearchers, in this case, chose to let these places stand and serve as appropriate emotional reminders and not be used for weddings. The interpretive programs that the community members created, including a group of 15-year-olds, were just amazing, especially in their ability to make people *feel*. Jimena remembered her grandfather telling her that, in his day, the primary objective of a museum or historic site was to "educate," which ignored most of the reasons people went to these places. Today, in 2073, everyone knows that historic sites are places where you go to *feel, experience,* and, especially, to *empathize*.

CHANGE MAKERS

This view into a hypothetical future, in which Jimena, a local city employee who is functionally equivalent to a local preservation planner, today, exemplifies most of the major concepts explored in this book. While I make no claims as to the accuracy of this future, it does demonstrate the possibilities in moving beyond orthodox built heritage conservation doctrine and policy. And, more than anything else, it shows that the job of future "historic preservationists" should not be to educate the public on the nature of reality. Instead, the work of this nascent professional should be to *understand* reality from the perspective of the public, and in the process, embrace local knowledge. This does not mean that future practitioners, and the policy which leads them, should be subservient to the wishes of the public, but rather, there needs to be a balance between the experienced reality of conventional experts and civil experts. In the interest of participatory democracy, the field needs to be engaging in discussions today on how to achieve this balance in order to create a better and more relevant future.

The changes, exemplified in the story of Jimena, may seem overly ambitious and idealistic, but there is a reason why they are within the context of a local municipality, which has to do with the way the US Constitution is structured. According to the tenth amendment of the Constitution, all powers not explicitly granted to the federal government are given to the states, which means that the states have the full and unique authority to regulate private property (Coyle, 1993). And, in the few states that are non-Dillon's Rule states, local municipalities do not need to seek state approval through enabling legislation to create their own local built heritage conservation policy (e.g., ordinance and guidelines); these are, in effect, states that allow "home rule" (Richardson, Gough, & Puentes, 2023). For the most part, these municipalities only need be concerned that their ordinances do not violate the US or their state's constitution. This would readily position municipalities, in these non-Dillon's Rule states, to be creative in how they might implement a local built heritage conservation program, yet this has never happened. Time and time again, in the past fifty years, as local municipalities have created their preservation ordinances, they chose to duplicate federal historic preservation policy, rather than implement public policy that represented their local residents' values and needs (Avrami, Leo, & Sanchez, 2018; Bronin & Irwin, 2023).

The ideas presented in this book provide a ready source of potential inspiration for these kinds of local municipalities to lead the United States to crafting the first people- and human-centered built heritage conservation ordinances and corresponding policies. In addition, there are Dillon's Rule states that allow certain municipalities to have home rule (e.g., Colorado,

Maryland, South Dakota) and that also have similar potentials in crafting their own version of local built heritage conservation policy. Of all the local municipalities in the United States, perhaps the one closest to this vision of crafting its own locally-contextual ordinance is the home rule city of Santa Fe, NM. In an insightful investigation, Sara Casten (2020) explains that Santa Fe crafted its first preservation ordinance in 1957, prior to the passage of the National Historic Preservation Act (NHPA). As a result, the local preservation policy that developed was unique to this city and its design guidelines, which emphasized an "adobe" aesthetic, were antithetical to the later federal policy (e.g., Secretary of the Interior's Standards). Indeed, the National Park Service (NPS) repeatedly threatened to withdraw Santa Fe's Certified Local Government status unless it changed its design guidelines to be compliant with federal policy; to date, this has not happened. But, Santa Fe's example does provide yet more evidence of the hegemony of federal preservation policy at all levels of government in the United States.

Change at the federal level in the United States is substantially more challenging. Of all the federal agencies that have influence over federal preservation policy, the NPS has the most, primarily because of its primary influence over the National Register of Historic Places, the Secretary of the Interior's Standards, the Secretary of the Interior Professional Qualifications Standards, its Preservation Briefs and National Register Bulletins, and the Certified Local Government system. But, the NPS is highly resistant to change for a number of important reasons. Anna Christina Mills (2014) performed an illuminating analysis of the NPS's work culture, based on interviews of NPS employees, which came to the following conclusions about this agency:

- A work culture defined by "fear of change" that reinforces static, positivistic thinking while rejecting "dynamic complexity";
- Employees, and especially leadership, are highly "risk adverse" and often "defer to others";
- Employees are consistently punished and denied advancement if they have engaged in risk-taking that did not go well;
- Poor communication between staff and leadership and between internal units; "highly siloed" culture and many "turf wars";
- All power in the NPS is centered in Washington, DC, in older employees (i.e., 30+ years of NPS employment) who are "disconnected from new ideas and practice";

- Internal NPS policy "stifles change"; there is a pervasive "perceived lack of a need for new policy."

This characterization of the NPS as resistant to change has apparently defined this agency for many decades. According to a 2001 report by the NPS Advisory Board, the NPS was criticized for being "a sleeping giant. Beloved and respected, yes. But perhaps too cautious, too resistant to change, too reluctant to engage the challenges that must be addressed in the 21st century." All these factors may be why, today, the NPS remains resistant to consider changing federal preservation policy, much less starting discussions on this need. To give the NPS credit, however, its recent work has increased a focus on how groups, long marginalized because of their racial, ethnic, gender, and sexual identities, can be better represented in the National Register and in its interpretive programs in the parks. While this focus on representation is sorely needed, the NPS is still resistant to conversations on the structural issues in its policies that continue to create social justice issues.

Many positive changes in federal preservation policy can be implemented, internally, in the NPS through subtle changes in its guidelines, which is a substantially easier task than rulemaking and certainly does not require the US Congress to be involved. For instance, many social justice advocates have pointed out that the way the NPS interprets its requirements for historical integrity in National Register nominations and in the determination of eligibility (especially critical for Section 106 review) is prejudicial against vernacular buildings and landscapes that are prone to many more modifications, over time, than are high-style buildings (Bronin, 2021; Roberts, 2019; Ryberg-Webster, 2020). But, a "fix" for this issue could be deceptively simple: The guidelines for preparing a National Register nomination (e.g., NPS, 1997) instruct preparers that they cannot make an argument for historical integrity only around the elements of "feeling" and "association," which do not require a direct relationship with historic fabric. By simply removing the few words in its guidelines that present this directive, much of the social justice issues around historical integrity issues in the United States could be largely eliminated, and without even needing to go through a rulemaking process. (For reference, the US Administrative Procedure Act requires that changes to *regulations* need to go through a public process; guidelines are not addressed in this act.) Similarly, while the names of the four criteria for historical significance are part of a regulation, the ways in which these criteria are defined are part of the NPS's guidelines and are much easier to change because, as guidance, they are not normally subject to the rulemaking process. Redefining what the four criteria are is a process that is highly amenable to the participatory methods outlined in chapter 4.

The Advisory Council on Historic Preservation (ACHP) is another federal agency with significant influence over federal preservation policy, primarily in regard to how Section 106 of the NHPA is implemented. Much of what is in 36 CFR 800 (the implementing regulations of Section 106) is beyond the direct control of the ACHP and highly referent to the NPS—specifically the National Register of Historic Places and its criteria for eligibility, which limits some of its influence. But, via the NHPA, the ACHP is officially charged to "recommend the conduct of studies in such areas as the adequacy of legislative and administrative statutes and regulations pertaining to historic preservation activities of State and local governments," which, to date, has not really been its focus. When Sara Bronin was the Chair of the ACHP, she began a focus on the power of policy research, which looked like a step in fulfilling the ACHP's directive. As of 2025, it is unknown if this will continue, however.

There are three national advocacy organizations that could also play an important role in advocating for people- and human-centered changes to federal preservation policy: the National Trust for Historic Preservation, Preservation Action, and the National Conference of State Historic Preservation Officers (NCSHPO). For decades, their advocacy has primarily focused on supporting existing federal historic preservation policy, especially as it relates to funding and the availability of financial incentives, such as fully funding the Historic Preservation Fund (as was promised in the NHPA) and keeping and/or strengthening the Federal Rehabilitation Tax Credit. More recently, this advocacy has also focused on increasing representation in the field through grant funding. Some examples in this latter case are funds for organizations to prepare National Register nominations that focus on the contributions of people with minoritized identities, improving interpretive programs, and funding the administrative costs of organizations who do this work.

But, even though the US National Trust recently created its vision for "Preservation for the People" (Meeks, 2017), none of these organizations have publicly embraced policy *change* that addresses people- or human-centered built heritage conservation, nor have they lobbied Congress for such changes. Similarly, the Preservation Caucus of the US House of Representatives represents the legislative interests of the federal government in historic preservation. Consisting of 74 members, including two cochairs, its legislative agenda is largely set by the work of the National Trust, Preservation Action, and NCSHPO, which means that at each yearly session of Congress, the focus of the Caucus is on funding and financial incentives and not on meaningful policy change. Clearly, all these entities have the potential for supporting people- and human-centered preservation/conservation, which is sorely needed to address the social justice issues that have been identified in this book.

Lastly, the role of higher education in creating future practitioners who understand BAOP and the need for people- and human-centered preservation/conservation should not be underestimated. In many ways, the students entering degree programs, today, will be the ones who actually will be able to make many of the needed policy changes explored in this book. But, as a former educator in four historic preservation degree programs in the United States, including an experience directing such a program at the graduate level, I see significant issues here, as well, that need to be addressed.

The largest issue for historic preservation degree programs is their severe lack of racial and ethnic representation in their students and faculty. According to the US Department of Education, most students in historic preservation degree and certificate programs are White/ non-Latinx; between July 1, 2019, and June 30, 2020, students in these programs identified as 0.7% American Indian, 1.9% Asian, 1.0% African American, and 4.1% Hispanic or Latino. In comparison, in 2021, the US population identified as 0.7% American Indian, 4.8% Asian, 12.3% African American, 16.4% Hispanic or Latino, and 1.8% multiracial.[1] In addition, based on my own (unpublished) research in which I analyzed course syllabi, there are very few authors and guest speakers with minoritized racial and ethnic identities represented

---

1. https://usafacts.org/data/topics/people-society/population-and-demographics/our-changing-population?endDate=2021-01-01&startDate=2010-01-01.

in historic preservation courses. Simiiarly, the racial and ethnic identities of faculty in these programs are less diverse than the students' identities (Wells, 2021). Much like orthodox historic preservation doctrine (see chapter 3), students and faculty in historic preservation degree programs exclude the perspectives and, especially, lived experiences outside of the dominant racial group.

More troubling is that, of the tenure-track faculty in these programs who have more than a 50% teaching appointment, only 2.0% of faculty have published research on topics related to community engagement, and only 6.8% have published on topics related to diversity, inclusion, equity, or social justice; less than 1% have published on policy change (Wells, 2021). And, 48.3% of *tenured* faculty in these programs have five scholarly publications or less (Wells, 2021). In terms of disciplinary background, most historic preservation faculty do not have degrees in historic preservation and self-identify primarily as architects, architectural historians, and (processual) archaeologists. A minority self-identify with planning or the social sciences. Based on this research, a picture emerges of the majority of tenure-track historic preservation faculty teaching in degree programs who are disconnected from the discipline's on-the-ground practice and the gains in people- and human-centered research in the field; this issue is compounded by the fact that many of these faculty fail to engage in scholarly research that would inform them about these topics.

In terms of curricula, there appears to be no historic preservation degree programs that require coursework in public policy, policy research/analysis, environmental psychology, or action research. In assembling this evidence, innovation, as it applies to policy change in historic preservation, is happening outside of the historic preservation discipline. This work is being undertaken largely by planners, anthropologists, and humanities and public administration specialists who do not have a teaching appointment to a historic preservation program (e.g., Adams & Edges, 2021; Aidoo, 2020; Brown, 2020; Cheong, 2021; Roberts, 2019; Samuels, 2018). And, these faculty are far more diverse, in terms of racial and ethnic identities, than tenure-track faculty in historic preservation programs. The natural conclusion is that without significant institutional changes, existing historic preservation programs are not going to be able to produce graduates who will lead policy change in the field. Others will likely take this mantle, instead. And, who might these "others" be?

Perhaps, based on this situation, in higher education, the logical answer to advancing policy change is to accept the need for specialization. Existing historic preservation degree programs, and their faculty emphasis on art/historical facts and materials conservation, should continue to provide this specialization to the approximately 20% of the historic preservation field in which this work occurs (Wells, 2018). For the 70% of the field which is driven by policy, existing degree programs in urban and regional planning and public administration should then take up the mantle of embracing and teaching people- and human-centered built heritage conservation. No such programs, exist, today, but why not? Awareness could go a long way toward gaining interest from these disciplines. Again, looking through the evidence, what other conclusion seems reasonable?

MOVING FORWARD

Table 6.1 summarizes the essential five major problems and five potential solutions for built heritage doctrine and policy that this book has explored, which are organized under the themes of lived experience, inclusion, practice, politics, and education. As one of the first voices in this space, I want to emphasize that these are, in many ways, inchoate ideas that need to be explored, discussed, and critiqued by academics, practitioners, policymakers, and the public. My hope is that this book has served its primary purpose, and that is to catalyze thinking about change in orthodox built heritage doctrine and policy, especially in the United States. I patiently await others to join this space and help the field move forward in a way that maximizes public benefit.

I want to conclude this book with a quote from the preamble of the US National Historic Preservation Act of 1966, which reminds us about the reasons why historic preservation is in the public interest:

> The historical and cultural foundations of the Nation should be preserved as a living part of our community life and development in order to give a sense of orientation to the American people. . . . The preservation of this irreplaceable heritage is in the public interest so that its vital legacy of cultural, educational, aesthetic, inspirational, economic, and energy benefits will be maintained and enriched for future generations of Americans.

What should strike the reader is how, in 1966, the nation's political leaders were already thinking in terms of how old places could contribute, in the

TABLE 6.1. Changing orthodox doctrine and policy: Five problems and five potential solutions

Category	Problem	Potential solution
Lived experience	No recognition of BAOP	Informing doctrine and policy with environmental psychology research that focuses on the person–patina relationship; participatory phenomenology ("old place meditation")
Inclusion	Voices of people with nondominant racial and ethnic identities were not part of creation of orthodox doctrine and policy	Inclusive, community-based participatory processes (e.g., action research) to inform doctrine and policy
Practice	Authorized heritage discourse	Recognition of civil experts and local knowledge in informing doctrine and policy
Politics	Policy stagnation	NPS needs to overcome its work culture; advocacy organizations need to make good on their "people-centered" promises and inform Preservation Caucus
Education	Educational stagnation	Specialization within historic preservation degree programs; assimilation of policy specialization (majority of practice) within regional and urban planning and public administration programs

present, to a living heritage and how built heritage should be leveraged for its "inspirational" benefits. More than fifty years after these words were written, federal preservation policy has not yet achieved these aspirations. Managing the magic of old places is one potential way to fulfill these promises.

Works Cited

Adams, A. C., & Edges, A. C. (2021). Advancing underrepresented preservation webs: A cross-case analysis for African American historic site planning. *Great Plains Research*, 31(1), 35-56.

Aidoo, F. (2020). The community foundations of allyship in preservation: Lessons from West Mount Airy, Philadelphia. In Avrami, E. (Ed.), *Preservation and social inclusion* (pp. 157-174). Columbia University Press.

Avrami, E., Leo, C.-N., & Sanchez, A. S. (2018). Confronting exclusion: Redefining the intended outcomes of historic preservation. *Change Over Time: International Journal of Conservation and the Built Environment*, 8(1), 102-120.

Bronin, S. C. (2021). Integrity as a legal concept. *Change Over Time: International Journal of Conservation and the Built Environment*, 10(2), 108-121.

Bronin, S. C., & Irwin, L. R. (2023). Regulating history. *Minnesota Law Review*, 108(1), 241-331.

Brown, M. A. (2020). Preservation's expanded field: The Hacking Heritage Unconference and the Fogarty Funeral. In S. Smulyan (Ed.), *Doing public humanities*. Routledge.

Casten, S. C. (2020). Santa Fe, "the city different": A brief look at preservation. University of Vermont. https://www.uvm.edu/histpres/HPJ/casten/SantaFe.htm.

Cheong, C. (2021). Preservation at a crossroads: The need for equity preservation. *Change Over Time: International Journal of Conservation and the Built Environment, 10*(1), 66–83.

Coyle, D. J. (1993). *Property rights and the constitution: Shaping society through land use regulation.* State University of New York Press.

Meeks, S. (2017, May 18). Presenting "Preservation for the people: A vision for the future." Preservation Leadership Forum, National Trust for Historic Preservation. https://forum.savingplaces.org/blogs/stephanie-k-meeks/2017/05/18/presenting-preservation-for-people-a-vision-for-the-future.

Mills, A. C. (2014). The US National Park Service: Organizational adaptation in an era of complexity, uncertainty, and change [Master's thesis, University of Montana]. https://scholarworks.umt.edu/cgi/viewcontent.cgi?article=5239&context=etd&httpsredir=1&referer=

National Park Service (NPS). (1997). *National Register bulletin: How to apply the National Register criteria for evaluation.* US Department of the Interior.

National Park Service Advisory Board. (2001). Rethinking the national parks for the 21st century. US Department of the Interior, National Park Service. https://www.nps.gov/subjects/policy/upload/Rethinking-the-National-Parks-for-the-21st-Century-2001.pdf.

Richardson, J. J., Gough, M. Z., & Puentes, R. (2023). Is home rule the answer? Clarifying the influence of Dillon's Rule on growth management. Brookings Institution Center on Urban and Metropolitan Policy.

Roberts, A. R. (2019). "Until the Lord come get me, burn it down, or the next storm blow it away": The aesthetics of freedom in African American vernacular homestead preservation. *Buildings & Landscapes: Journal of the Vernacular Architecture Forum, 26*(2), 73–97.

Ryberg-Webster, S. (2020). Toward an inclusive preservation: Lessons from Cleveland. In E. Avrami (Ed.), *Preservation and social inclusion* (pp. 23–34). Columbia University Press.

Samuels, K. S. (2018). *Mobilizing heritage.* University Press of Florida.

Wells, J. C. (2018). Challenging the assumption about a direct relationship between historic preservation and architecture in the United States. *Frontiers of Architectural Research, 7*(4), 455–464.

———. (2021). Does intra-disciplinary historic preservation scholarship address the exigent issues of practice? Exploring the character and impact of preservation knowledge production in relation to critical heritage studies, equity, and social justice. *International Journal of Heritage Studies, 27*(5), 449–469.

APPENDIX A

Authors of Built Heritage Conservation Doctrine (Sorted by Year of Birth)

This appendix is a comprehensive list of all the individuals who created key European and American preservation doctrines and public policies over the past 200 years, as referenced in chapter 3. In addition to their names and dates of birth and death, each person's education, expertise, area of influence, and contributions are noted. Lastly, any documented racial or ethnic bias, by a particular individual, is briefly described. Refer to chapter 3 for the methodology used to assemble this list.

(BEGINS ON FOLLOWING PAGE)

APPENDIX A

Last	First	Gender identity	Racial identity	Birth/death	Nationality	Education	Expertise	University professor?
Carter	John	man	White	1748–1817	England	Architectural apprenticeship	Architecture	
Didron	Adolphe Napoleon	man	White	1806–1867	France	Studied law, but later completed seminary studies at Meaux and Reims	Archaeology	
Bourassé	Jean-Jacques	man	White	1813–1872	France	Ecclesiastical studies in Paris	Archaeology	Professor
Viollet-le-Duc	Eugène Emmanuel	man	White	1814–1879	France	Graduate of the College de Bourbon	Architecture	
Ruskin	John	man	White	1819–1900	England	Degrees from Christ Church, Oxford, and King's College, London	Art critic	
Morris	William	man	White	1834–1896	England	Studied classics at Oxford University	Architecture	
Lubbock	John	man	White	1834–1913	England	Studied mathematics at Cambridge University	Politics	

Doctrine or policy contribution	Area of influence	Influence	Documented racial or ethnic bias	Source(s) that establish the influence of this individual
	Method	Influential and early proponent of preservation over restoration as a treatment.		Jokilehto (1999)
	Method	Well known for his recommendation that "regarding ancient monuments, it is better to consolidate than to repair, better to repair than to restore, better to restore than to rebuild, better to rebuild than to embellish; in no case must anything be added and, above all, nothing should be removed"; the early National Park Service often quoted this passage as policy for how historic buildings should be treated.		Jokilehto (1999)
	Method	Published works that theorized about the degree and extent to which restoration is acceptable.		Jokilehto (1999)
	Method	While initially respected in the nineteenth century by many architects for his theory on restoration, his perspective on "scraping" back later layers of building fabric was increasingly vilified throughout the early twentieth century; as such, his work is often used as the "bad" or "improper" foil for Ruskin's imperative to preserve as found.	Viollet-le-Duc wrote, "The human races are not equal and, to speak only of the two extremes, it is obvious that the White races that have covered Europe for three thousand years are infinitely superior to the Negro races that have lived since time immemorial in a large part of Africa" (Ramey, 2014, p. 23).	Jokilehto (1999); Lee (1950)
	Method	Established the foundation for the widely accepted way the older built environment is valued for its age and for how buildings should be properly treated to preserve their authenticity.	Ruskin defended the enslavement of African peoples and expressed racist attitudes toward Indian people (Arthur, 2001; Brantlinger, 1996).	Jokilehto (1999); Lee (1950)
	Method	Author of the Repair of Ancient Buildings, which helped translate the theory of the SPAB Manifesto into practice; significant contributor in writing the Athens Charter.	Nora Hanagan (2019) explains that the Arts and Crafts Movement led by Morris was, in part, designed to reify White supremacy; Morris, in particular, wrote pejoratively about Chinese culture.	Jokilehto (1999)
Ancient Monuments Act of 1882	Policy	Sir John Lubbock introduced the Bill for Parliament that created the Ancient Monuments Act of 1882.		Jokilehto (1999)

Last	First	Gender identity	Racial identity	Birth/death	Nationality	Education	Expertise	University professor?
Boito	Camillo	man	White	1836–1914	Italy	Studied at the Accademia di Belle Arti di Venezia	Architecture	Professor
Colvin	Sidney	man	White	1845–1927	England	Educated at Trinity College, Cambridge	Art critic	Professor
Bacchelli	Giuseppe	man	White	1849–1914	Italy	Bachelor's degree (lauria)	Politics	
Cloquet	Louis	man	White	1849–1920	Belgium	University education as a civil engineer	Architecture	Professor
Beltrami	Luca	man	White	1854–1933	Italy	Studied at Politecnico in Milan and Brera Academy	Architecture	
Dunning	William Archibald	man	White	1857–1922	USA	PhD in history from Columbia University	History	Professor
Riegl	Alois	man	White	1857–1905	Austria	Studied philosophy and history at the University of Vienna	Art history	
Lethaby	William Richard	man	White	1857–1931	England	Studied at the Barnstaple Art School	Architecture	Professor
Boni	Giacomo	man	White	1859–1925	Italy	Studied architecture at the Accademia di Belle Arti	Archaeology	
Harcourt-Smith	Cecil	man	White	1859–1944	England	Studied at Winchester College	Archaeology	
Horta	Victor Pierre	man	White	1861–1947	Belgium	Studied at the Royal Academy of Fine Arts in Brussels	Architecture	Professor
Destrée	Jules	man	White	1863–1936	France	PhD in Law from the Université Libre de Bruxelles	Law	

APPENDIX A

Doctrine or policy contribution	Area of influence	Influence	Documented racial or ethnic bias	Source(s) that establish the influence of this individual
	Method	Architect who published ideas on how government should implement a preservation/conservation policy, which became a standard reference; promoted a philosophical approach to interventions that emphasized careful objectivity.		Jokilehto (1999)
	Method	Colvin summarized and refined Ruskin's ideas on preservation and anti-restoration.		Jokilehto (1999)
	Method	Politician who published Giú le mani! dai nostri monumenti antichi ("hands off from our antique monuments") in 1910. Promoted scientific restoration/conservation.		Jokilehto (1999)
	Method	Cloquet presented his theories on the appropriate treatments of "dead" and "living" monuments to the International Congress of European and American architects in Madrid in 1904.		Jokilehto (1999)
	Method	Protégé of Camillo Boito; widely published architect who promoted the need for the scientific documentation of buildings to accurately restore them.		Jokilehto (1999)
	Method	Helped normalize historical positivism in public history and, by extension, historic preservation.	White supremacist (Smith & Lowery, 2013; Soleim, 2021).	Soleim (2021)
	Method	Created and published the first systematic analysis of heritage values.		Jokilehto (1999)
	Method	Leader of SPAB and widely published the views/beliefs from this organization's manifesto.		Jokilehto (1999)
	Method	Published extensively on maintaining the authenticity of historic buildings and on scientific principles for conservation.		Jokilehto (1999)
Athens Charter	Doctrines	Significant contributor to the Athens Charter using his expertise in museums and archaeology.		Jokilehto (1999)
Athens Charter	Doctrines	With Giovannoni, Horta argued to expand the scope of the Athens Charter from single monuments to places/landscapes.		Allais (2018)
Athens Charter	Doctrines	Chaired the meeting in Athens in 1931 that produced the Athens Charter.		Jokilehto (1999)

Last	First	Gender identity	Racial identity	Birth/death	Nationality	Education	Expertise	University professor?
Croce	Benedetto	man	White	1866–1952	Italy	Studied law at the University of Naples	Philosophy	
Balanos	Nikolaos	man	White	1869–1943	Greece	Studied at the Ecole Nationale des Ponts et Chaussées	Architecture	
Goodwin	William Archer Rutherford	man	White	1869–1939	USA	Divinity degree from Virginia Theological Seminary	History	
Merriam	John Campbell	man	White	1869–1945	USA	PhD, University of Munich	Paleontology	Professor
Wissler	Clark	man	White	1870–1947	USA	Doctoral degree in psychology from Columbia University	Archaeology	Professor
Giovannoni	Gustavo	man	White	1873–1947	Italy	University degrees in civil engineering and public hygiene	Architecture	Professor
Léon	Paul	man	White	1874–1962	France	Studied at the Lycée Condorcet	Architectural history	Professor
Appleton	William Sumner	man	White	1874–1947	USA	Graduate of Harvard College	Architecture	
Chierici	Gino	man	White	1877–1961	Italy	Graduate studies at the Royal Institute of Fine Arts in Bologna	Architecture	Professor

APPENDIX A   227

Doctrine or policy contribution	Area of influence	Influence	Documented racial or ethnic bias	Source(s) that establish the influence of this individual
	Method	Created a theory of aesthetics based on Hegel/gestalt psychology that guided later ideas by Italian critical theorists.		Jokilehto (1999)
Athens Charter	Doctrines	Significant contributor to the Athens Charter on theories related to anastylosis; used this technique in the controversial restoration of the Parthenon.		Allais (2018); Jokilehto (1999)
	Method	Originator of the idea of Colonial Williamsburg and its approach to building interventions and interpretations.		Jokilehto (1999)
National Register of Historic Places	Policy	Former head of the Carnegie Institution (DC); Chair of the NPS Advisory Board on National Parks, Historic Sites, Buildings and Monuments in the early 1930s where he helped develop early policies that led to the National Register.	When he was head of the Carnegie Institution, Merriam substantially increased funding to the Eugenics Record Office.	Lee (1950)
National Register of Historic Places	Method	As a member of the NPS Advisory Board, Wissler developed the thematic framework approach that was eventually adopted in the National Register process.	Wissler was a "blatant racist" who helped the US Government to turn away victims of the Nazi genocide (Shapiro, 2010).	Sprinkle (2014)
Athens Charter	Doctrines	A proponent of Boito, he was an influential founder of the "scientific" method for restoration/conservation with a broad focus, including less significant buildings and urban landscapes; a significant contributor to the 1931 Athens Charter.	Member of the steering committee of the Institute of Roman Studies that promoted fascism (Aramini, 2020).	Allais (2018); Jokilehto (1999)
Athens Charter	Doctrines	Contributed his expertise in the history of monumental arts to the writing of the Athens Charter.		Allais (2018); Jokilehto (1999)
	Method	Translated concepts from SPAB, the English National Trust, the French Monuments Historiques, and the Skansen open-air museum in Stockholm to a US context through his work as the founder of the Society for the Preservation of New England Antiquities. Promoted scientific restoration/preservation.	Appleton was a documented eugenicist who used historic sites associated with northern Europeans to "prove" that White culture was superior to others (Lindgren, 1996).	Hosmer (1965); Jokilehto (1999)
	Method	Proponent of scientific restoration/conservation.		Jokilehto (1999)

APPENDIX A

Last	First	Gender identity	Racial identity	Birth/death	Nationality	Education	Expertise	University professor?
Leland	Waldo Gifford	man	White	1879–1966	USA	BA from Brown University; MS in history from Harvard University	History	
Powys	Albert Reginald	man	White	1881–1936	England	Studied at the Regent Street Polytechnic	Architecture	
Perry	William Graves	man	White	1883–1975	USA	Undergrad degree from Harvard, architecture degree from MIT and L'Ecole des Beaux Arts	Architecture	
Morison	Samuel Eliot	man	White	1887–1976	USA	PhD in history from Harvard University	History	Professor
Kimball	Sidney Fiske	man	White	1888–1955	USA	Bachelor's and master's degrees in architecture from Harvard University	Architecture	

APPENDIX A 229

Doctrine or policy contribution	Area of influence	Influence	Documented racial or ethnic bias	Source(s) that establish the influence of this individual
National Register of Historic Places	Policy	Chair of 1948 report from the National Council for Historic Sites and Buildings (precursor to the National Trust) that helped to establish the basic criteria—especially architectural—that became incorporated into the National Register; Chairman of the Advisory Board of the NPS from 1935 to mid-1950s where he led efforts to establish historical/architectural significance and integrity criteria used in the NPS.		Sprinkle (2014)
Athens Charter	Doctrines	Author of the Repair of Ancient Buildings, which helped translate the theory of the SPAB Manifesto into practice; significant contributor in writing the Athens Charter.		Jokilehto (1999)
	Method	Lead architect at Colonial Williamsburg; extensively published on his theoretical observations.		Jokilehto (1999)
	Method	Morison was the author of The Growth of the American Republic (1930), one of the most influential books on American history through the mid-century. It would have likely been a core textbook for courses on American history, which mid-twentieth-century preservationists would have used to establish the process of documenting the historical significance of buildings and places.	Morison expressed consistent racial bias in his writings toward people of African descent, especially in relation to their enslavement. Morison's work is considered to be part of the "Phillips school" of slavery historiography, named after Ulrich Bonnell Phillips (1877-1934) and noted for its benign or positive portrayal of slavery in American history (Gilmore, 1978). The NAACP publicly called out Morison's bias in his textbook in 1944 (Jumonville 1999, p. 147).	Zimmerman (2004)
National Register of Historic Places	Method	Prominent architect who helped create Colonial Williamsburg and consulted on the restoration of Monticello, Gunston Hall, and Stratford Hall; contributed to theories on differentiating old and new building fabric. Most active member of the Advisory Board on National Parks, Historic Sites, Buildings (NPS) in the 1930s, where he helped shaped policy that would form the foundation for the National Register.		Hosmer (1965); Jokilehto (1999); Sprinkle (2014)

APPENDIX A

Last	First	Gender identity	Racial identity	Birth/death	Nationality	Education	Expertise	University professor?
Balbás	Leopoldo Torres	man	White	1888–1960	Spain	Architecture degree from Higher School of Architecture in Madrid	Architecture	
Collingwood	Robin George	man	White	1889–1943	England	Degree in the classics from University College, Oxford	History	Professor
Benjamin	Walter	man	White	1892–1940	Germany	Studied at the University of Berlin	Philosophy	
Newsome	Albert Ray	man	White	1894–1951	USA	PhD in History from the University of Michigan	Public history	Professor
Chatelain	Vern	man	White	1895–1991	USA	Doctoral degree in history from University of Minnesota	History	Professor
Schneider	John Thomas	man	White	1895–1976	USA	Graduate of Harvard Law School	Law	
Pane	Roberto	man	White	1897–1987	Italy	Graduate of the University of Rome	Art history	Professor
Plenderleith	Harold James	man	White	1898–1997	Scotland	Doctoral degree in chemistry from University College, Dundee	Art conservation	Professor
Kieslinger	Alois	man	White	1900–1975	Austria	Doctoral degree from the University of Vienna	Geology	Professor

APPENDIX A   231

Doctrine or policy contribution	Area of influence	Influence	Documented racial or ethnic bias	Source(s) that establish the influence of this individual
Athens Charter	Doctrines	Curator and Chief Architect in charge of the conservation of Alhambra who contributed his expertise on scientific restoration to help write the Athens Charter.		Jokilehto (1999)
	Method	Influential historian who promoted historical positivism (i.e., doing history "scientifically").		Jokilehto (1999)
	Method	Published on ways to maintain the authenticity of older buildings, especially in relation to the differences between the original and a copy.		Jokilehto (1999)
	Method	First President of the Society of American Archivists (1936-1939); influenced development of local history techniques.		Soleim (2021)
National Register of Historic Places	Policy	As first Chief Historian of the NPS, developed and implemented policies used in the Historic Sites Survey in the 1930s; created the basic framework for historical significance later adopted for the National Register.		Sprinkle (2014)
National Register of Historic Places	Policy	Normalized basing NPS preservation policy on European precedents through his report on The Preservation of Historic Sites and Buildings (1935); chapter 3 in this book contained a recommended bill for Congress to introduce that included many of the ideas originally adopted in the 1966 National Historic Preservation Act.		Mackintosh (1986); Sprinkle (2014)
Venice Charter	Doctrines	Proponent of Giovannoni's scientific restoration and of "critical restoration," which respected all layers of fabric in a building; expert in the art of the Renaissance and regional monuments in Italy; coauthor of the Venice Charter.		Jokilehto (1999)
Venice Charter	Doctrines	Plenderleith was the first director of ICCROM; coauthor of the Venice Charter.		Jokilehto (1999)
Athens Charter	Doctrines	Kieslinger specialized in the decay of stones used in monuments and contributed this expertise to the drafting of the Athens Charter.	Kieslinger is documented as assisting the Nazi regime in operating the quarry at the Mauthausen concentration camp (Mertz, 2020) during WWII.	Allais (2018)

Last	First	Gender identity	Racial identity	Birth/death	Nationality	Education	Expertise	University professor?
Zachwatovicz	Jan	man	White	1900–1983	Poland	Architecture degree from the Warsaw University of Technology	Architecture	Professor
Rains	Albert McKinley	man	White	1902–1991	USA	Law degree from the University of Alabama	Politics	
Crittenden	Charles Christopher	man	White	1902–1969	USA	PhD in History from Yale University	Public history	Professor
Benavente	Luis	man	White	1902–1993	Portugal	Architecture degree from Escola de Belas Artes do Porto	Architecture	
Pavel	Jakub	man	White	1903–1974	Czechoslovakia	Graduate of the Univerzity Karlovy	History	
Boskovic	Djurdje	man	White	1904–1990	Yugoslavia	Architecture degree from the University of Belgrade	Architecture	Professor
Bannister	Turpin Chambers	man	White	1904–1982	USA	Master's degree from Columbia University; PhD from Harvard University	Architectural history	Professor
Kahler	Herbert E.	man	White	1904–1993	USA	Degree from the University of Minnesota	History	

APPENDIX A   233

Doctrine or policy contribution	Area of influence	Influence	Documented racial or ethnic bias	Source(s) that establish the influence of this individual
Venice Charter	Doctrines	Codirector of the Warsaw Reconstruction Office; Coauthor of the Venice Charter.		Jokilehto (1999)
National Register of Historic Places	Policy	Rains was a congressman who served in the US House of Representatives from 1945 to 1965, representing Alabama's fifth district; he was the chairman of the Special Housing Subcommittee, where he used his influence to push for the introduction of a bill that became the National Historic Preservation Act of 1966; Rains led the special committee that resulted in the publication of the book With Heritage So Rich, which he coauthored with Laurence G. Henderson and which contains the text that was included in the Preservation Act.	Rains vigorously supported segregation and the annihilation of Native Americans while opposing public school integration; he saw preservation as a tool for supporting Southern White supremacy (Haeuser, 2018).	Glass (1990); Mackintosh (1986)
	Method	Founder and first President of the American Association for State and Local History; helped create the National Trust for Historic Preservation; significant contributor to historical research methods relevant to public history.		Soleim (2021)
Venice Charter	Doctrines	Benavente was the Director of Monuments in Portugal and a restoration architect; coauthor of the Venice Charter; founding member of ICOMOS.		Jokilehto (1999)
Venice Charter	Doctrines	Proponent of historic cities; founding member of ICOMOS; coauthor of the Venice Charter.		Jokilehto (1999)
Venice Charter	Doctrines	Expert in medieval architecture; coauthor of the Venice Charter.		Jokilehto (1999)
National Register of Historic Places	Policy	Significant contributor to 1948 report from the National Council for Historic Sites and Buildings (precursor to the National Trust) that helped to establish the basic criteria—especially architectural—that became incorporated into the National Register; preeminent architectural historian of his era.		Sprinkle (2014)
National Register of Historic Places	Policy	As Chief Historian of the NPS, he led the effort to develop the seven aspects of integrity which were eventually incorporated into the National Register.		Sprinkle (2014)

APPENDIX A

Last	First	Gender identity	Racial identity	Birth/death	Nationality	Education	Expertise	University professor?
Finley	John Huston, Jr.	man	White	1904-1995	USA	Bachelor's and doctoral degrees from Harvard University	Classics	Professor
Lee	Ronald F.	man	White	1905-1972	USA	Undergraduate and graduate degrees in history from University of Minnesota	History	
de Campos	Deoclecio Redig	man	Latin American	1905-1989	Brazil	University studies in art history in Rome	Art history	
Brew	John Otis	man	White	1906-1988	USA	Doctoral degree from Harvard University	Archaeology	
Peterson	Charles Emil	man	White	1906-2004	USA	Bachelor's degree in architecture from University of Minnesota	Architecture	
Brandi	Cesare	man	White	1906-1988	Italy	Graduate of Literature from University of Florence	Art conservation	Professor
Feiss	Carl	man	White	1907-1997	USA	Degree in architecture from the University of Pennsylvania	Architecture	Professor
Alexander	Edward Porter	man	White	1907-2003	USA	PhD in history from Columbia University	Public history	Professor

APPENDIX A   235

Doctrine or policy contribution	Area of influence	Influence	Documented racial or ethnic bias	Source(s) that establish the influence of this individual
Athens Charter	Doctrines	Finley contributed his expertise in the classics to help write the Athens Charter.		Allais (2018)
National Register of Historic Places	Policy	Chief Historian of the National Park Service, Lee had a fundamental influence on the development of federal preservation policy in the US by studying European (especially English) and doctrinal (e.g., Athens Charter) precedents and adapting them to the US context; he was especially influential in drafting early versions of significance and integrity criteria that were later incorporated into the National Register.		Glass (1990); Jokilehto (1999); Mackintosh (1986)
Venice Charter	Doctrines	Director of the Vatican Pinacoteca; expert in art museums; coauthor of the Venice Charter.		Jokilehto (1999)
National Register of Historic Places	Policy	Former Director of Harvard's Peabody Museum; helped finalize NPS policy for the National Register; was a member of the three-person "Special Committee on Historic Preservation" organized by George B. Hartzog in 1966.		Glass (1990); Mackintosh (1986)
National Register of Historic Places	Policy	Created the Historic American Building Survey (HABS) program in 1933 in the National Park Service, which provided the first policy basis for what became the National Register of Historic Places.		Jokilehto (1999)
	Method	Well-known proponent of "critical restoration theory" based on gestalt psychology; worked closely with Argan; published Teoria del restauro in 1963, which was highly influential.		Jokilehto (1999)
National Historic Preservation Act	Policy	Feiss was an architect, professor, and political activist who helped define and promote the passage of the National Historic Preservation Act of 1966; he helped raise funds with Albert Rains and Laurence Henderson to support their special committee's publication of With Heritage So Rich; he was particularly concerned about the way "inappropriate" treatments of buildings presented a "false" history.		Feiss (1964); Sprinkle (2014)
	Method	Served as Vice-President for interpretation at Colonial Williamsburg (1946–1972) and founded the Museum Studies program at the University of Delaware.		Soleim (2021)

Last	First	Gender identity	Racial identity	Birth/death	Nationality	Education	Expertise	University professor?
Gazzola	Piero	man	White	1908-1979	Italy	University degree in civil engineering with specialization in architecture	Architecture	
Gray	Gordon F.	man	White	1909-1982	USA	Law degree from Yale University	Law	
Ireland	Clifford (Casey)	man	White	1909-1988	USA	Degree in law from Kent College in Chicago	Politics	
Argan	Giulio Carlo	man	White	1909-1994	Italy	College education	Art conservation	Professor
Merlet	Jean	man	White	1910-1976	France	Graduate of the École nationale supérieure des Beaux-Arts	Architecture	
Sorlin	Francois	man	White	1911-1995	France	University studies	Architecture	
Bonelli	Renato	man	White	1911-2004	Italy	Degree in architecture from University of Rome La Sapienza	Architecture	Professor
Stikas	Eustathios	man	White	1912-1983	Greece	Architecture degrees from the National Technical University of Athens and the Sorbonne	Architecture	
Zbiss	Slimane-Mustapha	man	White	1913-2003	Tunisia	University studies in archaeology	Archaeology	

APPENDIX A 237

Doctrine or policy contribution	Area of influence	Influence	Documented racial or ethnic bias	Source(s) that establish the influence of this individual
Venice Charter	Doctrines	Chairman who helped draft the Venice Charter; emphasized how "the ensemble of things," old and new, that make up an urban environment contribute to its authenticity.		Jokilehto (1999)
National Register of Historic Places	Policy	Gray was the Chairman of the Board of the National Trust for Historic Preservation from 1962 to 1973.	As Secretary of the Army, Gray wanted to maintain racial segregation in the Army; as the President of UNC Chapel Hill, Gray resisted integrating the campus (Poole, 2014).	Glass (1990); Mackintosh (1986)
National Register of Historic Places	Policy	Ireland was legislative assistant to Rep. William B. Widnall (R-NJ) and helped set up the travels for the Rains Committee to investigate preservation work in eight European countries in 1965; based on these trips, Ireland, along with Carl Feiss, drafted recommendations for US preservation policy.		Glass (1990)
	Method	Founder of the Central Institute of Restoration (Istituto Centrale del Restauro). Promoted scientific restoration/conservation in partnership with Brandi.	Member of the National Fascist Party (Argan, 1931)	Jokilehto (1999)
Venice Charter	Doctrines	Served as the Chief Architect of Historic Monuments; coauthor of the Venice Charter.		Jokilehto (1999)
Venice Charter	Doctrines	Was the General Inspector of Historic Monuments in France; coauthor of the Venice Charter.		Jokilehto (1999)
	Method	Principal theorist of "critical restoration" school.		Jokilehto (1999)
Venice Charter	Doctrines	Was Director of Conservation of the Ministry of Education in Greece; coauthor of the Venice Charter.		Jokilehto (1999)
Venice Charter	Doctrines	Widely considered to be a "pioneer" of archaeological practice in Tunisia, especially for his emphasis on scientific accuracy; coauthor of Venice Charter.		Jokilehto (1999)

APPENDIX A

Last	First	Gender identity	Racial identity	Birth/death	Nationality	Education	Expertise	University professor?
Sonnier	Jean-Léon	man	White	1913–2004	France	Architecture degree from École nationale supérieure des Beaux-Arts	Architecture	
Tripp	Gertrud	woman	White	1914–2006	Austria	Doctoral degree in art history	Art history	
Hussey	John A.	man	White	ca. 1915–?	USA	PhD in history from University of California, Berkeley	History	
de Vrieze	Piet L.	man	White	1917–1987	Netherlands	University studies in architecture	Architecture	
Langberg	Harald	man	White	1919–2003	Denmark	Master's degree in art history from the Efterslægtselskabets School	Architectural history	
Hartzog	George B., Jr.	man	White	1920–2008	USA	Bachelor's degree from American University	Law	
Daifuku	Hiroshi	man	Japanese American	1920–2012	USA	Doctoral degree in archaeology from Harvard University	Archaeology	Professor

APPENDIX A 239

Doctrine or policy contribution	Area of influence	Influence	Documented racial or ethnic bias	Source(s) that establish the influence of this individual
Venice Charter	Doctrines	Was the Chief Architect of Historic Monuments (1949–1982) in France; coauthor of the Venice Charter.		Jokilehto (1999)
Venice Charter	Doctrines	Was Director of the Federal Monuments Office in Austria; coauthor of the Venice Charter.	Tripp appeared to help the Nazis in their efforts to steal artwork from Jewish people; in 1941, she was responsible for cataloguing the "seized [art] collection" belonging to Stephan Mautner. (https://www.lexikon-provenienzforschung.org/en/tripp-gertrude)	Jokilehto (1999)
National Register of Historic Places	Policy	Appointed by Robert M. Utley, Chair of the "Historic Preservation Task Force" in 1966; Hussey, along with five other NPS employees, independently created the criteria for the National Register of Historic Places, which was finalized in 1967.		Glass (1990); Mackintosh (1986)
Venice Charter	Doctrines	Coauthor of the Venice Charter.		Jokilehto (1999)
Venice Charter	Doctrines	Was the Secretary of the Association for the Preservation of Old Buildings (Denmark); coauthor of the Venice Charter.		Jokilehto (1999)
National Register of Historic Places	Policy	Hartzog was director of the National Park Service from 1964 to 1972 and helped to steward the creation of the National Historic Preservation Act of 1966 and its policy and procedural implementation; it was through Hartzog's influence on the Rains Committee that the National Park Service became the home of the National Register of Historic Places.		Glass (1990); Mackintosh (1986)
Venice Charter	Doctrines	Worked at UNESCO, specializing in the protection of historic monuments; coauthor of the Venice Charter; helped create ICOMOS and ICCROM.		Jokilehto (1999)

Last	First	Gender identity	Racial identity	Birth/death	Nationality	Education	Expertise	University professor?
Connally	Ernest Allen	man	White	1921–1999	USA	Doctoral degree in architectural history from Harvard University	Architectural history	Professor
Garvey	Robert Robey, Jr.	man	White	1921–1996	USA	Degree from Davidson College	Public administration	
Lemaire	Raymond Martin Marie Ghislain	man	White	1921–1997	Belgium	Doctoral degree in art history and archaeology from Catholic University of Louvain	Architectural history	Professor
Henderson	Laurence G.	man	White	1923–1977	USA	Undergraduate degree from the University of Virginia. Graduate studies at Bard College, Harvard University, University of Paris, and University of Edinburgh	Urban planning	
Murtagh	William J.	man	White	1923–2018	USA	PhD in history from the University of Pennsylvania	History	
Philippot	Paul	man	White	1925–2016	Belgium	Studied law and art history at Ecole du Louvre	Art conservation	Professor

APPENDIX A 241

Doctrine or policy contribution	Area of influence	Influence	Documented racial or ethnic bias	Source(s) that establish the influence of this individual
National Register of Historic Places	Policy	As the first head of the NPS's Office of Archaeology and Historic Preservation, Connally helped finalize NPS policy for the National Register; was a member of the three-person "Special Committee on Historic Preservation," organized by George B. Hartzog in 1966.		Mackintosh (1986); Sprinkle (2014)
National Register of Historic Places	Policy	Garvey was the founder of US/ICOMOS; he was Executive Director of the National Trust for Historic Preservation from 1960 to 1967 and the first Executive Director of the Advisory Council on Historic Preservation; Garvey played a significant role in the creation of the National Historic Preservation Act of 1966 and its regulatory implementation, especially Section 106.		Glass (1990); Mackintosh (1986)
Venice Charter	Doctrines	Lemaire, a Baron, was the rapporteur to the working group of the Charter of Venice that produced the Venice Charter in 1964; he helped found ICOMOS.		Jokilehto (1999)
National Register of Historic Places	Policy	Henderson was instrumental in helping to fund the special historic preservation committee led by Albert M. Rains that led to the publication of the book With Heritage So Rich, which he coauthored with Albert Rains. The text in this book was introduced in Congress as the National Historic Preservation Act in 1966.		Glass (1990)
National Register of Historic Places	Policy	As the first Keeper of the National Register, Murtagh helped establish the fundamental guidelines for preparing acceptable National Register nominations that became NPS policy; prior to this role, Murtagh contributed to the 1964 National Trust report on "Principles and Guidelines for Historic Preservation in the United States" that helped lead to the 1966 National Historic Preservation Act.		Mackintosh (1986); Sprinkle (2014)
Venice Charter	Doctrines	Philippot helped bring the Italian scientific restoration school to US practice, which influenced policy implemented by the National Park Service (e.g., Secretary of the Interior's Standards); protégé of Brandi; wrote the introductory page to the Venice Charter of 1964.		Jokilehto (1999)

Last	First	Gender identity	Racial identity	Birth/death	Nationality	Education	Expertise	University professor?
Bradley	Zorro Allen	man	White	1925–2010	USA	Graduate degree in archaeology from University of New Mexico	Archaeology	Professor
Nelligan	Murray Homer	man	White	ca. 1926–?	USA	PhD in history from Columbia University	History	
Nelson	Lee H.	man	White	1927–1994	USA	Master's degree in architecture from University of Illinois at Urbana-Champaign	Architecture	
Pimentel Gurmendi	Victor	man	Latin American	1928–	Peru	Undergraduate architecture degree from the National School of Engineering (Peru); Master's degree in urban planning and construction technology from Sapienza University of Rome	Architecture	Professor
Utley	Robert Marshall	man	White	1929–2022	USA	MA in history from Indiana University	History	

APPENDIX A

Doctrine or policy contribution	Area of influence	Influence	Documented racial or ethnic bias	Source(s) that establish the influence of this individual
National Register of Historic Places	Policy	Appointed by Robert M. Utley, Chair of the "Historic Preservation Task Force" in 1966; Bradley, along with five other NPS employees, independently created the criteria for the National Register of Historic Places, which was finalized in 1967.		Glass (1990); Mackintosh (1986)
National Register of Historic Places	Policy	Appointed by Robert M. Utley, Chair of the "Historic Preservation Task Force" in 1966; Nelligan, along with five other NPS employees, independently created the criteria for the National Register of Historic Places, which was finalized in 1967.	Nelligan was well known as an expert and afficionado of the social life of Arlington House, Robert E. Lee's home, upon which he based his doctoral dissertation; in his work, he consistently refers to enslaved people at the home as "servants"; "slave" or "slaves" appears less than a handful of times (Chornesky, 2015; Nelligan, 1951)	Glass (1990); Hosmer (1965); Mackintosh (1986)
National Register of Historic Places	Policy	Author of NPS Preservation Brief 17, Architectural Character: Identifying the Visual Aspects of Historic Buildings as an Aid to Preserving Their Character, dating from 1982, which influenced how the preparers of National Register nominations describe the "character-defining features" in a building; cofounder of the Association for Preservation Technology; established the NPS's Preservation Brief series, which provided federal government policy guidelines for historic preservation practice.		Lee (1988); Mackintosh (1986)
Venice Charter	Doctrines	Studied under Robert Pane and Cesare Brandi; proponent of Italian school of scientific and critical restoration; coauthor of the Venice Charter.		Jokilehto (1999)
National Register of Historic Places	Policy	As Chief Historian of the NPS, Utley put in place the first policy for National Historic Landmark criteria which influenced the development of the National Register.		Mackintosh (1986); Sprinkle (2014)

APPENDIX A

Last	First	Gender identity	Racial identity	Birth/death	Nationality	Education	Expertise	University professor?
Thomas	Kathryn (Kay)	woman	White	ca. 1930–	USA	?	Administration	
Bassegoda-Nonell	José	man	White	1930–2012	Spain	Doctoral degree from Polytechnic University of Catalonia	Architecture	Professor
Brown	William Edward	man	White	1930–2016	USA	Bachelor's degree in history from Whittier College	History	
Flores Marini	Carlos	man	Latin American	1937–2015	Mexico	Graduate of the Universidad Nacional Autónoma de México	Architecture	Professor
Morton	Woolridge Brown, III	man	White	1938–	USA	Bachelor of architectural history from the University of Virginia; Diplomé Etudes Supérieures de l'Histoire, de la Construction, et de la Conservation des Monuments Anciens, Ministère des Affaires Culturelles, Service des Monuments Historiques, Paris	Architectural history	Professor
Keune	Russell V.	man	White	1938–2015	USA	Master's degree in architecture from University of Illinois at Urbana-Champaign	Architecture	Professor

Doctrine or policy contribution	Area of influence	Influence	Documented racial or ethnic bias	Source(s) that establish the influence of this individual
National Register of Historic Places	Policy	Thomas was an Employee Relations Specialist at the Western Office of Design and Construction of the NPS; Appointed by Robert M. Utley, Chair of the "Historic Preservation Task Force" in 1966; Thomas served as secretary and was joined by five other NPS employees who independently created the criteria for the National Register of Historic Places, which was finalized in 1967.		Mackintosh (1986)
Venice Charter	Doctrines	Founding member of ICOMOS and coauthor of the Venice Charter; contributed his expertise on the restoration of buildings designed by Gaudí.		Jokilehto (1999)
National Register of Historic Places	Policy	Appointed by Robert M. Utley, Chair of the "Historic Preservation Task Force" in 1966; Brown, along with five other NPS employees, independently created the criteria for the National Register of Historic Places, which was finalized in 1967.		Glass (1990); Mackintosh (1986)
Venice Charter	Doctrines	Flores was a well-known defender of Latin American patrimony; coauthor of the Venice Charter.		Jokilehto (1999)
Secretary of the Interior's Standards	Policy	Lead author of the Secretary of the Interior's Standards (1977), codified into 36 CFR 68, which were a translation of the Venice Charter into an American context to serve as evaluative criteria for the Federal Rehabilitation Tax Credit, but now widely mandated in all areas of preservation practice in the US; lead author of the 1979 booklet that interpreted these standards, which helped established NPS administrative guidelines that were promulgated to state historic preservation offices; served as Chairman of the United States National Committee of ICOMOS (US/ICOMOS) from 1975 to 1979; historic preservation professor at the University of Mary Washington.		Hudgins (2012); Mackintosh (1986)
National Register of Historic Places	Policy	Appointed by Robert M. Utley, Chair of the "Historic Preservation Task Force" in 1966; Keune, along with five other NPS employees, independently created the criteria for the National Register of Historic Places, which was finalized in 1967; founding member of US/ICOMOS; helped create the Advisory Council on Historic Preservation.		Glass (1990); Mackintosh (1986)

Last	First	Gender identity	Racial identity	Birth/death	Nationality	Education	Expertise	University professor?
Shull	Carol D.	woman	White	ca. 1945–	USA	MA in American history from University of Texas in Austin	Public history	
Jandl	H. Ward	man	White	1946–1995	USA	Degree in art history from Yale University; graduate certificate in historic preservation from Columbia University	Architectural history	
McClelland	Linda F.	woman	White	ca. 1955–	USA	MA in history from University of Massachusetts	Architectural history	
Andrus	Patrick W.	man	White	ca. 1957–	USA	MA in history from Louisiana State University	Public history	

Works Cited

Allais, A. (2018). *Designs of destruction: The making of monuments in the twentieth century*. University of Chicago Press.

Andrus, P. W. (1990). *National Register bulletin: How to apply the National Register criteria for evaluation*. US Department of the Interior, National Park Service.

Aramini, D. (2020). A racist and anti-Semitic Romanità: The Racial Laws of 1938 and the Institute of Roman Studies. *Trauma and Memory*, 8(2), 161-196.

Argan, G. C. (1931). La teoria di architettura di Sebastiano Serlio. Tesi datt. Torino: Regia Università, Facoltà di Lettere e Filosofia.

Arthur, T. (2001). Economics, slavery and Victorian reformers. *Economic Affairs*, 21(2), 49-52.

Brantlinger, P. (1996). A postindustrial prelude to postcolonialism: John Ruskin, William Morris, and Gandhism. *Critical Inquiry*, 22(3), 466-485.

Chornesky, M. B. (2015). Confederate island upon the Union's "most hallowed ground": The battle to interpret Arlington House, 1921-1937. *Washington History*, 27(1), 20-33.

Feiss, C. (1964). Preservation of historic areas in the United States. *Historic Preservation*, 16, 133-149.

Doctrine or policy contribution	Area of influence	Influence	Documented racial or ethnic bias	Source(s) that establish the influence of this individual
National Register of Historic Places	Policy	Shull presided over and influenced the development of many of the implementation policies of the National Register from 1972 until her retirement from the NPS in 2015.		Mackintosh (1986); https://protectnps.org/centennial-biographies-2/carol-d-shull/
National Register of Historic Places	Policy	Author of Preservation Brief 18, Rehabilitating Interiors in Historic Buildings: Identifying and Preserving Character-Defining Elements (1988), which established federal government policy on "character-defining features" in historic buildings; as Deputy Chief, Technical Preservation Services Branch in the Preservation Assistance Division of the NPS, Jandl had a great deal of influence on federal preservation policy.		Jandl (1988)
National Register of Historic Places	Policy	Author of the 1977 (and, as revised) National Register Bulletin, published by the NPS, on How to Complete the National Register Registration Form.		McClelland (1977)
National Register of Historic Places	Policy	National Register Historian at the NPS; primary coauthor of the National Register Bulletin, published by the NPS in 1990, on How to Apply the National Register Criteria for Evaluation (based on a 1983 draft).		Andrus (1990)

Gilmore, A. T. (Ed.). (1978). *Revisiting Blassingame's The slave community: The scholars respond*. Greenwood Press.

Glass, James A. 1990. *The beginnings of a new national historic preservation program, 1957 to 1969*. American Association for State and Local History.

Haeuser, E. N. (2018). *A tricky chessboard: Albert Rains, New Deal liberalism, and southern progressivism in Alabama* [Master's thesis, Auburn University].

Hanagan, N. (2019). The citizen, the baker, and the candlestick maker: What Democrats can learn from the Arts and Crafts and Slow Food movements. *American Political Thought: A Journal of Ideas, Institutions, and Culture*, 8(4), 479–503.

Hosmer, C. B. (1965). *Presence of the past: A history of the preservation movement in the United States before Williamsburg*. Putnam.

Hudgins, C. (2012). *Transcription of W. Brown Morton III, Hon. AIA, interview*. Clemson/College of Charleston Historic Preservation Graduate Program.

Jandl, H. W. (1988). *Rehabilitating interiors in historic buildings: Identifying and preserving character-defining elements*. US Department of the Interior, National Park Service.

Jokilehto, J. (1990). *History of architectural conservation*. Butterworth-Heinemann.

Jumonville, N. (1999). *Henry Steele Commager: Midcentury liberalism and the history of the present.* University of North Carolina Press.

Lee, R. F. (1950). Historical and architectural monuments in the United States. National Park Service.

Lee, N. (1988). *Preservation brief 17: Architectural character: Identifying the visual aspects of historic buildings as an aid to preserving their character.* US Department of the Interior, National Park Service.

Lindgren, J. M. (1996). *Preserving historic New England: Preservation, progressivism, and the remaking of memory.* Oxford University Press.

Mackintosh, B. (1986). The National Historic Preservation Act and the National Park Service: A history. US Department of the Interior, National Park Service.

McClelland, L. F. (1977). *How to complete the National Register registration form.* US Department of the Interior, National Park Service.

Mertz, G. (2020). "Das braun der erde". Die träger der Haidinger-Medaille der Geologischen Bundesanstalt und der Nationalsozialismus. *Jahrbuch der Geologischen Bundesanstalt*, 160(1-4), 359-408.

Nelligan, M. (1951). The building of Arlington House. *Journal of the Society of Architectural Historians*, 10(2), 11-15.

Poole, A. H. (2014). The strange career of Jim Crow archives: Race, space, and history in the mid-twentieth-century American south. *The American Archivist*, 77(1), 23-63.

Ramey, L. T. (2014). *Black legacies: Race and the European Middle Ages.* University Press of Florida.

Shapiro, W. (2010). Some implications of Clark Wissler's race theory. *The Australian Journal of Anthropology,* 15(1), 1-17.

Smith, J. D., & Lowery, J. V., (Eds.). (2013). *The Dunning school: Historians, race, and the meaning of reconstruction.* University Press of Kentucky.

Soleim, S. A. M. (2021). "To make history the living force": The professionalization of public history—1880-2000 [Doctoral dissertation, North Carolina State University].

Sprinkle, J. H. (2014). *Crafting preservation criteria: The National Register of Historic Places and American historic preservation.* Routledge.

Zimmerman, J. (2004). Brown-ing the American textbook: History, psychology, and the origins of modern multiculturalism. *History of Education Quarterly*, 44(1), 46-69.

APPENDIX B

Conducting a Guided First-Person Existential Phenomenology

PURPOSE: Guide a group of interested residents from an identified neighborhood/community through a first-person existential phenomenology. The purpose is to help each person understand their emotional and experiential relationship with where they live, perhaps for the first time.

GOAL: Each participant should understand the experience of being in their neighborhood with a focus on their own, individual, lived experience. Or, in another sense, each participant will be exploring the nature of being in their neighborhood.

OBJECTIVE 1: Invite, by phone, email, and in person, residents to participate in this phenomenological exercise. Choose a common place and meeting time.

OBJECTIVE 2: Have the participants record, on paper, their experiences, which can then be summarized and shared with the larger group in a workshop meeting.

SUMMARY OF STEPS

The research should be based on what van Manen (1990, pp. 30–31) proposes as a general "methodological structure for human science research":

- turning to a phenomenon which seriously interests us and commits us to the world;

- investigating experience as we live it rather than as we conceptualize it;
- reflecting on the essential themes which characterize the phenomenon;
- describing the phenomenon through the art of writing and rewriting;
- maintaining a strong and oriented pedagogical relation to the phenomenon;
- balancing the research context by considering parts and whole.

HOW TO IMPLEMENT VAN MANEN'S METHOD

Step 1: The phenomenon under study is the experience of being in a particular neighborhood.

Step 2: Instruct the participants to experience their neighborhood as if it is the first time they have ever experienced it. Some suggestions in instructing people:

- Tell participants to pretend that they are a child and experience the world with a "childlike wonder" that you see when a little boy or girl experiences something for the first time.
- Use the more well-known concept of "meditation" and ask the participants to meditate on their neighborhood. The participants should only pay attention to the very first instance of a thought as it flashes into their mind.
- Tell participants that they should focus on the bare, essential essences of what they are experiencing.
- For instance, these are phenomenological descriptions: "the leaves make a sound when the wind passes through them"; "the garden smells damp"; "I feel very relaxed standing by this building"; "I want to close my eyes and smell the neighborhood." These phrases represent the very first instance of a meaning that appears in someone's head. The goal of the participants should be to write down the most bare, basic essences of meanings as they first appear without thinking too much about them.
- These are not phenomenological descriptions: "I like the building because of its architectural style"; "people tell me they like the garden because of its fruit"; "I would like to build a house here." These descriptions are the result of more intensive thinking and building relationships between meanings, which is not what a phenomenological approach tries to understand, at least not at this stage of gathering data.
- Have the participants write down their phenomenological descriptions in a notebook or on a piece of paper.

APPENDIX B   251

Steps 3 through 6: van Manen's description is complicated, but I will attempt to summarize it in a way that can be described to participants:

- After the participants have recorded the essential meanings of their experiences, ask them to try and organize their meanings into similar themes. For instance, if many of the meanings that a participant records are related to smell, they should create a theme for "smell" and summarize the meanings associated with it. Tell the participants to reflect on their experiences and try to not only describe the details of their experiences, but also how it relates to the larger idea of what the neighborhood is and its relationship to people.

Resources
van Manen, M. (1990). *Researching the lived experience*. University of Western Ontario.

INDEX

Page numbers in **bold** refer to figures.

academic audience, 7
academic inquiry, 150
academic research, 173, 177
academics, 8, 29, 51, 53, 175, 179, 195, 218
accessibility, 149, 165
ACHP. *See* Advisory Council on Historic Preservation
ACHS. *See* Association for Critical Heritage Studies
Advisory Council on Historic Preservation, 37, 176, 204, 215
advocacy, 37, 53, 115–17, 165, 176, 199, 204, 210, 215, 219
aesthetics: of adobe, 213; and appeal of decay, 99, 100; of high-style buildings, 127; and inferiority of non-Western architecture, 130; qualities of, 55, 73, 131; value of, 60, 63, 64, 130; and value by a community or cultural group, 74; of vernacular places, 28; that are undesirable, 132

Africa, 51, 54, 129, 130
African American people, 24, 27, 28, 179, 216
African people, 26, 129, 132
AHD. *See* Authorized Heritage Discourse
AHRC. *See* Arts and Humanities Research Council (UK)
AIA. *See* American Institute for Architects
Alabama, 232, 247
Alberta, Canada, 78
Alexander, Edward Porter, 234
Alhambra, Spain, 231
Allentown, Pennsylvania, 15, 27
American Institute for Architects, 6, 7
American Planning Association, 6
American Psychological Association, 7, 199
American Scenic and Historic Preservation society, 131
ancestors, 9, 22, 54, 104, 177
Andersen, Hans Christian, 111

Anderson, South Carolina, 14, 15
Andrus, Patrick W., 246
Anglo-American, 130
Anglo-Saxon, 129, 131, 132
anthropologists, 58, 63, 80, 106, 201, 217
anthropology, 5, 10, 11, 30, 33, 46, 56, 57, 61, 62, 81, 126, 201, 209
anti-intellectual agenda, 192
antiquarian, 7, 30, 58
antique, 95, 97
anti-scrape theories for restoration/preservation, 19, 114
Appleton, William Sumner, 122, 131, 226
archaeological theory, 10
archaeologist, 57, 117, 168
archaeologists, 4, 30, 31, 55–58, 63, 80, 117–19, 122, 126, 132, 217
archaeology, 10, 11, 33, 55–57, 61, 63, 75, 77, 78, 91, 118, 121, 122, 126, 128, 149, 178
architects, 4, 6–8, 19, 20, 30, 37, 48, 56, 62, 77, 80, 114, 117–19, 120, 122, 126, 129, 132, 217

architectural conservation, 16, 46, 56, 90, 92
architectural conservationists, 53
architectural conservation theory, 90, 92
architectural history, 75, 168, 194
architectural materials conservation, 194
architectural styles, 94
architecture, 6–9, 12, 21, 27, 53, 56, 61, 75, 78, 91, 99, 128–30, 138, 169
archival research techniques, 73
archives, 168
Argan, Giulio Carlo, 130, 236
art, 4, 9, 10, 11, 13, 22, 35, 67, 90, 91, 93, 97, 99, 111, 117, 119, 126, 128, 131, 138, 218
artifacts, 57, 60, 95
Arts and Crafts movement, 114, 130
Arts and Humanities Research Council (UK), 195, 196
Asia, 51, 54, 68, 130

253

Asian American people, 24, 27, 216
Association for Conservation of National Treasures (Japan), 53, 81
Association for Critical Heritage Studies, 7, 9, 10, 11, 12, 61
Association for the Preservation of Virginia Antiquities, 131
Athens, Greece, 4, 48
atmosphere, 36, 91, 105, 154, 180
attorney, 118
audience, 6, 7, 154, 155, 196
Australia, 33, 55, 61, 67, 69, 71–76, 79, 195, 196, 199
Australian Research Council, 196
Austria, 224, 230, 238, 239
authenticity: and ability to perceive it, 95; based on age, 34; in art, 138; of building fabric, 35, 112; constructivist ideas on, 119; and differentiating new from old, 119; as experienced, 93; of fabric, 2, 10, 24, 26, 30, 31, 33, 35, 47–50, 51, 54, 56, 57, 66, 68, 79, 92, 112–23, 126, 128, 138, 139, 167, 177, 184, 203, 214; and genuine condition, 116; and how building materials naturally change and degrade, 95; and historical authenticity, 34, 49, 76, 93, 113, 116, 121; and historical integrity, 4, 16, 28, 113, 116, 117, 125, 214; and historical significance, 53, 125; ignores emotional responses, 117; and necessity of decay, 95; and original building fabric, 122; and original reality, 122; and original state, 48, 53, 97; as personal experience, 30; of place, 30; and protection from adulteration, 35, 112, 113, 115, 116, 120, 122, 167; psychological experience of, 31
Authorized Heritage Discourse, 30, 31, 35, 62, 63, 112, 219

Bacchelli, Giuseppe, 224
Balanos, Nikolaos, 226
Balbás, Leopoldo Torres, 230
Ballarat, Australia, 67–71
Ballarat Imagine, 69
Baltimore, Maryland, 99, 179
Bannister, Turpin Chambers, 232
BAOP. *See* Being Affected by Old Places
Bassegoda-Nonell, José, 244
Battle of the Plains of Abraham (Canada), 24
beauty, 9, 20, 22, 34, 94, 99, 168
Bede, Saint, 1
behavior, 5, 7, 12, 13, 46, 51, 62, 65, 79, 100, 112, 116, 127, 138, 139, 159, 160, 162, 176, 201, 210
Being Affected by Old Places: and the ambiguity of perception, 105, 174; and design guidelines, 210; and emotions, 89–94; and fantasy, 37, 105, 106; and imagined places, 93; and mediation through environmental patina, 94–101; and mystery, 105; and spontaneous fantasy, 101–6
belief, 4, 25, 29, 77, 115, 116, 139, 150
belonging, 9, 26
Beltrami, Luca, 224
Benavente, Luis, 232
Benjamin, Walter, 230
bias, 7, 9, 14, 28, 29, 35, 37, 38, 48, 59, 124, 128, 129, 132–34, 137, 164, 201, 209
biodiversity, 73, 79
blood, 24
Boito, Camillo, 19, 47, 117, 119, 224
Bolivia, 26
Bonelli, Renato, 236
bones, 1, 4, 115
Boni, Giacomo, 224
Boskovic, Djurdje, 232
Boston, Massachusetts, 24, 118
bottom-up, grassroots approaches, 5, 13, 27, 56, 57, 148
Bourassé, Jean-Jacques, 222
Bradley, Zorro Allen, 242
Brandi, Cesare, 47, 119, 138, 139, 234
Brew, John Otis, 234
British Standards Institution, 47, 76
Brown, William Edward, 244
Bulgaria, 21
business, 15, 69, 70, 156, 181, 183

Camden, New Jersey, 99
Canada, 23, 33, 55, 61, 72, 74–79, 80, 120
Canberra, Australia, 61, 196, 196
Capone, Al, **100**
Carbonara, Giovanni, 47
Caribbean, 178
Carter, John, 222
cathedrals, 19, 90, 129
Celtic, 15, 24
cemetery, 21, **60**

ceremonial buildings, 26
Chaco Culture National Historical Park, New Mexico, 21, 64
Chandler, Joseph, 121
Charleston, South Carolina, 15, 91, 94
charm. *See* magic
Chatelain, Vern, 230
chemistry, 192
Chicago, Illinois, 99
Chierici, Gino, 226
childcare, 165, 210
childlike behavior, 172, 250
children, 22, 105, 178
Chile, 61
China, 50–54, 60, 61, 130
Christianity, 4, 111, 114, 115, 169
church, 15, 21, 118, 154, 165
civil experts, 36, 148–52, 167, 212, 219
climate change, 8, 192, 193, 209
Cliver, Blaine, 37
Cloquet, Louis, 224
Coatepec, Mexico, 18
cognition, 2, 7, 13, 103, 173
cognitive dissonance, 2
cognitive psychology, 13
Coherit Associates LLC, 178
collaboration, 16, 68, 150
Collingwood, Robin George, 230
Colonial America, 16
colonialism, 9, 62
Colonial Williamsburg, 122, 229
colonization, 24, 25, 51, 54, 133
colonize, 25, 49
colonizer, 24, 25, 33, 54
Colorado, 181, 212
Colvin, Sidney, 224
communication, 63, 154, 213
communities, 26–28, 63, 64, 68, 81, 151, 159, 164, 178, 179, 184, 195, 200
community engagement, 64, 69, 192, 217
community engagement methods: and active listening, 156; and brainstorming, 157; and empowering participants to lead process, 150; and facilitation techniques, 152, 160, 161; and facilitator role, 71, 148, 156, 164, 209; and meeting room setup, 154, 155, 159; and nonparticipant observation, 63, 151; and participant rules, 160; and participatory processes, 36, 166, 211, 219; and role playing, 158, 164; and round robin discussion, 158; and safety, 162; and techniques for engaging participants, 157; as workshops and charrettes, 36, 36, 63, 67, 149, 152–54, 157–63, 167, 173, 174
community-based participatory research: and action research, 149, 178, 184, 198, 217, 219; and archaeology, 57, 149, 178; as community engagement's first step, 166; and community-driven recommendations, 36; as community-led change, 149; and the consensus of meanings, 64; as the coproduction of knowledge, 152; coresearchers role in, 149, 151, 178, 210, 211; and coresearching with local residents, 209; and cultural differences, 162; evaluation of, 151; in general, 36, 148, 149–53, 158, 162, 166, 173, 174, 177, 178, 185; as grassroots community research, 198; as interdependent science, 150; and process, 70, 209; and reports created by a community, 210; as self-research, 150; and vision creation, 69; and workplans, 166
comprehensive and small area plans, 36, 57, 69, 70, 153, 179, 181, 182, 183
conflict, 10, 13, 61, 62
Connally, Ernest Allen, 240
connoisseurship, 9, 30, 47
consecration of old places, 23, 115, 132
conservation practitioners, 5, 8, 51, 106
conservation theory, 19, 35, 51, 53, 90, 92, 125, 139
conservators, 36, 48, 51, 97, 114, 117, 119, 126, 126, 138, 168
consumer, 7, 45
control of heritage, 30, 33, 37, 58, 59, 71, 76, 149, 180, 183, 215. *See also* Authorized Heritage Discourse
conventional experts, 3, 27, 36, 71, 139, 148–52, 166, 167, 180, 185, 212
Córdoba, Mexico 17, 18, **19**
corpse, 1
cosmic and spiritual significance, 54
Cove Fields, Canada, 24
craftsmanship, 77, 78, 91
Cram, Mildred, 91

critical heritage studies, 7, 9-13, 30, 33, 61, 62, 64, 195
critical theory, 47
Crittenden, Charles Christopher, 232
Croce, Benedetto, 226
Cuba, 21
Cuetzalan del Progreso, Mexico, 17
Cuitzeo del Porvenir, Mexico, 17
cultural heritage, 3, 54, 60, 62, 65, 66, 77, 80, 126, 181-84, 196, 197
cultural history, 73, 74
cultural landscapes, 16, 31, 64, 106
cultural mapping, 70
cultural meanings, 10, 29, 74, 173
cultural memory, 93
cultural resource management, 127
cultural significance, 54, 75
cultural traditions, 16, 25, 26

Daifuku, Hiroshi, 238
Damascus, Syria 21
dark histories, 211
dark tourism, 139
database, 16, 175
Daughters of the American Revolution, 131
Deadwood, South Dakota, **60**
death, 1, 34, 60, 98
de Campos, Deoclecio Redig, 234
democracy, 36, 69, 151, 154, 212
Denmark, 238, 239
Denver, Colorado 181
Derrida, Jacques, 171
desecration, 25, 113
designers, 45, 103
Destrée, Jules, 48, 224
destruction of cultural heritage, 60
Detroit, Michigan, 99
developers, 7, 80, 183
de Vrieze, Piet L., 238
Didron, Adolphe Napoléon, 117, 222
difficult memories, 60
disability access, 159
disciplinary bias, 59
disciplines, 11, 12, 35, 36, 55-57, 58, 63, 103, 104, 111-13, 117-19, 125-28, 138, 156, 169, 192, 193, 200, 201, 217
disease, 120, 178
Disneyfication, 103
diversity, equity, inclusion: and ability, 165, 209; and cultural diversity, 26; and diversity of Americans, 138; and disempowerment, 80, 151; and the diversity deficit, 28; and the dominant racial group, 217; and excluded histories, 28; in general, 27, 28, 29, 42, 65, 141, 192, 207, 217, 19, 220; and Indigenous belief systems, 54, 74, 150; and Indigenous peoples, 17, 24, 26, 75, 132; and intersectionality, 209; and marginalized communities, 164; and marginalized cultures, 53; and marginalized groups, 24, 28, 126, 127, 164; and minoritized identities, 26, 124, 134, 177, 215; and racial and ethnic identity, 28, 35, 137, 139, 216, 217, 219; and sexual identity, 209, 214; and social justice, 13, 37, 65, 81, 151, 192, 197, 214, 216, 217; and socioeconomic class, 9, 130
divinity, 4
doctrines: and art/historical values, 13; Athens Charter, 4, 36, 47-50, 55, 92, 130; Burra Charter, 76, 79, 81; challenges to, 58; and colonization, 49, 51-54; definition, 3, 4; and demographics of its creators, 24, 33, 128-38; and exclusion of emotions and subjective experiences, 31, 90, 94; and exclusion of community participation, 50; and exclusion of historical significance, 55; and exclusion of lived experience, 106; and exclusion of magic and charm, 5, 19, 20, 105; and exclusion of meanings and values, 9; and exclusion of normal human experiences, 5, 19; and expectations for public to use doctrines in communication, 31; in general, 3, 4, 20, 29, 33, 35, 45-47, 49, 50, 53, 56, 58, 81, 102, 105, 106, 111, 113, 117, 120, 125, 126, 134, 137, 138, 139, 218; and intersection with policy, 9, 28, 29, 34, 35, 111; and material/fabric-based authenticity, 10, 30; Nara Document on Authenticity, 53, 55, 68; and need to benefit people, 147; norms of, 128; and numinism, 2; and objectification of history, 102; and parallels with religious belief, 115; philosophy of, 47; and punishment for failing to use, 57; and purity, 111-40;

INDEX 257

as received wisdom, 47; stasis of, 81; and values-centered preservation, 63; Venice Charter, 4, 16, 33, 47–51, 53–55, 68, 76, 79, 92, 116, 117, 119, 120, 130, 131, 168, 184; and ways to change it, 212, 218, 219
downtown revitalization, 14, 70
Dunning, William Archibald, 20, 133, 224
Dunning School of historiography, 133

Eastern State Penitentiary, Pennsylvania, **100**, 101
economic diversity, 210
economic growth and revitalization, 70
economy, 8, 17, 63, 69, 70, 165, 184, 192, 198, 210, 218
ecosystems, 79
Edinburgh, Scotland, 21, 240
EDRA. *See* Environmental Design Research Association
educated elite, 151
elitism, 9
emic or insider perspective, 64
empathy, 9, 164, 209, 211
empirical evidence, 7, 12, 35, 65, 67, 94, 118, 121, 133, 137, 139, 148, 172, 180, 202
empiricist-positivist ontological paradigm, 121
empowering communities, 151, 153
engineering, 78
England, 8, 14, 55, 56, 64, 76, 118, 120, 121, 122, 131
Enlightenment, 25
environmental conservation, 3, 127, 128, 149, 178, 185
environmental conservationists, 129
environmental cues, 200
Environmental Design Research Association, 65, 176, 199
environmental experiences, 167
environmental psychologists, 175, 178, 201, 202, 210
environmental psychology, 12, 13, 15, 33, 46, 62, 65, 66, 81, 126, 175, 176, 180, 200, 202, 204, 209, 217
environment and behavior research, 65, 79, 127, 138, 210
epistemological agnosticism, 150
epistemological purity, 35, 113, 125–28, 138
epistemology, 125, 139, 150, 200
ethnographic perspective, 5, 13
ethnographies, 13, 150, 172
eugenics, 128, 129, 131, 133
Europe, 24, 49, 51, 68, 129, 131, 176, 195, 196, 202
European Commission, 196

fabric purity, 35, 113–17, 119, 125
Facebook, 69
fascism, 130
fear, 25, 26, 165, 213
Feilden, Bernard, 96
Feiss, Carl, 234
filial piety, 51
financial incentives, 4, 70, 215, 216
Finley, John Huston, Jr., 234
First Nations, 75
Florence, Italy, 21, 234
Flores Marini, Carlos, 244
folklore, 15, 54, 158
forgery, 98, 120
Foucault, Michel, 106, 112, 171
France, 48, 114, 117
Friedländer, Max, 117, 119
frontier thesis, 132
funding for social science/people-centered research, 16, 28, 37, 54, 127, 179, 195–97, 200, 202, 204, 215, 216
fungus, 98
future, 72, 176, 211, 212

gardens, 99, 105, 131
Garvey, Robert Robey, Jr., 240
gatekeepers, 128
Gazzola, Piero, 236
Geertz, Clifford, 57
generalizability, 29, 64
genius loci, 23, 169
gentrification, 27
geographers, 58, 90, 169
Gestalt psychology, 90, 97, 105, 119, 120, 126, 138
Giovannoni, Gustavo, 130, 226
Goodwin, William Archer Rutherford, 226
Gothenburg, Sweden, 61
Gothic architecture, 19, 90, 91, 129, 130
Grant, Madison, 133
Gray, Gordon F., 236
Greece, 4, 48
guidelines, public policy: and changes to improve federal policy, 214; definition, 3, 4; for design guidelines, 79, 179, 180, 184, 210, 213; Guide to the Principles of the Conservation of Historic Buildings (UK), 76; and

guidelines, public policy (*cont'd*):
exclusion of people's lived experiences, 125; for historical theme studies, 125; National Register Bulletins, 124, 213; for the Pueblos Mágicos program in Mexico, 18; for preparing a National Register nomination, 214; and potential to improve through environmental psychology, 179; Principles of Repair (England), 76; Secretary of the Interior's Professional Qualifications Standards, 213; Secretary of the Interior's Standards, 2, 4, 28, 35, 36, 47, 50, 68, 73, 76, 79, 116, 117, 120, 130, 137, 168, 180, 184, 213; Standards for the Treatment of Historic Properties, 4; for significance statements, 123; and special architectural or historical interest (UK), 55, 73; and support for historical positivism, 124; Standards and Guidelines for the Conservation of Historic Places in Canada, 76, 120

HABS. *See* Historic American Building Survey
hallowed ground, 22, 23, 24
Halloween, 100
Harcourt-Smith, Cecil, 224
Harlem, New York, 27
Hartzog, George B., Jr., 238
Havana, Cuba, 21
Hegel, Georg Wilhelm Friedrich, 169
hegemony, 180, 201, 213
Heidegger, Martin, 90, 170, 171
Henderson, Laurence G., 240
heritage environments, 199, 202
heritage industry, 58
heritage practitioners, 7, 111
high-style buildings, 214
historians, 4, 11, 19, 20, 22, 30, 31, 55, 56, 59, 62, 80, 91, 118, 119, 123, 124, 126, 131, 132, 133, 217
historical accuracy, 121
historical research methods, 123, 233
historical significance, 15, 25, 51, 53-55, 63, 69, 75, 77-79, 92, 94, 102, 106, 113, 124, 125, 131, 134, 168, 203, 214

Historic American Building Survey, 55, 123
Historic Buildings and Monuments Commission (England), 55, 57
Historic Environment Knowledge Network, 65
historic preservation discipline, 127
historic preservation education: and curricula, 46, 47, 133, 176, 209, 217; emphasizes teaching orthodox doctrines, 46; faculty do less scholarly research than average, 192, 217; and higher education, generally, 37, 47, 126, 192, 197, 216, 218; historic preservation degree and certificate programs, 27, 176, 192, 197, 216, 216, 217, 218, 219; Historic Preservation Education Foundation, 176; Institute for Historic Building Conservation (UK), 46, 47; and the ivory tower, 191, 203; and the lack of racial and ethnic diversity in students and faculty, 216; National Council for Preservation Education, 46, 47; and overemphasis on the theories of educated White men, 47; and preservation education programs, 37; and recommended changes, 176, 177; and resistance to change, 192; and the role of higher education, 216; syllabi, 47, 216; teaching, 27, 37, 133, 149, 204, 217, 218; teaching policy analysis, 204; treats doctrine as received wisdom, 47; tenure-track faculty, 27, 202, 217; textbooks, 133
historic preservation field, 27, 37, 114, 191-93, 218
historic preservation practitioner, 36, 164
historic structure reports, 192
Historic Urban Landscape approach, 67-69
historiography, 133
Hollywood, California, 21
Hong Kong, China, **52**
Horta, Victor Pierre, 224
Hosmer, Charles, 131
HUL. *See* Historic Urban Landscape approach
human-centered practice and policy, 5, 33, 34, 45, 46, 56, 64-66, 71, 72, 79, 81, 212, 215-18
human flourishing, 7, 103

humanistic geographers, 58, 90, 126, 169
humanistic geography, 57, 58, 90, 169
humanities, 48, 56, 57, 209, 217
Husserl, Edmund, 169, 170, 171
Hussey, John A., 238

IAPS. *See* International Association of People-Environment Studies
ICCROM. *See* International Centre for the Study of the Preservation and Restoration of Cultural Property
ICOMOS. *See* International Council on Monuments and Sites
IHBC. *See* historic preservation education: Institute for Historic Building Conservation
Illinois, 242, 244
India, 50, 54, 130
Indonesian people, 26
industry, 58, 99, 203
infrasound, 105
intangible heritage, 16, 36, 47, 65, 68–70, 126, 167, 181, 184, 196
International Association of People-Environment Studies, 176, 199
International Centre for the Study of the Preservation and Restoration of Cultural Property, 37, 65, 176
International Council on Monuments and Sites, 47, 48, 51, 53, 54, 68, 79, 92, 130, 176
Internet Movie Database, 16
interpretation, 14, 20, 22, 28, 29, 47, 49, 57, 97, 106, 123, 132–34, 139, 170, 171, 185
I'On, South Carolina, 94
Ireland, 21, 89
Ireland, Clifford (Casey), 236
Italian School of architectural conservators, 36, 130, 168
Italy, 4, 19, 21, 36, 48, 65, 117, 130, 131, 138, 168
Izamal, Mexico, 21

Jacobs, Jane, 136
Jamestown, Virginia, 20, 131
Jandl, H. Ward, 246
Japan, 25, 53, 54, 179
Japanese Association for Conservation of Architectural Monuments, 53
Japantown, San Francisco, California, **182**
Johnson, Lady Bird, 135

Kahler, Herbert E., 232
Kant, Immanuel, 169
Kenya, 54

Keune, Russell V., 244
Kieslinger, Alois, 131, 230
Kimball, Sidney Fiske, 228
King Edward Park, Canada, 24

Labrador, Canada, 78
Landmarks, 77, 78, 183, 193, 202
landscapes, 2, 6, 16, 29, 31, 54, 64, 67–69, 77, 78, 95, 96, 98, 99, 101–4, 113, 117, 177, 192, 214
Langberg, Harald, 238
language, 13, 54, 118, 120, 129, 160, 173
Laos, 25
Latinx people, 24, 27, 216
laws: Administrative Procedure Act (US), 214; Ancient Monuments Consolidation and Amendment Act (UK), 54; Ancient Monuments Protection Act (UK), 54; Antiquities and Monuments Act (Kenya), 54; Canadian Environmental Assessment Act (US), 79; Endangered Species Act (US), 127; Environment Protection and Biodiversity Conservation Act (Australia), 73, 79; Listed Building Act (UK), 56, 73; National Environmental Policy Act (US), 79; National Historic Preservation Act (US), 55, 68, 79, 127, 135, 192, 195, 213, 215, 218; Rehabilitation Tax Credit (US), 4, 73, 215
laypeople, 5, 9, 10, 13–15, 19, 31, 45, 46, 57, 67, 91
leaders, 9, 16, 51, 54, 61, 68, 130, 161, 165, 168, 176, 178, 179, 180, 181, 184, 197, 202, 218
leadership, 149, 176, 213
League of Nations, 48
Lee, Ronald F., 234
Leland, Waldo Gifford, 228
Lemaire, Raymond Martin Marie Ghislain, 240
Léon, Paul, 48, 48, 226
Lethaby, William, 120, 120, 224
lived experience: and affect, 29, 102, 105, 112; and exclusion from preservation/conservation doctrine and policy, 139; and anthropological research, 201; in general, 139, 171, 201, 218, 219; and imagined heritage, 112; and

lived experience (*cont'd*): standardized historical themes/contexts, 125; and minoritized identities, 139, 217; in relationship to naked heritage, 139; in relationship to magic and charm and spontaneous fantasies, 139
Liverpool, England, 21
living heritage, 219
local history research, 132
local knowledge, 150, 212
Los Angeles, California, 67, 99
Lowenthal, David, 57, 61
Lubbock, John, 222

Macau, China, **52**
magic: and apparitions, 18; and authenticity, 15; belief in, 14; and belief in spirits or ghosts, 29; and relationship to bewitchment, 14; and charm, 5, 14–16, 19–22, 24, 26, 27, 29–31, 98, 139, 147, 148, 174, 185, 209; and charm management, 148; and embedded spirits found in objects and places, 1, 19, 23, 25, 26, 115; and emotion, 15; and enchantment, 14, 15, 19, 20, 21, 23, 24, 105; and folklore and "thin" places, 15; and ghosts, 20, 29, 95, 104, 105, 139, 167; and ghost stories, 139; and hallowed ground, 23, 24; and haunted places, 105; heretical perspective on, 31; in legends, 16, 18, 22, 106; and lived experience, 139; and movies, 20; is missing from heritage places, 1; and numinism, 2, 5; older places, and association with, 15, 19; and orthodox conservation doctrine, 19; outside of the dominant culture, 24–29; and the paranormal, 14; and place attachment, 15; and places defined by magic and charm, 14–24; and poetic nature of ruins, 99; and policy, 19; and reality of others, 14; and rejection by professionals, 25, 31, 191; and ruins and ghost towns, 99–105; and social media, 21; and spontaneous fantasy, 105; and time travel, 22; as a universal human characteristic, 29; the veracity of which is not important to people, 14

Main Street program, 70, 71
Man-Environment Research Association (JAPAN), 199
Manitoba, Canada, 77
Marquesas Islands, 26
Marxism, 9
material culture, 24, 30
material fetish, 115. *See also* purity, fabric
McClelland, Linda F., 246
Medieval, 99
meditation, 174, 219
melancholia, 99
memories, 1, 60, 70, 93, 103, 105, 106, 172, 202, 211
memory, 9, 24, 59, 93, 105, 138
Merleau-Ponty, Maurice, 92
Merlet, Jean, 236
Merriam, John Campbell, 226
Methodologies for research, 94, 123, 150, 162, 173, 175
Michigan, 230
Michoacán, Mexico, 17
military, 15
Mississippi, 168
Modernism, 49, 118, 120
Modernist architects, 120
Montreal, Canada, 61
monuments, 4, 48, 49, 53, 56, 60, 79, 93, 99, 131

morality and treatment of tangible heritage, 35, 60, 112, 116, 118, 120, 131
Morison, Samuel Eliot, 133, 228
Morocco, 21
Morris, William, 47, 114, 116, 130, 222
Morton, Woolridge Brown, III, 4, 50, 244
Murtagh, William J., 240
museum curators, 59
Mussolini, Benito, 131
mystery, 26, 91, 105
mystical heritage, 15
myth, 20
mythical heritage, 94, 104, 129, 168
mythology, 51

naked heritage, 35, 111–39, 167, 180
Naples, Italy, 22
narrative, 59, 60, 103, 104, 128, 131–33
National Conference of State Historic Preservation Officers, 28, 204, 215, 216
National Park Service: and central role in public policy, 194, 204; and conflict with Santa Fe, NM over design review, 213; and exclusion of lived experience in establishing significance,

125; in general, 4, 28, 37, 64, 113, 117, 123–25, 137, 176, 194, 204, 213–15, 219; and need to consider how people are affected by older places, 176; and resistance to change, 214; and the team that created the "integrity" and "significance" criteria, 137; and use of values-centered management, 64; work culture in, 213
National Trust (UK), 202
National Trust for Historic Preservation (US), 9, 65, 70, 176, 202, 204, 215, 216
Native American people, 26, 27, 216
natural and cultural environments, 79
natural environment, 139, 199
Nazi regime, 130, 131
NCPE. *See* historic preservation education: National Council for Preservation Education
NCSHPO. *See* National Conference of State Historic Preservation Officers
negotiation, 13, 61
Nelligan, Murray Homer, 242

Nelson, Lee H., 242
NEPA. *See* laws: National Environmental Policy Act
neurobiology, 210
neuroscience, 12, 178, 202, 202
Newark, New Jersey, 99
Newfoundland, Canada, 78
newness, 95
Newsome, Albert Ray, 230
NHPA. *See* laws: National Historic Preservation Act
Nigeria, 54
Norberg-Schulz, Christian, 169
Northumbria, United Kingdom, 1
Nostalgia, 7, 93, 103
Notre Dame Cathedral, France, 113
Nova Scotia, Canada, 75, 77
NPS. *See* National Park Service
numinism, 1, 2, 4, 5, 15, 114, 115
Nunavut, Canada, 75, 78
nursing research, 90, 93, 169, 171, 172

objectification, 20, 102
objectivity, 5, 23, 36, 38, 58, 81, 111, 112, 115, 118, 122, 123, 125, 131, 169

Ohio, 23, 38
Old South Meeting House, Massachusetts, 24
Ontario, Canada, 77
ontological and epistemological orientations, 35, 111, 112
ontological purity, 35, 113–25, 138
ontology, 35, 50, 81, 111, 112, 113, 115, 117, 118, 119, 121, 123, 125, 138, 171
ornamentation, 96
Oswald, King, 1

pain, 90, 169
paintings, 60, 97, 151, 158
paleontology, 78
Palermo, Italy, 21
pandemic, 61
Pane, Roberto, 230
paradigm, 35, 111, 121
Paris, France, 101
participatory democracy, 27, 36, 66, 68, 69, 148, 149, 151, 154, 157, 185, 198, 212
patina or decay: and affect, 97; and animals, 94, 98; and antiquing process, 95, 97; and appearance of aged surfaces, 34, 91; and artifice, 98, 99; and artificial aging, 96; and building and landscape materials,

95; compared, 5, 16, 34, 92; and corrosion, 97; definition, 97; and disintegration, 34, 95; and environment, 34, 89, 94, 100, 177; and experiential qualities, 92; and the "golden stain of time," 91, 96, 100, 138; and materials' change over time, 96; and melancholy decay, 100; and patination, 97, 98; perception of, 94, 95, **96**, **97**, 98, 99; and pleasing appearance, 96, 97; and rust, 96, 97; and tendency to dissolve shape and color, 95; and value, 99
patriarchal, 130
patriotism, 23, 128
Pavel, Jakub, 232
Pennsylvania, 15, 27, 100
people-centered preservation/conservation, 33, 45, 46, 56, 65, 66, 69, 71, 71, 72, 81, 219
perfection, 122
Perry, William Graves, 122, 228
Peterson, Charles Emil, 234
phenomenologies: and approach to inquiry, 92, 171, 168, 174, 174, 250; and being-affected-by-the-past,

phenomenologies (cont'd): 103; and body as an instrument, 138, 173; and body's reaction to an experience, 173; and bracketing, 90; bracket cognition and higher-order thought processes, 103; and illusions, 93; and being in the world, 90, 170, 171, 173; and decline in popularity, 93, 94; definition, 169–71; and essences of individual human perception, 65, 97, 170; existential type, 90, 173, 210; experience the phenomenon on its own terms, 172; experience the world prereflectively, 139, 170; and experiential meanings as we live them, 170; and explication of phenomena as they present themselves, 170; first-person existential phenomenology type, 171, 172, 210; and first-person phenomenological reduction, 138; hermeneutical phenomenology type, 169, 170; and higher-order cognitive processing, 172, 173; historical creation of, 90; and the impossibility of experiencing the world without your body, 173; and informing policy, 168, 174–77; and interface between body and environment, 90; and lack of interest for researching old places, 34; and the lifeworld, 89, 94, 102, 106, 106, 171; and noumena, 169, 169; and reduction, 34, 36, 90, 138, 139; and research, 170, 171; and precognitive nature, 36, 90, 168, 172; and preontological ramifications, 170; and raw description, 173; third-person phenomenology type, 171; transcendental phenomenology type, 170; and understanding emotion, 169; and use by laypeople, 173, 174; and use in understanding experience of environmental patina, 94

phii, 25

Philadelphia, Pennsylvania, 99, 100, 101, 121, 179

Philippot, Paul, 47, 97, 117, 119, 240

Phillips, Wendell, 24

Phillips school of slavery historiography, 133

philosophy, 12, 47, 90, 116, 118, 171, 199

photographs, 121, 122, 174

physical age of places, 89, 103

physical age of the built environment, 38

physical sensation, 168

physical stimuli, 115

Pimentel Gurmendi, Victor, 242

pirate, 21

place attachment: and affect/emotional attachment, 14, 29, 31, 34, 35, 65, 89–91, 93, 101–3, 105, 112, 147, 169, 174, 177, 178; and emotional connection/bond with place, 34, 70, 168; and emotional experience of being in certain places, 169; and emotional experience of being in the world, 171; and emotional responses to the environment, 173; and emotional state, 15, 91, 92; and lack of interest by critical heritage studies researchers, 12; and lack of studies on the psychological impact of historic environment, 200; and patina and decay, 34, 107; and personal attachment, 103; and policy, 174, 175; and relationship with magic of old places, 15; and spontaneous fantasy, 101–6; and subjective human experiences influenced by the environment, 58

place conservation manager, 209

place identity, 12, 200

planners, 6, 7, 36, 63, 89, 153, 164, 179, 182, 183, 217

plants, 100, 177

Plenderleith, Harold James, 230

pluralism, 50, 68, 123, 124, 201

poetic, magical places, 99

poetry, 158

Poland, 179

policy, public: analysis of, 37, 127, 176, 193–98; and adaptive regulatory systems, 72; and administrative law, 72, 185; agencies, 4, 57, 74, 127, 213; Australia, 68–70, 73–79; and building code enforcement comparison, 81, 183; Canada, 75–80; Certified Local Government,

213; China, 51; and codifying regulations, 70, 180, 184, 185; and Congress, 48, 92, 121, 130; definition, 3, 4; and demographics of its creators, 24, 33, 128-38; and Dillon's Rule states, 212; directives, 148; drives majority of paid work in preservation/conservation, 56, 57, 72, 203; and diversity, equity, and inclusion, 27-29; and efficiency, reproducibility, and predictability, 148, 197; and elected officials, 4, 154, 155, 179, 180, 183, 197; emphasis on fabric over people, 10, 30, 57; and environmental psychology, 63; and European influence, 118; and exclusion of human experiences, 5; and exclusion of place attachment, 169; fails to consider people's needs, 46; and failure of critical heritage studies to address, 62; and government, 4, 8, 16, 28, 38, 48, 53, 54-57, 60, 64, 69, 70, 73-76, 124, 125, 152, 154-56, 164-68, 176, 178, 180, 181, 183, 185, 194, 195, 197, 198, 202, 212, 213, 215, 216; and government officials, 16, 76; Historic Preservation Fund, 215; and historic preservation, 37, 119, 127, 134, 137, 139, 147, 168, 176, 180, 183, 193, 195, 212, 215; Historic Urban Landscape approach 68-70; Japan, 51, 53; Kenya, 54; and legislation, 68, 166, 183, 185, 212, 216; and local government, 37, 56, 74-76, 69, 75, 159, 164, 176, 181-83, 185, 194, 209, 212, 213, 215; Mexico, 16-18; needed changes, 5, 19, 69, 72, 148, 178, 191, 212-18; and numinism, 2; ossification of, 37, 66, 81, 125, 180, 191, 197; reliance on the written record, 59; overemphasis on historicity, 127; and Parliament (UK), 54, 223; and religious belief, 115; and policy makers, 4, 6, 38; and positivism, 49, 123; and reform challenges, 37; research, 37, 195, 215, 217; and policy-making, 166, 196; and political manipulation, 17; political process, 72; and powers granted to the states, 212; Preservation Caucus of the US House of Representatives, 216; and public benefits, 36, 152; and regulatory environment, 57, 72, 183; and regulatory systems, 33, 72; is referential to the Venice Charter, 50; rulemaking process, 214, 215; Rwanda, 54; and sanitization of the past, 59; and staff reports, 210; State Historic Preservation Office, 73, 168, 245; United Kingdom, 54, 73. *See also* guidelines, laws, regulations

policy enforcement: through compliance, 17, 33, 57, 72, 194; through fines, 76; though imprisonment, 76; inspections, 181, 183, 237; police, 148, 149

positivism (as reflected in doctrines and policy): and archaeological reading of buildings, 121; assumes facts exist independently of interpretation, 123; and buildings as a document, 121; and empiricist-positivist paradigm, 119, 120, 121, 126; eviscerates subjectivity, 118; avoids a "false sense of history," 49, 102, 117, 119, 125; defined through its emphasis on absolute "facts" and objectivity, 19, 20, 25, 33, 48, 67, 73, 89, 93, 122-25, 127, 173, 210; and factual histories, 67, 127; and false history, 102; and false image, 38; and false newness, 95; and false objects, 49; and fallacy that professionals use an objective "truth", 59; and false veil of objectivity, 36, 111; and falsified historical record, 120; and falsification of testimony, 120; focus on a singular, "true" history, 58; forms the basis of doctrines and policy, 50; and hierarchy of truth and accuracy, 122; historical facts, 9, 20, 35, 67, 75, 106, 111, 127, 203, 218; historical positivism, 123-26; and its history, 91; ignores

positivism (*cont'd*):
culturally relative nature of facts, 124; objectification of history, 102; objective descriptions, 94; objective past, 12, 101; objective purity, 119; objective scientist, 119; objectively read buildings, 121; objectivity and scientific principles, 115; and Modernism, 49; makes assessment of significance easier, 64; needs to avoid making buildings and objects prevaricate, 49, 95, 117; privileges scientism and objectivity, 81; and reductive nature, 124; rejects people's everyday experiences, values, and meanings, 33, 34, 58, 102, 122; and scientific accuracy, 91, 121, 123, 237; and scientific analysis of the building fabric, 122; and scientific basis, 92; and scientific conservation, 49; and scientific facts to guide restorations, 122; and scientific theory of conservation, 115, 166, 119; and scientifically pure approach, 122;
and scientism, 47, 81, 92, 118, 121, 123, 125; and the "true" nature of historical objects, 116–25
post-modernism, 57, 123, 124
postmodern perspective on history, 124
postmodern turn, 57, 123
postoccupancy evaluations, 12, 199
postprocessual archaeologists, 58
power, social, 36, 126, 126, 148–52, 156, 164
Powys, Albert Reginald, 228
prehistoric, 78
Preservation Action, 204, 215, 216
preservation ethic, 116
Preservation for the People, 65, 215
private property, 27, 194, 212
private property owners, 27
private property rights, 194
processual archaeologists, 126, 217
processual archaeology, 57
processual versus postprocessual archaeological debate, 57
professionalism, 116, 128
proper care of heritage, 30, 118, 119

Protestant Reformation, 25
psychological, 7, 199
psychological approach to built heritage, 202
psychological constructs, 46, 200
psychological health, 65
psychological impact of built historic environments, 200
psychological perspective, 8, 13, 30, 35, 76
psychological phenomena, 23, 29
psychological relationship with older places, 33, 35, 63, 89
psychologist, 139, 175, 202
psychologists, 80, 93, 139, 175, 178, 200, 201–2, 210
psychology discipline's lack of environmental interest, 200
public administration, 209
public consciousness, 48
public consumption, 59
public health, 149, 178, 191, 198
public history, 11, 15, 132, 133
Puebla, Mexico, 17
Pueblos Mágicos (Mexico), 16–18
purification of a discipline, 112

qualitative data, 17, 64, 166, 172, 198
quality of life, 69
quantitative data, 64, 166, 198
Quebec, Canada, 24, 75

racial bias, 35, 128, 129, 133, 137
racial, ethnic, religious, or other marginalized groups, 126
racism, 124, 130, 165, 198
Rains, Albert McKinley, 232
rationalistic arguments, 47, 94
rationalistic perspective, 139
reenactors, 15
reflexive practitioner, 148, 164
regulations: and basis for listing buildings and places, 75; certificate of appropriateness, 59, **60**, 183; and criteria used in the National Register of Historic Places, 123; and design review, 27, 28, 33, 72, 76, 79, 185, 203; and designation of historic buildings, 56, 72; and determination of eligibility, 214; and environmental assessments, 33, 79, 80; and environ-

mental review, 27, 28, 29, 72, 79, 127, 184; environmental review processes, 127; and heritage impact assessments, 76, 196; historical registers, 74, 124; and listed building consent, 76; and listing buildings, 28, 74, 167; listing rules and process for historic buildings and places, 73, 75; local landmark regulations, 193; local historic preservation ordinances, 180, 181, 191, 211-13; National Register of Historic Places, 28, 35, 55, 73, 79, 114, 123, 124, 132, 137, 192-94, 203, 213-15, 220; National Register of Historic Places criteria, 132, 137, 220; National Register of Historic Places nominations, 73, 55, 124, 192, 194, 203, 214, 215; National Register of Historic Places criteria, 28, 35, 79, 132, 137, 215; National Register of Historic Places nominations, 28; Section 106 (environmental review), 27, 79, 164, 203, 214, 215; and social impact assessments, 79; and statements of significance, 63
relativism, 62
relics, 1, 114, 115, 121
religion, 22, 25, 115
resistance to research, 37, 192-204
Revere, Paul, 48, 121
revitalization culture, 14
rhetoric, 7, 64, 118, 125, 126
Richmond, Virginia, 21
Riegl, Alois, 19, 47, 91, 92, 95, 224
Roman, 131
Romania, 21
Romantic Period of the nineteenth century, 104
Rome, Italy, 37
ruin, 22, 102, 103, 105
ruinmood, 34, 38, 99
ruins, 22, 25, 26, 29, 91, 99, 100, 102-5
Ruskin, John, 19, 47, 90, 91, 92, 94, 96, 99, 114, 115, 129, 138, 222
Rwanda, 54

sacred, 9, 15, 23, 26, 115, 118, 132
Santa Fe, New Mexico, 213
Santiago, Chile, 61
Saskatchewan, Canada, 75, 77

Schneider, John Thomas, 230
scientific accuracy, 123, 124
scientific approaches, 48
scientific arguments, 60
scientific conservation, 49
scientific disciplines, 57
scientific evidence, 122
scientific knowledge, 150
scientific methods, 92, 121, 125
scientific progress, 51
scientific theory of conservation, 115-19
Scotland, 21, 195
scrape and anti-scrape theories, 19, 116, 120
semiotic qualities, 132
senescent environments, 5, 6, 12, 30
sense of place, 65, 69, 89, 169, 179. *See also* place attachment
sentimental treatment of heritage, 119, 121
Shinto religion, 25
SHPO. *See* policy, public: State Historic Preservation Office
Shull, Carol D., 246
Sicily, Italy, 21
situated knowledge, 150
skyscrapers, 99
slavery, 129, 132, 133
smells, 70, 172, 172, 250
social impacts, 80
social purity, 35, 113, 119-38

social science approaches, 9, 65
social science disciplines, 12, 201
social science evidence, 5
social science funding, 197
social science methods and methodologies, 45, 80, 150
social science perspectives, 30, 81, 200, 201
social science research, 8, 204
social sciences, 7, 8, 12, 48, 56, 57, 128, 209, 217
social scientists, 6, 80
Society for Environmental, Population and Conservation Psychology, 199
Society for the Protection of Ancient Buildings (England), 116, 118, 120
sociocultural meanings, 46, 70
sociocultural norms, 134
sociology, 5, 81, 126, 201, 209
Sonnier, Jean-Léon, 238
Sorlin, Francois, 236
sounds, 26, 70, 105
SPAB. *See* Society for the Protection of Ancient Buildings
SPAB Manifesto, 116, 120

specialization, 10, 112, 119, 218, 219
spirituality, 9, 26, 54, 74, 77, 129
spontaneous fantasy: and connecting with ancestors, 104; definition, 101-6; and ghost towns and ruins, 104, 105; as an imaginative act, 103; as imagined history, 103; as imagined narratives, 103; and involuntary perception, 105; and natural landscapes, 106; as opposed to objective focus of orthodox doctrine, policy, and practice, 102; as opposed to premeditated fantasy, 103; and relationship with emotional attachment to place, 177; and relationship with patina, 103
stakeholders, 13, 36, 45, 57, 67, 70, 71, 80, 81, 152, 196
stereotypes, 27, 130
Stikas, Eustathios, 236
storytelling, 18, 166, 210
stylistic restoration, 48, 51
SurveyLA, 67
symbolism, 16
symmetrical buildings, 132
Syria, 21

tangible heritage, 47, 69, 70, 183
tapu, 26, 26
teleological, 123
territorialization, 125
Thailand, 25
thin places, 15
Thomas, Kathryn [Kay], 137, 244
top-down approaches, 13, 33, 45, 56, 148
tourism, 16, 139
tradition, 4, 15, 16, 18, 25, 26, 50, 74, 118, 127, 129, 149, 171, 183, 191, 203
traditional knowledge, 54
Tripp, Gertrud, 131, 238
Turner, Frederick Jackson, 132

UNESCO. *See* United Nations Educational, Scientific and Cultural Organization
United Kingdom, 15, 33, 46, 55, 63, 64, 68, 72-76, 79, 195
United Nations Educational, Scientific and Cultural Organization, 48, 54, 67-69
urban planning, 33, 56, 136, 182, 219
Utley, Robert Marshall, 242

values: and age of building or place, 19, 34, 92-95; aesthetic, 28, 55, 60, 63, 64, 73, 74, 77, 78, 91, 99, 100, 127, 130-32, 213, 218; archaeological, 55; art/historical, 9, 10; artistic, 51, 53, 77, 96, 98, 151; associative/symbolic, 63; and the Authorized Heritage Discourse, 30, 31, 62, 112, 119; and beliefs, 18, 26, 115, 173; community, 68-70; cultural, 74, 76, 173; disciplinary, 56, 57, 62, 138; economic, 63; experiential 75, 103, 106, 174; fabric, 113-17; high-style, 127, 214; historical, 19, 53, 64, 77, 92 ; informational, 63, 63, 126; and lack of agreement, 9; and orthodox value assessments, 127; public perspective on, 27, 33, 49, 56, 57, 140, 148; rarity, 55, 73; in relation to policy, 194, 195, 212; religious, 4, 25, 26, 114, 115, 118, 126, 209; sociocultural, 64; and storytelling, 168; typology, 63; as used for listing historic buildings and places, 75; values-centered conservation/preservation, 33, 45, 63, 64
Veracruz, Mexico, 18
vernacular architecture, 28, 214, 220
vernacular, non-Western architecture, 130
vicarious experience, 22. *See also* spontaneous fantasy
Viollet-le-Duc, Eugène Emmanuel, 47, 114, 129, 222
Virginia, 20, 21, 131

Waco, Texas, 21
Warsaw, 179
Washington, DC, 121, 213
White House, Washington, DC, 48, 121
White supremacy, 24, 29, 128-33
wisdom, 47
Wissler, Clark, 226
World Heritage, 52, 53, 54, 68, 79
World Heritage Convention, 53, 54, 68

Yukon, Canada, 78

Zachwatovicz, Jan, 232
Zbiss, Slimane-Mustapha, 236
zócalo, 16, **16**, 17

www.ingramcontent.com/pod-product-compliance
Lightning Source LLC
Chambersburg PA
CBHW081433070526
44586CB00020B/2572